MW00657394

Farewell-to Spring

Wildflowers of Southern Oregon

by John Kemper

Photographs by the Author

With a Foreword by Dr. Frank Lang

Outdoor Press
Medford, Oregon

This book is dedicated to
MY WIFE, BARBARA
my wildflower-hunting companion

ACKNOWLEDGEMENTS

I would like to express my deep appreciation to a number of people who helped me in finding and identifying wildflowers in Southern Oregon, and in preparing this book. Outstanding among these was Dr. Frank Lang, retired chairman of the Biology Department at Southern Oregon University, who read the manuscript and made a great number of helpful suggestions. He also graciously consented to write a foreword for the book. While his work helped me enormously, in improving the book and avoiding mistakes, it seems to be inevitable that some mistakes will get through anyway, and for these I take full responsibility. Others who helped me were Bob Claypole, Dick Heintz, Ed Hoover, Roger Hutchings, Norm Jensen, Boyd Kline, Bob Korfhage, Alex Maksymowicz, Margaret Meierhenry, Jean Miller, Jeanne Moore, Lewis Owen, Veva Stansell, Molly Sullivan, Kay Wylie, and Lawson Wylie.

OTHER NATURE BOOKS BY THE SAME AUTHOR

Exploring Southern Oregon's Beautiful Places
2003, Outdoor Press

Southern Oregon's Bird Life
2002, Outdoor Press

Birding Northern California
1999, Globe Pequot Press

Discovering Yolo County Wildlife
1996, Yolo Audubon Society and Yolo Basin Foundation

Copyright 2006
by John Kemper

ISBN 0-9722509-2-1

Foreword

"I am new to Southern Oregon and love wildflowers. What book should I use for identification?" was one of my most frequently asked questions (FAQ). Until John Kemper put this book together, I told them there was no book for beginners covering all of Southern Oregon.

Don Begnoche's *Siskiyou Sundays* includes the Siskiyous and the coast, but does not include Crater Lake and the rest of the Cascades. Other field guides include *Plants of the Northwest Coast,* by Pojar and MacKinnon, and *A Field Guide to Pacific States Wildflowers*, by Niehaus and Ripper. Unfortunately, the area included in Pojar and MacKinnon extends only as far south as Eugene, and the region covered by Niehaus and Ripper is so vast that many Southern Oregon species don't get included. Eugene Kozloff's recent book, *Plants of Western Oregon, Washington & British Columbia* includes many plants in our area. But it is heavy and will not fit in a pocket. Many people prefer something smaller to carry into the field. And, as with any book that covers such a large region, many of its species don't occur in Southern Oregon, and some of our species are not included.

The botanical "bible" for many years was Morton Peck's classic work, *A Manual of the Higher Plants of Oregon.* But Peck's 1961 book was written for a scientific audience, and is now out of print and out of date. Much of the Oregon market for an Oregon flora vanished when Hitchcock and Cronquist's *Flora of the Pacific Northwest,* which covers the Northwest as far south as the 44th parallel, was published. Other books long out of date and expensive, but illustrated with line drawings, are LeRoy Abram's four-volume *Illustrated Flora of the Pacific States,* Hitchock and others' five-volume *Vascular Plants of the Pacific Northwest.*

The best current book, oddly enough, that covers most, but not all of the plants in our region, is *The Jepson Manual -- Higher plants of California,* James Hickman, editor. But, because the book covers all of California, most of its species do not occur in Oregon. Furthermore, the book is very large, weighs five pounds, and would not be considered a field guide by most persons. In addition, it is directed to a scientific audience and beginners often find it difficult to use.

John Kemper's wildflower book satisfies the need for a wildflower field guide that specializes in our area, written primarily for a non-scientific audience. His book includes 698 species found in our region, with 443 color photos arranged by flower color. A brief text describing important features and the place and time of year the photo was taken accompanies each photograph. Although it doesn't include everything, most commonly encountered native plants, a few weeds, some flowering shrubs, and plants with eye-catching fruits are included. There is an illustrated glossary and synopsis of plant families. The geographical area includes Coos, Curry, Douglas, Jackson, Josephine, and Klamath counties. Thanks to John Kemper, I have an answer to my most FAQ, *Wildflowers of Southern Oregon.*

Dr. Frank Lang
Ashland, Oregon

CONTENTS

How to Use This Book

The book is organized by flower color, since color is the most obvious thing a person generally notices about a plant. A problem, of course, is that color is only useful during the time a plant is in flower. Nevertheless, I think most readers of this book with find organization by color to be helpful.

Within color groupings, the arrangement is alphabetical by family (scientific names), and then alphabetical within the families (again, by scientific names). The advantage of arranging plants by family is that many species that bear resemblances to each other are grouped in proximity. There are limitations to this advantage, because members of the families will often have different colors.

Grouping by color has other problems, because the flowers in a species many range in color from white, to blue, to pink, for example. The placement within a given color group has been largely controlled by the color of the flower in the photo that is being used, with supplemental information in the accompanying text material, to describe possible variations. In many cases, as with the color *violet,* it may be difficult to decide whether the dominant color is reddish, in which case it goes into the "Red to Pink" section, or is purple, in which case it goes into the "Blue to Violet" section. With some flowers, I have simply had to make an arbitrary decision, and the reader may not always agree with my decisions.

An effort has been made to avoid the use of scientific terms as much as possible. However, in many cases, as with words such as *bract, corolla, involucre, perianth, petiole,* and *sepal,* the words are so useful, and come up so frequently, that I have used them anyway, because their equivalents in "ordinary language" would be lengthy and cumbersome. Thus, the Glossary (next section) is vital, to assist in understanding. Likewise, the pages that follow the Glossary, which illustrate the various flower and leaf parts, are also essential to understanding the terms used in the descriptions.

The problem of common names, with any book on wildflowers, soon becomes apparent. For most species, many different common names have cropped up in general usage. Worse, in many cases, the same common names have been applied to entirely different species. For the species in this book, I tried to uncover as many common names as I could, and have listed those that seemed to be useful.

Scientists prefer to use metric units, in order to correspond with international usage. In fact, scientific journals universally require that metric units be used in articles. However, the members of the general audience to whom this book is addressed are more likely to be familiar with English units, such as inches and feet. Thus, English units are used herein.

Many plants, some of them with attractive flowers, are non-native. These are included, because the user may encounter them, feel them to be attractive, and want to know what they are. In each case, I have given the original source -- usually from Europe -- and placed the common name(s) in bold face italics.

Information concerning the range of a species has been included in a general way. For this, I have mostly relied upon Peck's wonderful book, *A Manual of the Higher Plants of Oregon* (2nd ed.), and secondarily on *The Jepson Manual -- Higher Plants of California.* The Jepson Manual includes information about the occurrence of plants in Oregon in a general way, but Peck's book is still the most useful reference for Oregon, even though it is out of date in some respects. In considering range, it is important to note that Southern Oregon is where certain botanical regions come together. In particular, many California species penetrate Southern Oregon, and many Great Basin species come west all the way to the Cascade divide, particularly in the Cascade-Siskiyou National Monument.

One of the most useful sources for writing this book came from the Internet: *The PLANTS Database, Version 3.5* (http.//plants.usda.gov), United States Department of Agriculture (USDA) Natural Resources Conservation Service. This database gives just one common name for each species. For the species accounts in this book, I have tried to include the USDA common names.

The USDA database I think is the most useful source for current scientific names. Scientific names do change over time, as taxonomists determine new relationships, leading to changes in genus names, or establish that certain species should be "split" into one or more newly-named species, or, conversely, that certain species should be "lumped" into one. In those cases where new names have supplanted the old, I have shown the older scientific names in square brackets. Such alternative names are known as "synonyms."

GLOSSARY and ABBREVIATIONS

achene (sometimes **akene**) Dry 1-seeded unwinged fruit, often appearing to be a naked seed.
acuminate Leaf with a long sharp tip, with concave sides.
acute Leaf with sharp tip, straight or concave.
AK Alaska.
alternate A leaf structure in which leaves (with or without petioles) are on opposite sides of the stem, on alternating sides. (Fig. 5)
angiosperm Plant with seeds in an ovary.
annual Completes life cycle in one growing season. See **biennial**.
anther Pollen-bearing part of a stamen. (Fig. 1)
appressed Lying flat on the surface.
aril A fleshy covering (perhaps covering only part) of a seed, that arises from the point of seed attachment.
auricle Ear-like lobe at the base of a leaf or petal. (See Fig. 5, for auriculate leaf.)
axil Angle between two organs, as between a leaf and a stem. (Fig. 6)
axillary Located at an axil.
BC British Columbia
banner Upper petal of a pea-like flower. See **standard**.
basal Refers to leaves at the base of a plant, near the ground.
berry Pulpy fruit with many seeds imbedded in the body of the fruit.
biennial Completes life cycle in two growing seasons, usually blooming in the second season. See **annual.**
binomial See **scientific name.**
bilateral Divisible into left and right mirror images, by running an imaginary vertical line down the middle.
bipinnate A pinnate leaf, in which the divisions are again pinnate. Same as 2-compound (see Fig. 4).
blade The more or less flat, expanded part of a leaf or petal. (Fig. 6)
bloom A whitish film on leaves or fruit that is usually easily rubbed off. Also, a flower.
bract Small leaf-like structure associated with an inflorescence. (Fig. 7) Also, a small leaf-like structure sticking out from behind the scale of a cone.
bractlet Relatively small secondary bract within an inflorescence. (Fig. 7)
bulb A short underground stem or branch surrounded by modified fleshy leaves.
CA California.
calyx A group of sepals.
carpel A simple pistil, or a unit of a compound pistil. The number of carpels is usually the same as the number of compartments in a compound pistil, or may be the same as the number of styles and stigmas.
catkin Long, thin, dense cluster of unisexual, apetalous flowers. Usually, drooping from a stem, but may be short and fat, as in a pussy willow.
cauline Refers to leaves on an above-ground stem, as opposed to **basal leaves.**
CG Campground.
chlorophyll Green pigment of plants, used for photosynthesis.
ciliate Refers to hairs along the edge.
clasping A term usually applied to a leaf that holds or surrounds the main stem tightly.
claw Narrowed stalk-like base of a petal.
Co. County
compound leaf In a 1-compound leaf, the leaf is divided into several leaflets connected by a stem; in a 2-compound leaf, the primary leaflets are divided into secondary leaflets. (Fig.4)
conifer A tree with cones, as in a pine. Usually evergreen, but some, such as larch, are deciduous.
cordate Heart-shaped. (Fig. 5)
corm A short modified stem, usually underground, that is fleshy and thickened.
corolla Collective term for all the petals in a flower.
corymb A flat-topped cluster of flowers with pedicels of unequal length. (Fig. 7)
crenate Having rounded teeth. (Fig. 5)
cyme Branched inflorescence in which the terminal flowers open before the lower flowers. (Fig. 7)
deciduous A plant that drops its leaves in winter.
decumbent Most of stem lying on ground, but with end curving up.
deltoid Shaped somewhat like a triangle. (Fig. 5)
dentate Having relatively sharp, coarse teeth, pointing outward. (Fig. 5)

GLOSSARY and ABBREVIATIONS

dia. Diameter.

dioecious Having male and female flowers on separate plants.

discoid head A flower head composed entirely of disk flowers, in the *Asteraceae* family. (See, also, **ligulate head.**)

disk flowers The tubular flowers in the center of the flower head, in members of the Sunflower Family (*Asteraceae*).

drupe Fleshy fruit with hardened stone, such as a cherry or a plum.

elliptic A leaf that is more or less in the form of an ellipse, with the sides of nearly uniform curvature. (Fig. 5)

emergent A plant that is rooted under water, but extends above water.

endemic Native to a particular geographic area.

entire Having smooth margins (i.e., without teeth).

evergreen A plant that does not lose all its leaves in winter, although it may shed some of its leaves at certain seasons.

exserted Protruding beyond any surrounding structure.

extirpated No longer surviving in a particular geographic area.

fascicle A bundle.

filament The stalk of a stamen bearing an anther. (Fig. 1)

filiform Very thin, thread-like.

floral tube The tube-like basal part of a flower, in which portions of the petals or sepals are more or less fused together.

FR Forest Road.

genus (*plural:* genera) A name belonging to a closely related group of plants, *not* the same thing as "family." (A plant family is made up of a group of closely related genera.) See **scientific name.**

glabrous Not hairy; smooth.

gland A small, usually spherical, structure that exudes a sticky substance.

glandular Having glands.

glaucous Having a whitish film that is usually easily rubbed off. See **bloom.**

gymnosperm A plant with seeds that are not borne in an ovary, but are borne in a structure like a cone.

habitat A plant community.

herb A plant generally with non-woody parts above ground, whose above-ground parts die back at the end of the growing season.

herbage The non-woody parts of a part, composed of stems and leaves, that are above ground.

hirsute Having short stiff hairs.

hypanthium An expansion of the floral axis, saucer-shaped, cup-shaped, rod-shaped, or tubular, that has the sepals, petals, and stamens attached to its upper margin.

inferior ovary An ovary that is beneath its flower, below the bases of the sepals, petals, and stamens.

inflorescence A term for the entire collection of flower parts, including bracts and pedicels.

involucel A small secondary involucre in a compound umbel. (Fig. 7)

involucre A group of bracts at the base of a flower cluster that more or less is held together as a unit. (Figs. 3 and 7)

irregular Having parts, such as petals, of different shapes, producing bilateral symmetry.

keel The lower, fused petals of a pea-like flower.

lacerate Irregularly and deeply cut.

lanceolate Elongated and narrow, tapering from base to tip. (Fig. 5)

leaflet One of the small leaves in a compound leaf. (Fig. 4)

legume A dry fruit with one carpel, that at maturity splits open along two sutures.

ligulate head A flower head composed entirely of ray flowers, or **ligules**, in the *Asteraceae* family. (See, also, **discoid head.**)

ligules The outer flowers in members of the Sunflower Family (*Asteraceae*) having strap-like shape. The flattened part of the corolla is referred to as a **ray**, or **ligule**. (Fig. 3)

limb The expanded, often lobed, part of a corolla at the end of a tube.

linear Long and narrow, of nearly uniform width. (Fig. 5)

monoecious Having both female and male flowers on the same plant.

Mt., Mtns. Mountain, Mountains.

mycotroph A plant, usually without chlorophyll, that gets its food from dead plant or animal material, usually with the help of a symbiotic relationship with a fungus. Plants of this type were called "saprophytes" in the past. See **parasite**.

nectary A structure or organ that produces nectar.

NM National Monument.

NP National Park.

node A point on the stem where a leaf or another stem is attached.

oblong A leaf in which the sides are more or less parallel for much of its length. (Fig. 5)

OR Oregon.

opposite A leaf structure in which leaves (with or without petioles) are in pairs on opposite sides of the stem. (Fig. 5)

ovary The part of the pistil, usually wider than the rest, containing the ovules that will become seeds after fertilization. (Fig. 1)

ovate Leaf that is more or less egg-shaped. (Fig. 5)

p. Page.

palmate Radiating from a common point, resembling the palm of a hand. (Fig. 4)

panicle Inflorescence with compound branching, in which the lower outer flowers open before the terminal flowers. (Fig. 7)

pappus In the Sunflower Family (*Asteraceae*), the structures arising from the top of the achene. May consist of hairs, bristles, or scales, in the location where the calyx generally occurs in other flowers. (Fig. 3)

parasite A plant, usually without chlorophyll, that gets its food directly (without fungi) from living plant material. See **mycotroph**.

pedicel Stalk of an individual flower or fruit. (Fig. 7)

peduncle Stalk of an entire inflorescence. (Fig. 7)

perennial Non-woody plant living more than two growing seasons.

perianth Sepals and petals collectively.

petal One of the inner leaf-like parts of a flower. (Figs. 1 and 2)

petiole Leaf stalk. (Fig. 6)

phyllary A bract of the involucre below a flower head, in the Sunflower Family (*Asteraceae*). (Fig. 3)

pinnate Having two rows of leaflets on opposite sides of a stem. (Fig. 4)

photosynthesis The formation of carbohydrates in plants, by exposure to light.

pistil The seed-bearing, female part of a flower, collectively, the ovary, style, and stigma. (Fig. 1)

pistillate A flower with fertile pistils, but without functional stamens.

pome A fleshy fruit with a papery wall surrounding the seeds, and a thick and fleshy outer layer, such as in an apple or a pear.

pubescent Having soft short hairs.

raceme Unbranched inflorescence of flowers with short pedicels of about equal length, with the lower flowers blooming first. (Fig. 7)

rachis Axis of a compound leaf, or of a flower cluster.

radiate head A flower head composed of both disk and ray flowers, in the *Asteraceae* family.

ray A primary axis, as in a radiating branch of a compound umbel. (Fig. 7) See, also, **ray flowers.** (Fig. 3)

ray flowers See **ligules.**

regular Having radial symmetry.

reniform Kidney-shaped.

rhizome An underground stem that usually grows horizontally.

runner See **stolon**.

SP State Park.

sagittate Arrowhead-shaped. (Fig. 5)

salverform A corolla with a narrow tube that spreads into a more or less flat limb

scape A flowering stalk without leaves, arising from the ground or from a group of basal leaves.

scientific name A unique name given to a plant (other organisms, as well) generally consisting of two words, called a **binomial**, written in Latin, and in italics. The first word, always capitalized, is the name of the **genus**; the second word, never capitalized even if it is derived from a proper noun, is the name of the **species**. Example: *Erythronium oregonum* (common name, Oregon Fawn Lily) in which *Erythronium* is the name of the genus, and *oregonum* is the name of the species. When two species of the same genus are being discussed, then the generic name of the second species may be abbreviated, as in *Erythronium oregonum,* and *E. klamathense.* For subspecies and varieties, a third Latin word is added. In formal usage, an abbreviation of the name of the author is included, as in L., for Linnaeus.

scorpiod Flowers in a coiled arrangement resembling a scorpion.

scurfy Covered with small scales.

sepal Leafy appendage beneath the petal, usually green, but sometimes colored and looking like a petal. (Figs. 1 and 2)

serrate Having margins of sharp teeth pointing toward tip. (Fig. 5)

sessile Without a stalk.

sheathing Generally applied to a leaf that partly or entirely surrounds the stem.

silicle A seedpod, in the *Brassicaceae* family, which is typically less than twice as long as wide.

silique A seedpod, in the *Brassicaceae* family, which is typically more than twice as long as wide.

simple leaf Composed of a single leaf (not compound).

SNA State Natural Area.

SP State Park.

sp. Species (singular).

spp. Species (plural).

spadix A thickened floral spike crowded with small flowers.

spathe A large bract surrounding a flower cluster, usually around a spadix.

spatulate Shaped like a flattened spoon. (Fig. 5)

species (Used for both singular and plural.) A name belonging to a particular kind of plant within a genus. See **scientific name.**

spike Unbranched inflorescence of sessile flowers, with the lower flowers opening first. (Fig. 7)

spur A narrow projection from the base of a calyx or corolla.

SRS State Recreation Site.

ssp. Subspecies (singular).

sspp. Subspecies (plural).

stamen The pollen-bearing, male part of a flower. (Fig. 1)

staminate A flower with fertile stamens, but without pistils.

staminode A stamen that doesn't produce pollen.

standard Upper petal of a pea-like flower. See **banner**.

stigma The part of the pistil that receives the pollen. (Fig. 1)

stipe A stalk.

stipules Leaf-like structures at the base of a petiole, with the parts often paired. (Fig. 4)

stolon An above-ground horizontal stem that may take root at the nodes and at the end.

style Stalk that connects the ovary to the stigma in a pistil. (Fig. 1) Note that a sigma may be sessile (no style).

subtend Immediately below.

superior ovary An ovary that is free from the perianth and sits above the bases of the sepals and petals, as in Fig. 1.

suture A line along which fruits may split.

sw Southwest.

tomentose Covered with dense, woolly hairs.

tube See **floral tube**.

umbel Inflorescence in which three or more pedicels radiate from the same point. (Fig. 7)

umbellet A secondary umbel of a compound umbel.

var. Variety.

WA Washington, or Wildlife Area.

whorl When more than two leaves are attached to the same point on a stem, it is called a **whorl**, as opposed to **opposite** or **alternate**.

wing A thin flat extension of a surface.

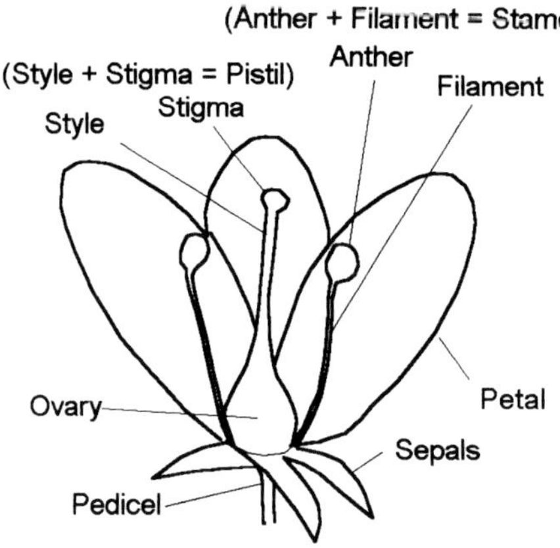

Fig. 1 FLOWER PARTS

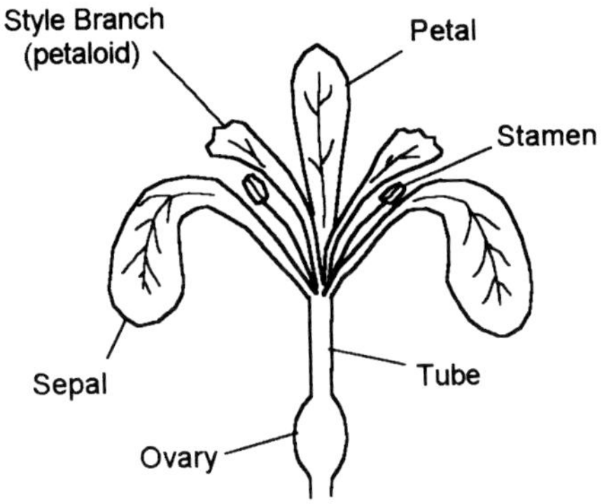

Fig. 2 IRIS

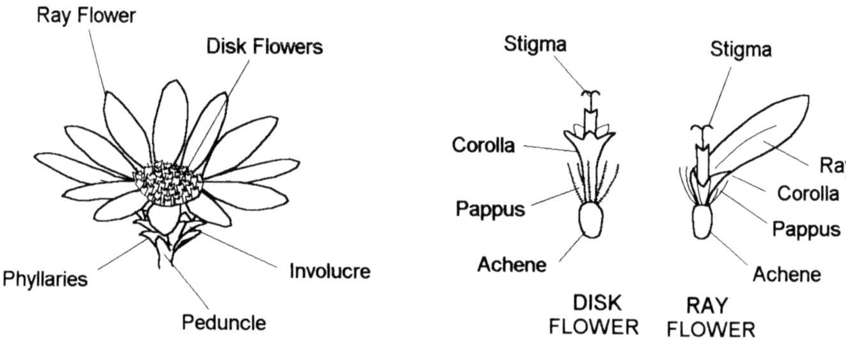

Fig. 3 PARTS OF FLOWERS IN SUNFLOWER FAMILY (*Asteraceae*)

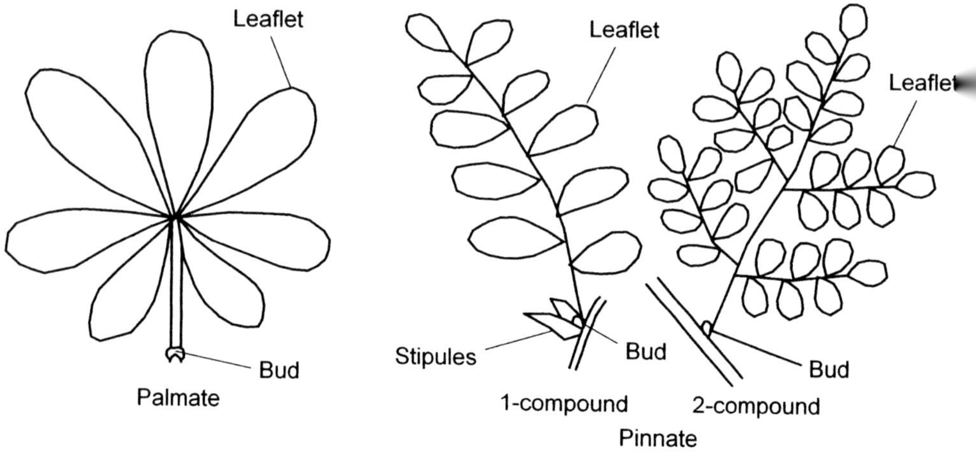

Fig. 4 TYPES OF COMPOUND LEAVES

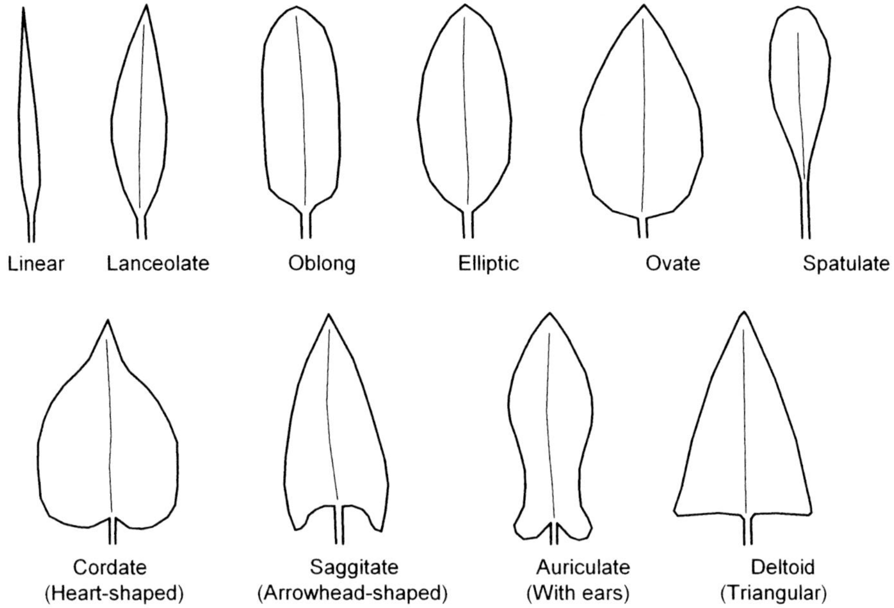

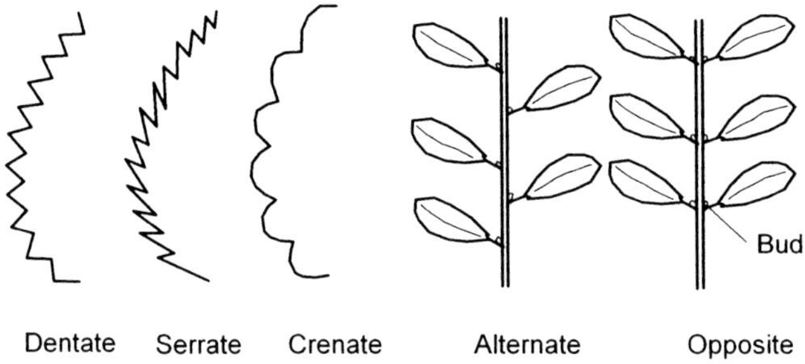

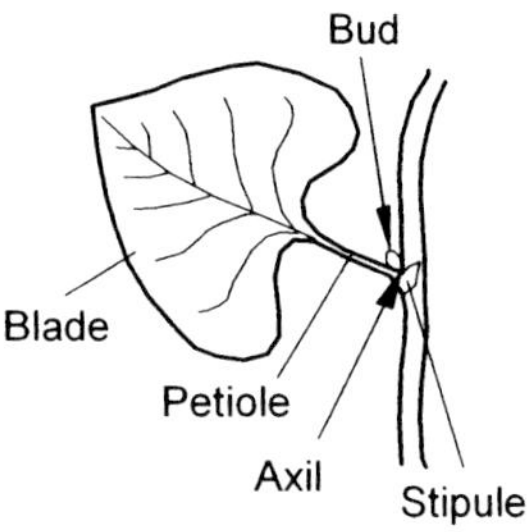

Fig 5 LEAF-SHAPES AND ARRANGEMENTS

Fig. 6
LEAF PARTS

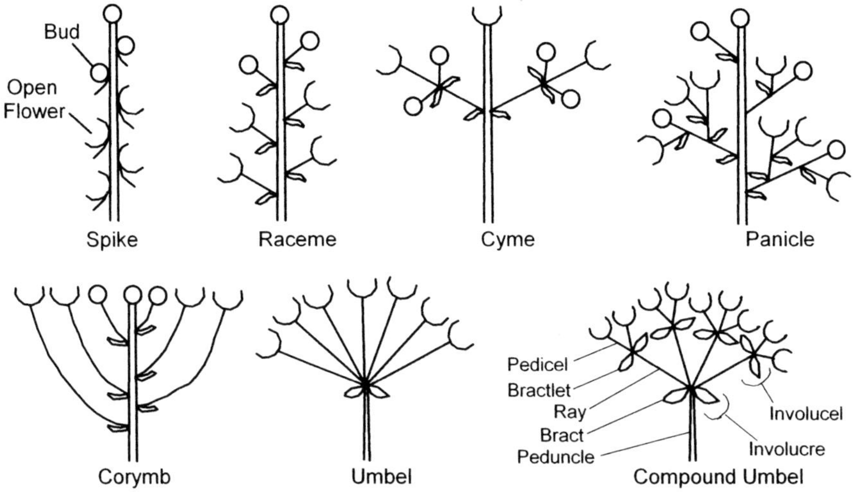

Fig. 7 FLOWER ARRANGEMENTS ON STEMS (INFLORESCENCES)

Plant Families

Some hints regarding identification of some of the important plant families are given here. Families which are represented in this book by only one species, such as ***Aizoaceae*** (Fig-marigold family), are not included. Botanically speaking, these clues are incomplete, but complete scientific description is beyond the scope of this book, which is intended for a general audience. Those characteristics that can be used in the field are emphasized, but it should be noted that such a brief listing may not succeed in identifying every member of every family. Also, there are always exceptions to the "rules". Nevertheless, the clues given below can be of help.

Apiaceae [*Umbelliferae*], **CARROT FAMILY** [Parsley Family]. Petals 5, stamens 5, ovary inferior. Usually has these characteristics: small white or yellow flowers in umbels, hollow stems, sheathing petioles, and often with feathery, many-divided compound leaves. Seed-like fruits split in half. Example: **QUEEN ANNE'S LACE,** *Daucus carota.*

***Apocynaceae*, DOGBANE FAMILY:** Corolla usually with 5 lobes, with a distinct tube. Leaves usually paired, entire, simple. Plants often have milky sap. Many are **TOXIC.** Example: **SPREADING DOGBANE,** *Apocynum androsaemifolium.*

***Asclepiadaceae*, MILKWEED FAMILY.** Flowers are usually in umbels, and have 5 sepals and 5 partially fused petals, with a complex central structure of stamens and stigma. Leaves are generally simple; plants have milky juice. Example: **SHOWY MILKWEED,** *Asclepias speciosa.*

Asteraceae [*Compositae*], **SUNFLOWER FAMILY** [Composite Family]. Our largest family. The flower heads are generally compact and composed of many tiny flowers, of two types: ray flowers (ligules), with straplike corollas, and disk flowers, with tubular corollas. Generally, the disk flowers are in a compact, often button-like, cluster at the center, and the ray flowers are arrayed around the outer edge, often resembling petals. In some species, the flower heads may consist of disk flowers only; in others the flower heads may consist of ray flowers only. Each of these flowers, whether disk flower or ray flower, is in fact a separate flower, sometimes complete with both pistils and stamens, sometimes only with pistils or only with stamens. Ovary inferior; the structures arising from the top of the ovary, called the *pappus,* may consist of hairs, bristles, or scales, in the location where the calyx usually occurs in other flowers. Generally, the flowers are enclosed by a leafy involucre, which is often mistaken for a calyx. Example: **EATON FLEABANE,** *Erigeron eatonii.*

***Berberidaceae*, BARBERRY FAMILY:** Flowers usually with 3 sepals and 3 petals, 6 stamens, the anthers usually opening by 2 valves (flaps), ovary superior. Leaves compound. Example: **OREGON-GRAPE,** *Berberis aquifolium.*

***Boraginaceae*, BORAGE FAMILY** [Forget-me-not Family]. Flowers usually in a scorpiod cluster, flower parts in 5s, corolla usually trumpet-shaped, 5 stamens, ovary superior, four nutlets. Leaves mostly rough-hairy, simple, entire. Example: **FIDDLENECK,** *Amsinckia menziesii.*

Brassicaceae [*Cruciferae*], **MUSTARD FAMILY:** Flowers with 4 petals, cross-shaped, usually in terminal racemes and often showy, 6 stamens, 2 short and 4 long, ovary superior. Leaves alternate. Seeds are often in a pod called a "silique," which typically is more than twice as long as wide, but may be in a pod called a "silicle," which is less than twice as long as wide. Example: **WESTERN WALLFLOWER,** *Erysimum capitatum.*

***Campanulaceae*, BELLFLOWER FAMILY** [Bluebell Family]. Corollas usually bell-shaped, 5-parted, leaves simple, with milky juice. Example: **SCOULER HAREBELL,** *Campanula scouleri.*

***Caprifoliaceae*, HONEYSUCKLE FAMILY.** Generally woody, with opposite leaves. Long, funnel-like flowers, with parts often in 5s, stamens poking far out of corollas. Ovary inferior. Leaves often united around stem, with stem "perforating" through. Example: **ORANGE HONEYSUCKLE,** *Lonicera ciliosa.*

***Caryophyllaceae*, PINK FAMILY.** Corollas usually with 5 petals, sometimes 4, may be deeply notched in some species, 5-10 stamens, ovary superior. Stem joints often swollen, leafs typically opposite, entire leaves. Example: **HOOKER INDIAN PINK,** *Silene hookeri.*

***Convolulaceae*, MORNING GLORY FAMILY.** Flowers in most cases funnel-shaped, stems climbing or twining, leaves usually more or less heart-shaped, simple, entire, alternate. Example: **FIELD MORNING GLORY,** *Convolvulus arvensis.*

***Cornaceae*, DOGWOOD FAMILY.** Often characterized by showy, petal-like bracts, surrounding a tight cluster of rather insignificant flowers, leaves opposite. Example: **PACIFIC DOGWOOD,** *Cornus nattallii.*

***Crassulaceae*, STONECROP FAMILY** [Sedum Family]. Flowers symmetrical, usually with 4 or 5 petals, often urn-like; leaves generally very fleshy. Example: **BROAD-LEAVED STONE-CROP,** *Sedum spathulifolium.*

***Ericaceae*, HEATH FAMILY.** Contains such disparate species as Manzanita, Rhododendron, Pine Drops, and Snow Plant, although these have sometimes been placed in their own families. Flowers urn-shaped, funnel-shaped, or flared, 5 petals, 10 stamens. Anthers open by terminal pores. Ovary may be inferior or superior. Leaves often evergreen, leathery, and sometimes needle or scale-like. Example: **WESTERN AZALEA,** *Rhododendron occidentale.*

Fabaceae [*Leguminosae*], **LEGUME FAMILY** [Pea Family]. Flowers irregular, with 1 large "banner petal" above, 2 "wing petals" to the sides, similar to each other, and two lower "keel petals," joined together to form the "keel," which encloses the stamens and pistil. In some species of *Lupinus* (lupine), an important characteristic may be whether the keel is ciliate (hairs along the edge) or not. Ovary superior. Leaves usually compound, some with tendrils. Example: **AMERICAN VETCH,** *Vicia americana.*

***Gentianaceae*, GENTIAN FAMILY.** Flowers usually 5-lobed, bell, salverform, or funnel-shaped. Leaves opposite, simple, glabrous. Example: **CENTAURY,** *Centaurium erythraea.*

***Gerianaceae*, GERANIUM FAMILY** [Crane's-bill Family]. Leaves often deeply lobed, flower parts generally in 5s, 5-10 stamens, ovary superior. Distinctive characteristic is the elongated pistil, leading to the name "crane-bill." Example: **FILAREE,** *Erodium cicutarium.*

***Grossulariaceae*, GOOSEBERRY FAMILY.** Example: **STICKY CURRANT,** *Ribes viscosissimum.*

***Hydrophyllaceae*, WATERLEAF FAMILY.** Flowers often in 1-sided scorpiod coils, corollas with 5 lobes, generally bell-like, 5 stamens, ovary superior. Leaves generally lobed. Example: **FENDLER WATERLEAF,** *Hydrophyllum fendleri.*

***Iridaceae*, IRIS FAMILY.** Perianth 6-parted, with 3 large petal-like sepals and 3 smaller, erect petals, or 6 more or less equal-sized petals, 3 stamens, ovary inferior. Flat, sword-like leaves. Example: **SLENDER-TUBED IRIS,** *Iris chrysophylla.*

Lamiaceae [*Labiatae*], **MINT FAMILY.** Two-lipped corolla, with 5 petals, 4 stamens, ovary superior, 4 nutlets. Inflorescence often whorled and spike-like. Stem usually 4-angled, leaves opposite or whorled. Often has strong, mint-like odor. Example: **NETTLELEAF HORSEMINT,** *Agastache urticifolia.*

***Liliaceae*, LILY FAMILY.** Sepals and petals usually in 3s, and colored similarly in most cases, (*Trillium* being a notable exception), 6 stamens. Ovary usually superior (i.e., perianth parts attached below ovary). Example: **OREGON FAWN LILY,** *Erythronium oregonum.*

***Linaceae*, FLAX FAMILY.** Flowers usually at the ends of stems, generally with 5 petals. In most cases, leaves are narrow, alternate. Example: **WILD BLUE FLAX,** *Linum lewisii*

***Malvaceae*, MALLOW FAMILY.** Flowers regular, 5 petals, stamens with filaments fused into a tube-like structure, with the anthers not fused. Stigma or stigmas protrude through the cluster of anthers. Ovary superior. Leaves often deeply lobed. Example: **OREGON SIDALCEA,** *Sidalcea oregana.*

***Nyctaginaceae*, FOUR O'CLOCK FAMILY.** Sepals fused into funnel-like corolla often with calyx-like involucre composed of colorful bracts; no true petals. Ovary superior. Example: **YELLOW SAND VERBENA,** *Abronia latifolia.*

***Onagraceae*, EVENING-PRIMROSE FAMILY.** Usually 4 sepals and 4 petals, 8 stamens, ovary inferior. Leaves usually opposite or whorled. Example: **TANSY-LEAF EVENING-PRIMROSE,** *Camissonia tanacetifolia.*

***Orchidaceae*, ORCHID FAMILY.** Flowers irregular, 3 sepals same color as petals, 2 lateral petals and a lower, larger lip petal. Stamen(s) and pistil united into a structure called a "column," highly variable, ovary inferior. Leaves linear to roundish, or bract-like. Example: **CALYPSO ORCHID,** *Calypson bulbosa.*

***Oxalidaceae*, OXALIS FAMILY** (Wood Sorrel Family). Calyx with 5 free sepals, corolla with 5 petals. Clover-like leaves. Example: **REDWOOD SORREL,** *Oxalis oregana.*

***Papaveraceae*, POPPY FAMILY.** Sepals fall off when flower opens; Petals 4 or 6, showy, many stamens, ovary superior. Milky sap, poisonous in some species. Example: **CALIFORNIA POPPY,** *Escholtzia californica.*

***Polemoniaceae*, PHLOX FAMILY.** Calyx with 5 lobes, corolla usually with a tube, expanding into 5-lobed salverform. Petals appear twisted in bud. Stamens 5, ovary superior. Leaf characteristics variable. Example: **GREAT POLEMONIUM,** *Polemonium carneum.*

***Polygonaceae*, BUCKWHEAT FAMILY.** Flowers mostly small, regular; clustered in racemes or umbels. Stem joints generally are swollen, often there are papery sheaths enclosing the stem at the petiole. Example: **WESTERN BISTORT,** *Polygonum bistortoides.*

***Portulacaceae*, PURSLANE FAMILY.** Usually 2 sepals, and mostly 5 petals, 5 stamens, ovary superior. Stems and leaves usually fleshy. Example: **WESTERN SPRING BEAUTY,** *Claytonia siberica.*

***Primulaceae*, PRIMROSE FAMILY.** Corolla with a tube and usually 5 spreading lobes, in a "pinwheel," or shooting star-like. Stamens borne opposite the petals. Somewhat fleshy leaves in basal rosette. Example: **HENDERSON SHOOTING STAR,** *Dodecatheon hendersonii.*

***Ranunculaceae*, BUTTERCUP FAMILY.** Large diverse family. Calyx often looks like a corolla, with 3 to many sepals, petals usually 3, to many. Flowers often regular, but may be irregular, with a spur, as in *Delphinium.* Stamens usually numerous. Ovary superior. Example: **COLUMBIA WINDFLOWER,** *Anemone deltoidea.*

***Rhamnaceae*, BUCKTHORN FAMILY.** Flowers usually in axillary clusters, small, generally with 5 petals, cup-shaped. Leaves generally simple. Example: **BUCKBRUSH,** *Ceanothus cuneatus.*

***Rosaceae*, ROSE FAMILY.** Flowers regular, usually with 5 petals and 5 sepals, and numerous stamens. Flower with cuplike structure bearing stamens, petals, and sepals. Cuplike structure may be free with pistils on raised center (strawberry), or with cuplike structure fused to ovary wall (apple), or with a fleshy wall and stone surrounding the seed (cherry). Leaves usually have stipules. Example: **WESTERN SERVICEBERRY,** *Amelanchier alnifolia.*

***Saxifragaceae*, SAXIFRAGE FAMILY.** Flowers regular, 4 or 5 petals, often very small, 5 or 10 stamens, ovary semi-inferior. Leaves often are palmately lobed, and lack stipules. Example: **HOWELL SAXIFRAGE,** *Saxifraga howellii.*

***Scrophulariaceae*, FIGWORT FAMILY** [Snapdragon Family]. Corollas often tubular, 5-lobed, 2-lipped, generally with 3 lobes on the lower lip. May be a wide tube, either 2-lipped or nearly regular, or a narrow tube with a narrow upper lip. Stigma generally 2-lobed. Ovary superior. Usually 4 stamens, plus 1 sterile stamen (staminode) in *Penstemon.* Example: **SISKIYOU PENSTEMON,** *Penstemon anguineus.*

***Valerianaceae*, VALERIAN FAMILY**. Cauline leaves opposite. Usually, flowers regular, small, tubular with spur, in clusters. Ovary inferior. Example: **ROSY PLECTRITIS,** *Plectritis congesta.*

***Verbenaceae*, VERVAIN FAMILY** [Verbena Family]. Resembles Mint Family [*Lamiaceae*], but without mintlike odor. Leaves opposite, flowers in dense spikes, somewhat 2-lipped. Fruit with 2 or 4 nutlets. Example: **WESTERN VERVAIN,** *Verbena lasiostachys.*

***Violaceae*, VIOLET FAMILY**. Flowers irregular, frequently nodding, 5 petals, usually 2 above, 2 side petals, and a lower lip petal, lower petal often spurred. Stamens 5, ovary semi-inferior. Leaves highly variable. Example: **WEDGE-LEAVED VIOLET,** *Viola cuneata*

Some Good Places for Wildflowers

In the descriptions below, some typical flowers are shown for each location. However, different species bloom at different times, so not all the species listed will be present at the same time. (Note that each photo in this book tells where and when it was taken.)

1. Table Rocks (At each rock, 2-3 mile hike, round trip): Upper and Lower Table Rocks lie north of Medford, via Table Rock Road, beyond the Rogue River. Follow signs. Look for shooting star, desert parsley, scarlet fritillary, buttercup, larkspur, plectritis, blue-eyed mary, pussy ears, camas, hound's tongue, fawn lily, miner's lettuce, and, of course, poison oak. On the top of Lower Table Rock, look for dwarf woolly meadowfoam, goldfields, miniature lupine, and popcorn flower.

2. Grizzly Peak (4 mile hike, round trip): The road that leads to the Grizzly Peak Trail is 2.9 miles on Shale City Road (see below) from Dead Indian Memorial Road, on the left. Some flowers to expect are lupine, windflower, trillium, woodland star, wild ginger, coralroot, tower delphinium, baneberry, stickseed, yellow salsify, bluehead gilia, and sulphur flower.

3. Rainie Falls (4 mile hike, round trip): The trail begins on the south side of the Grave Creek Bridge, which lies about 23 miles from Merlin on the Merlin-Galice Road. In places, the trail consists of narrow rocky ledges that have literally been hacked out of the cliffs. It is not a place for small children. Look for fawn lily, shooting star, spring gold, saxifrage, larkspur, and pink redwood sorrel.

4. Otter Point (1 mile hike, round trip): This state park wayside lies about 3 miles north of Gold Beach, on Old Coast Highway. The short hike to the sea cliffs has flowers such as paintbrush, azalea, sea-thrift, angelica, kinnikinnick, salal, man-root, seaside daisy, beadruby, fairybell, and blue blossum.

5. Mount Ashland and Siskiyou Crest (auto): Follow I-5, south of Ashland, and turn off to the Mount Ashland ski area. The pavement ends at 9.1 miles, and the road becomes one-way. Grouse Gap is about 2 miles further, and the best wildflowers lie in this stretch. Some flowers are lupine, paintbrush, penstemon, stonecrop, owl-clover, bog-orchid, scarlet gilia, marsh marigold, leopard lily, yellow monkeyflower, shooting star, wallflower, coyote mint, yarrow, woolly sunflower, sulphur flower, pussy ears, spreading phlox, blue flax, cow parsnip, balsamroot, columbine, and pussypaws. It is possible to hike short stretches of the Pacific Crest Trail, in this region.

6. Little Hyatt Lake Road (auto): The road begins at Green Springs Summit, east of Ashland, on State Highway 66. It is about 4.5 miles, on gravel road, to the paved road at Hyatt Lake. Some flowers are delphinium, buttercup, paintbrush, cinquefoil, yellow bells, great polemonium, checker lily, slender-tubed iris, Henderson fawn lily, dwarf waterleaf, dwarf hesperochiron, balsamroot, ookow, checkermallow, columbine, death camas, white hyacinth, and woolly sunflower.

7. Shale City Road (auto): Shale City Road is about 7 miles on Dead Indian Memorial Road from Ashland. It makes a ten-mile loop, partly paved, and returns to Dead Indian Memorial Road just on the east side of the crest. Some flowers are trillium, plectritis, Henderson fawn lily, Klamath fawn lily, Washington lily, larkspur, blue-eyed mary, pussy ears, shooting star, dwarf waterleaf, and dwarf hesperochiron.

8. Crater Lake Rim Drive, and Cloudcap (auto): At the park headquarters, take Rim Drive East, to **Castle Crest Wildflower Garden.** The trail is about 1/4 mile long. Some flowers are Lewis monkeyflower, yellow monkeyflower, wandering daisy, white bog-orchid, elephant heads, bleeding hearts, lupine, scarlet gilia, spreading phlox, and sulphur flower. Along the Rim Drive, and at Cloudcap (12 miles from the Headquarters area), look for plants such as pasque flower, pearly everlasting, ballhead ipomopsis, volcanic daisy, lupine, cut leaf daisy, rock cress, penstemon, buckwheat, and knotweed.

Oregon Fawn Lily

WHITE or CREAM-COLORED FLOWERS

Flowers in which the white color appears to dominate are included in this section, even if the flowers sometimes are pinkish, bluish, or greenish. Flowers sometimes start out to be white, but may become pinkish or reddish as they age. Thus, it may upon occasion be necessary to check not only this section, "White or Cream-Colored," but also the sections "Red to Pink," and "Blue to Violet," to find the flower wanted. In the case of **Western Trillium,** the color variations can be so pronounced that it is included *both* in the "White or Cream-colored" section and the "Red to Pink" section.

POISON OAK

Toxicodendron diversilobum [*Rhus diversiloba*]
(Sumac family, *Anacardiaceae*)
(Photo: Limpy Creek, Josephine Co., late May)

Poison Oak (*T. diversilobum*) is widely distributed in western Oregon, and a form of Poison Ivy (*T. rydbergii*) is found in the extreme eastern part of the state. Highly variable, usually a shrub or tree-like, and sometimes as a vine. Leaflets almost always in 3s, with wavy or slightly lobed margins. Leaflets turn an attractive red in the fall. Flowers very small, greenish-white (see photo). **TOXIC. Contact can cause severe dermatitis at any season.**

SEA-WATCH
SEACOAST ANGELICA

Angelica lucida (Carrot family, *Apiaceae*)
(Photo: Otter Point, Curry Co., mid May)

May grow to 5' tall. Stems stout, not hairy. Leaves compound, divided 2 or 3 times in 3s, leaflets more or less oval, 1½"-3" long, toothed, both surfaces green. Flowers small, white, in dense compound umbels, no bracts below main umbel, but conspicuous bractlets, ¼"-½" long, below the umbellets. Coastal bluffs and beaches, to AK and CA. **Henderson Angelica** (*A. hendersonii*), also coastal, is similar, but the bractlets are absent or inconspicuous, and leaflets are whitish and hairy below. **Shining Angelica** (*A. arguta*), found west of Cascades, is similar to *A. hendersonii*, but leaflets are not whitish and hairy below.

BUR-CHERVIL
BEAKED PARSLEY

Anthriscus caucalis [*A. scandicina*]
(Carrot family, *Apiaceae*)
(Photo: Near Shady Cove, Jackson Co., early May)

Plants 20"-36" high, somewhat branched, hairy, leaves up to 6" long, doubly compound, very lacy appearing, final segments 1/16"-3/16" long. Flowers in loose umbel, 3-7 flowered, with a few small, narrow bractlets at the base. Petals 5, tiny, white. Plants are aromatic. Native of Europe. Stream banks and open woods, to CA.

WHITE or CREAM
Apiaceae

WESTERN WATER HEMLOCK
DOUGLAS WATER HEMLOCK

Cicuta douglasii (Carrot family, *Apiaceae*)
(Photo: Lake Tahkenitch, Douglas Co., late July)

Stem stout, often reddish, to 6' high, branched. Leaves compound, mostly twice-pinnate, petioles sheathing, leaflets ½"-6" long, narrow, sharply toothed. Flowers small, white, in compound umbels, rays 1"-3" long. **TOXIC.** Wet areas, to AK and CA. Similar to **Water Parsley** (*Oenanthe sarmentosa*), also **TOXIC,** except in *C. douglasii,* lateral veins on leaflets end at bases of the notches between teeth, instead of at tips. **Poison Hemlock** (*Conium maculatum*), see below, also **TOXIC**, has more finely-divided leaves, and stems with purple blotches.

POISON HEMLOCK

Conium maculatum (Carrot family, *Apiaceae*)
(Photo: Rogue Valley, Jackson Co., late May)

Tall, stout, fleshy stems, up to 10' high, many-branched, stems purple-mottled. Leaves up to 2' long, doubly compound, the final leaflets about ½" long, deeply lobed. Tiny white flowers in compound umbels. **TOXIC;** has been responsible for many human deaths. Widespread, especially in disturbed ground at lower elevations. Native of Europe.

QUEEN ANNE'S LACE
WILD CARROT

Daucus carota (Carrot family, *Apiaceae*)
(Photo: near Susan Creek Falls, Douglas Co., late June)

The name refers to the lacy appearance of the flowers, although the name "Wild Carrot" is older. Plants may be up to 3' high on stout hairy stems. Leaves are twice pinnate, dissected into short narrow lobes. Flowers are in conspicuous umbels 2"-4" across, with narrow leafy bracts below, divided into small umbellets containing the flowers. Flowers are tiny, with 5 white petals that are sometimes pink or purple. As the flower heads age, they become cup-like, resembling a bird's nest. Widespread at lower elevations, especially on roadsides and disturbed places. Introduced from Europe. **American Wild Carrot** (*D. pusillus*), a native plant, differs in being shorter, and having umbels 1" across or less.

COW PARSNIP

Heracleum maximum [*H. lanatum*]
(Carrot family, *Apiaceae*)
(Photo: Humbug Mt. SP, Curry Co., mid May)

Very tall, up to 8' high, with stout, hairy stems. Large compound leaves, each with 3 large leaflets, and inflated petioles sheathing the stems. Leaflets 4"-16" wide, hairy, deeply lobed and toothed, resembling maple leaves. Flowers in large, compound umbels, with 15-30 unequal rays 2"-4" long. Flowers white, very small, < ¼" dia., 5 petals. Moist places, shaded or open, to 8000', to AK and CA.

YAMPA
FALSE CARAWAY

Perideridia sp. (Carrot family, *Apiaceae*)
(Photo: Denman Wildlife Area, Jackson Co., late June)

Tall, up to 3' or 4' high, with slender stems and mostly with grass-like leaflets. Flowers small, white, in compound umbels, usually with 7-16 rays. Widely distributed, open flats, grasslands, pine forest, from BC to CA. **Gairdner Yampa** (*P. gairdnerii*) has mostly pinnate leaves, leaflets linear or nearly so, and fruits about 1/16" long. **Oregon Yampa** (*P. oregana*) is similar, but has 10-30 rays in the umbel, and fruits about 1/8" long. **Howell Yampa** (*P. howellii*) has twice-pinnate leaves, with deeply toothed oval leaflets, leaflets crowded, and 17-20 rays in the umbel.

YARROW
MILFOIL

Achillea millefolium [*A. borealis, A. lanulosa*]
(Sunflower family, *Asteraceae*)
(Photo: Shale City Road, Jackson Co., late May)

Typically 1'-3', but can grow higher; stems and leaves somewhat hairy. Leaves triply compound, highly and finely dissected, reduced in size upward. At first glance, the flowers look like ordinary flowers, in a more or less flat-topped cluster, but each one is composed of both ray flowers and disk flowers. The ray flowers, usually 3 to 8, are typically round, about 1/8" long, white or pink. The disk flowers, 15-40, are tiny, and also are white or pink. Highly variable, once divided into many species, but now considered one species with 85 subspecies. Widespread, in many habitats, from sea level to fairly high elevations.

WHITE or CREAM
Asteraceae

BLOW WIVES

Achyrachaena mollis (Sunflower family, *Asteraceae*)
(Photo: Rogue Valley, Jackson Co., mid May)

Flowers yellow-orange, but tightly closed and inconspicuous. When heads open up and display their spectacular pappus, they appear white, and have been mistaken for white Corn Flowers. Stems 3"-16" high, branching, hairy, with narrow leaves 1"-4" long, entire, clasping, hairy. Flowers originally are enclosed in tight involucres 1/2"-3/4" long, appearing honeycomb-like on the ends. When open, the white, shining oblong pappus scales resemble flower petals, and are in two unequal series of 5 scales each, one set about 5/16" long, the other half as long. Open, dry grasslands west of Cascades, to CA.

PEARLY EVERLASTING

Anaphalis margaritacea
(Sunflower family, *Asteraceae*)
(Photo: Crater Lake NP, near Headquarters, Klamath Co., early August)

Stems rise 8"-36", woolly. Leaves alternate, 2"-3" long, without a stalk, narrow, woolly. Flowers in branched clumps, sometimes congested. Flowers about ¼" dia., with a few yellow disk flowers in center, surrounded by multiple layers of thin, papery, pearly white bracts. Common in open woods and along roadsides, to AK and CA.

DOG FENNEL
MAYWEED
STINKING CHAMOMILE

Anthemus cotula (Sunflower family, *Asteraceae*)
(Photo: Fairy Glen Botanical Park, Butte Falls, Jackson Co., early July)

Stems 10"-20" tall, branched, disagreeable odor. Leaves 1½"-2½" long, dissected into small linear divisions, somewhat lacy. Flowering heads daisy-like, about 1" diameter, 10-15 white ray flowers, rounded or shallowly notched, central disk about ¼" dia. Widespread, fields and roadsides at moderate and low elevations. Native of Europe. **Field Chamomile** (*A. arvensis*) is similar, but lacks the strong disagreeable smell, has 15-20 ray flowers, and leaves are less dissected.

ENGLISH DAISY

Bellis perennis (Sunflower family, *Asteraceae*)
(Photo: Lake in the Woods, Douglas Co., mid June)

English daisies, also called "lawn daisies," are familiar features of lawns. The white flowers are solitary, on short stems, rising above clusters of basal leaves. Leaves spoon-shaped, 1"-2" long, somewhat hairy, scalloped on the edges, petioles about as long as the blades. Flowers 1" or so in diameter, with many thin white rays, often pink-tinged. Native of Europe.

BLEPHARIPAPPUS ROUGH EYELASH

Blepharipappus scaber
(Sunflower family, *Asteraceae*)
(Photo: Near Old Siskiyou Summit, Cascade-Siskiyou NM, Jackson Co., early June)

The scientific name, in Greek, means "eyelash pappus," referring to the eyelash-like fringes on the pappus. Slender stems 3"-16" tall, branched, with thin linear leaves mostly less than 1" long. Flower heads numerous, each terminating a branch, with 2-8 white ray flowers, each 1/8"-5/16" long, deeply 3-lobed, purple-veined underneath. In the center are 6-25 tiny disk flowers with purple anthers. Dry open areas and pine forest, 3000'-9000', east of Cascades and in southwestern OR, to WA and CA.

DUSTY MAIDEN HOARY CHAENACTIS

Chaenactis douglasii [*C. rubricaulis,* in part]
(Sunflower family, *Asteraceae*)
(Photo: Near Star Flat, Josephine Co., late June)

May have several stems 6"-16" tall, reddish in some subspecies, white-woolly below, in others. Leaves less than 6" long, bipinnate, with many short segments, white-woolly. Involucre more or less bell-shaped, about ½" high, bracts narrow and hairy. Flowers all disk-type. Corollas whitish or pinkish, about 5/16" long, stamens generally exserted. Dry open ground, southern Douglas Co. to CA.

FEW-LEAVED THISTLE
WEAK THISTLE

Cirsium remotifolium
(Sunflower family, *Asteraceae*)
(Photo: Odell Lake, Klamath Co., late June)

A native thistle. Stems 1'-5' tall, somewhat hairy, less than ¾" diameter at base, branched, flowering heads 1 to several. Leaves 6"-20" long, lobed, dentate, spiny. Flowers often on long peduncles, with a few bract-like leaves below heads. Involucre hemispheric or bell-shaped, ½"-1½" dia., bracts loosely appressed, many spine-tipped. Flowers all disk-type, about 1" long, white to creamy-white or yellowish (sometimes purple). Grassy areas and forest openings, both sides of Cascades, below 6500 feet.

CUT LEAF DAISY
DWARF MOUNTAIN ERIGERON

Erigeron compositus (Sunflower family, *Asteraceae*)
(Photo: Cloudcap, Crater Lake NP, Klamath Co., mid July)

Flowering stems 2"-10" tall. Leaves crowded, 3/4"-2" long, hairy, 2-3 compound, the leaflets irregularly cut, the upper stem leaves smaller and less incised. Involucre about 5/16" high, hairy, the tips of the bracts purplish and sharp. Rays 30-60 (sometimes none), white to pink or lavender, ¼"-½" long, very narrow. Fairly high elevations in Cascades, to BC and CA.

EATON FLEABANE
EATON DAISY

Erigeron eatonii (Sunflower family, *Asteraceae*)
(Photo: Hyatt Meadows, Jackson Co., early June)

Clustered stems 6"-12" high, sometimes decumbent. Leaves linear, almost grass-like; basal leaves 3"-6" long, slender petioles, stem leaves smaller. Heads on long stems, hairy involucres about 5/16" high. Ray flowers white or light blue, 15-39 in number, less than ½" long. Open grassland or dry woods, east of Cascades. **Meadow Fleabane** (*E. decumbens*) similar, but involucre is less hairy, and stem leaves more numerous.

DAISY FLEABANE
PRAIRIE FLEABANE

Erigeron strigosus (Sunflower family, *Asteraceae*)
(Photo: Near White City, Jackson Co., early June)

Stems erect, 12'-32" high, often branched above, hairy. Leaves 1"-3" long, narrow, mostly entire, upper leaves smaller. Involucre sparsely hairy, with narrow sharp bracts. Rays 60-110, white or sometimes lavender, narrow, less than ¼" long. Open ground, western OR to WA and CA. **Spreading Fleabane** (*E. divergens*), in the sagebrush regions of eastern OR, is 6"-12" tall, has leaves 1"-2" long, and 75-150 very thin rays, white to purple.

WHITE HAWKWEED

Hieracium albiflorum
(Sunflower family, *Asteraceae*)
(Photo: Near Mill Creek CG, Jackson Co., late June)

Stems 20"-48" tall, branching, stems hairy below, hairless above. Leaves 2½"-6" long, the lower leaves more or less oval and pointed, hairy, edges wavy, leaves reduced above. Inflorescence open, with many flowering heads, each composed of 15-20 white ray flowers about 1/4" long, squared and 5-lobed on ends. Dry open woods, to BC and CA.

OXEYE DAISY
COMMON DAISY

Leucanthemum vulgare
(Sunflower family, *Asteraceae*)
(Photo: Port Orford Wetlands, Curry Co., late July)

The latin name *vulgare* means "common," not "vulgar." Stems rise to 20", with leaves that are heavily lobed, lower leaves with long petioles, upper ones with none. Flowers 1¼"- 2¾" dia., the rays white, 20 or so in number. Disk is bright yellow. Common in fields, meadows, and roadsides, at elevations up to 6000 feet. Escaped from cultivation. **Shasta Daisy** (*L. maximum*) is similar, but has larger flowers and leaves that are toothed, rather than lobed.

WESTERN COLTSFOOT
SWEET COLTSFOOT

Petasites frigidus var. *palmatus*
[*P. palmatus, P. speciosus*]
(Sunflower family, *Asteraceae*)
(Photo: Humbug Mtn. SP, Curry Co., late March)

Flowering stems appear first, and the maple-like basal leaves appear later, arising separately from the rootstock, seeming to come from separate plants. Flowering stems stout, to 2' high, with clasping leaves. Basal leaves up to 8" across, cleft into 7-9 divisions, the divisions dentate, on petioles to 8" long. Inflorescence is a dense cluster, with 10-20 small white flowers on slender stems up to 2" long. West of the Cascades, in shady woods, streambanks.

VANILLA LEAF
SWEET-AFTER-DEATH

Achlys triphylla (Barberry family, *Berberidaceae*)
(Photo: National Creek Falls Trail, Jackson Co., early June)

Widespread; often one of the main components of the understory in shady woods, west of the Cascades. Typically, there is a single leaf stalk and a single flowering stalk up to 20" tall, rising together from the root. Flowers tiny and white, crowded together in a spike. Leaf palmately compound, 3 leaflets, each coarsely toothed, one of them generally 3-toothed. The foliage has a sweet smell when dried. **California Vanilla Leaf** (*A. californica*) is similar, but all the leaflets are generally 6 to 8-lobed

NORTHERN INSIDE-OUT FLOWER
WHITE INSIDE-OUT FLOWER

Vancouveria hexandra
(Barberry family, *Berberidaceae*)
(Photo: Limpy Creek Botanical Area, Josephine Co., mid May)

Flowering stems leafless, rising 8"-20". Leaves rise from the base, about half as high as flowering stems, compound, leaflets roundish, often shallowly lobed, 1"-1½" broad. Few-flowered, slender pedicels. Sepals 6, white, about 3/16" long, petals 6, white, shorter than sepals, sepals and petals bent back, then arched outward. Stamens join in a point. Shady forests west of Cascades, to WA and CA. **Redwood Inside-out Flower** (*V. planipetala*), in Curry Co., has much smaller flowers.

ALPINE CRYPTANTHA
WALLOWA CRYPTANTHA

Cryptantha sobolifera [*C. subretusa*]
(Borage family, *Boraginaceae*)
(Photo: Cloudcap, Crater Lake NP, Klamath Co., mid July)

Stems 2"-8" tall, hairy. Leaves ½"-1½" long, lance-shaped to spoon-shaped, sometimes notched, hairy and bristly. Flowering head dense, more or less round. Calyx hairy, corolla tube about 1/8" long, white, 5-lobed, lobes round, about 1/8" across, throat yellow. Dry slopes at high altitudes in the southern Cascades, Wallowas, Steens, and to CA.

CALIFORNIA STICKSEED
CALIFORNIA STICKWEED

Hackelia californica (Borage family, *Boraginaceae*)
(Photo: Near Hyatt Lake, Cascade-Siskiyou NM, Jackson Co., late June)

Stems 16"-36" high, stout, hairy. Leaves more or less lance-shaped, generally pointed, 3"-6" long, somewhat hairy, the upper leaves sessile and partly clasping, smaller than lower. Flowers generally scattered, white, about 1/2" dia., 5 rounded lobes, the yellowish crests in the center prominent. The seeds have hooked prickles, hence the common names. **Greater Showy Stickseed** (*H. bella*) is similar, but the flowers are larger, the calyx lobes are generally more than 1/8" long (1/8" or less, in *H. californica*), and the appendages on the yellowish crests in the center are generally longer than wide, vs. wider than long, in *H. californica.* Open woods in the mountains of Southern OR to CA.

RUSTY POPCORNFLOWER

Plagiobothrys nothofulvus
(Borage family, *Boraginaceae*)
(Photo: Agate Desert Preserve, Jackson Co., late April)

Stems 6"-16" high, with flowers in loose scorpiod coil. Leaves mostly in basal rosette, linear to narrowly oval, 1"-4" long, stem leaves smaller. Stems and leaves somewhat hairy. Flowers white, 5 petals, 3/16"-3/8" broad, yellow at center. Dry open ground west of Cascades, to CA. **Stalked Popcornflower** (*P. stipitatus*) is shorter, lacks basal rosette, and favors vernal pools and other wet sites. There are several other species, most with tiny flowers 1/8" across or less.

SHEPHERD'S PURSE

Capsella bursa-pastoris
(Mustard family, *Brassicaceae*)
(Photo: Beekman Arboretum, Jackson Co., mid April)

Stems 8"-20" high, erect, capped by long racemes, pedicels 3 times as long as the fruit. Leaves mostly basal, clustered or in a rosette, 1½"-4" long, dentate or deeply lobed, stem leaves smaller, clasping. Petals 4, very small, white or pinkish. Fruits heart-shaped, flat, about 2 times as long as wide, shallowly notched at apex. Abundant in disturbed sites, widely distributed. Native of Europe.

MILKMAIDS
TOOTH WORT

Cardamine californica [*Dentaria californica*]
(Mustard family, *Brassicaceae*)
(Photo: Illinois River Canyon, Josephine Co., early March)

One of the earliest of wildflowers. Flowers are in clusters at the tops of stems 6"-15" tall. Stem leaves are alternate and compound, usually with 3 linear leaflets. Leaflets are almost without petioles, typically about 1" long. Flowers have 4 petals, white to pink, each petal about ½" long.

BITTERCRESS

Cardamine sp.
(Mustard family, *Brassicaceae*)
(Photo: Rogue Valley, Jackson Co., early March)

Slender stems up to 12" long. Leaves pinnate, 3-13 leaflets. Flowers have 4 white petals in a cross, each petal ranging from 1/16" to 5/32", depending on species. Fruits are slender, erect. When ripe, the seeds may be scattered explosively. ***Hairy Bittercress*** (*C. hirsuta*) and **Little Western Bittercress** (*C. oligosperma*) resemble each other. Both have basal rosettes of leaves, and the compound leaflets are mostly roundish. In *C. oligosperma,* the stems are few and erect, and the petals are 3/32"-5/32" long. In *C. hirsuta* the outer stems are usually decumbent, the leaflet petioles are hairy, and the petals are about 1/16" long. **Pennsylvania Bittercress** (*C. pensylvanica*) does not have a basal rosette, and the compound leaflets are mostly linear.

HOARY CRESS
WHITE TOP

Cardaria draba (Mustard family, *Brassicaceae*)
(Photo: Near Merrill, Klamath Co., early June)

Stems rise to 20", generally branched, somewhat hairy. Stem leaves oval, entire or slightly toothed, clasping; basal leaves petioled. Flowers in dense racemes, 4 white petals about 1/16" long. Seedpods more or less heart-shaped. Disturbed places, fields, roadsides, especially east of Cascades. Considered a noxious weed; native of Eurasia. This species has been called **Heart-podded Hoary Cress.** Another species, **Lens-podded Hoary Cress** (*C. chalepensis*) is similar, but has roundish seedpods. **Hairy Cress** (*C. pubescens*) has hairy seedpods, and more heavily-toothed leaves.

SPRING WHITLOW GRASS

Draba verna (Mustard family, *Brassicaceae*)
(Photo: Rogue Valley, Jackson Co., early March)

This little plant could be overlooked except, in early spring, the tiny white flowers mass together and make conspicuous white patches in moist open spaces. The plants are only 1"-2" high, and each cluster of 2 or 3 flowers is at the end of a slender stem, sometimes branched. Leaves are all basal and in a rosette perhaps only 1" dia. Each leaf is ½"-¾" long, usually without teeth, sometimes with a few coarse teeth. There are 4 white petals in a cross. Each petal is about 1/8" long, deeply cleft almost half way

SWEET ALYSSUM

Lobularia maritima (Mustard family, *Brassicaceae*)
(Photo: Emigrant Lake, Jackson Co., late April)

Multiple stems, often in clumps, 4"-16" high. Simple leaves, entire, ½"-2" long, about 1/8" wide, tips pointed. Flowers in clusters, white, fragrant, 4 petals about 1/8"-5/16" long, more or less oval-shaped. Waste places at lower elevations. Escaped ornamental, native of Eurasia. ***Small Alyssum*** (*Alyssum alyssoides*), also a native of Eurasia, is generally not as tall, with mostly shorter, rounded, leaves.

WATERCRESS
WHITE WATERCRESS

Rorippa nasturtium-aquaticum
(Mustard family, *Brassicaceae*)
(Photo: Near Fall Creek Falls, Douglas Co., late June.)

Found in slow-moving streams, springs, and lake margins; stems fleshy and sprawling, up to 2' long. Most of the leaves are compound, 3-7 leaflets, 3/8" long or so, but with terminal leaf larger, 1½" long. Flowers are tiny, with 4 white petals, in a cluster, the outer flowers blooming before those in the center. Widespread. Native of Europe.

PERENNIAL PENNYCRESS
WILD CANDYTUFT

Thlaspi montanum
[*T. alpestre, T. fenderli, T. glaucum*]
(Mustard family, *Brassicaceae*)
(Photo: Rough and Ready, Josephine Co., late March)

Stems 5"-15" tall, each with a cluster of white flowers. Basal leaves ½"-1" long, oval-shaped, more or less entire, petioled. Stem leaves less than ¾" long, clasping, entire or shallowly dentate. Flowers white or pinkish, about ½" dia., 4 petals, in clusters. Moderate to low elevations throughout the west. ***Field Pennycress*** (*T. arvense*), a native of Europe, has smaller flowers, larger leaves, and flat round seedpods, more or less shaped like pennies.

FIELD CHICKWEED
MEADOW CHICKWEED

Cerastium arvense (Pink family, *Caryophyllaceae*)
(Photo: Rough and Ready, Josephine Co., early April)

Plants are more or less clump-forming, stems decumbent, and flowering stems rising 4"-12". Leaves opposite, narrow, pointed, entire, 3/8"-1¾" long. Petals white, 5, about 3/8" long, deeply cleft, so deeply that it may appear on first inspection that there are 10 petals. Rocky, grassy places, from AK to CA. ***Common Chickweed*** (*Stellaria media*), a garden pest, and a native of Europe, has long spreading stems that form dense mats; the white petals are about 3/16" long.

STICKY CHICKWEED
STICKY MOUSE-EAR

Cerastium glomeratum [*C. viscosum*]
(Pink family, *Caryophyllaceae*)
(Photo: Near Bandon, Coos Co., early May)

Stems 3"-16", branching, hairy, generally sticky. Leaves opposite, more or less oval, ½"-1" long, somewhat pointed, hairy. Flowers mostly in congested clusters at tops of stems. Calyx hairy, the sepals narrow and pointed, about same length as petals. Petals white, 5, cleft on ends, about ¼" long. Widespread through much of U.S. Introduced from Europe.

DOUGLAS SANDWORT
DOUGLAS STITCHWORT

Minuartia douglasii [*Arenaria douglasii*]
(Pink family, *Caryophyllaceae*)
(Photo: Near Star Flat, Josephine Co., late June)

Slender stems 3"-10" high, branched. Leaves few, more or less thread-like, ½"-1" long, often curled. Sepals 5, about 1/8" long; petals 5, white, rounded or sometimes notched, twice as long as sepals. Dry places, southern counties from Klamath Co. westward, to CA. **Slender Sandwort** (*M. tenella*) similar, but is generally shorter, and petals are less than twice as long as sepals.

BELL-SHAPED CATCHFLY
SLENDER CAMPION
RED MOUNTAIN CATCHFLY

Silene campanulata (Pink family, *Caryophyllaceae*)
(Photo: Near Hyatt Meadows, Jackson Co., early July)

Stems to 16", mostly erect, much branched, hairy and sticky. Leaves generally 2" long, opposite, narrowly ovate, pointed, hairy. Flowers both axillary and terminal, nodding. Calyx about 3/8" long, bell-shaped, with 5 lobes. Petals 5, white to greenish, sometimes pinkish, strongly clawed, spreading, blades lobed 6-8 times into slender lobes. Stamens reach to level of petals, with 3 exserted styles. Coniferous forests, Douglas Co. to CA. **Lemmon Catchfly** (*S. lemmonii*), similar, but calyx tube is cylindric, and the stamens and styles are strongly exserted.

WHITE CAMPION
EVENING LYCHNIS

Silene latifolia [*Lychnis alba*]
(Pink family, *Caryophyllaceae*)
(Photo: Hog Creek Recreation Site, Lower Rogue River, Josephine Co., mid April)

Plants to 3' tall, stout hairy stems. Leaves narrow, to 3" long, lower leaves with petioles, upper ones smaller and without petioles. Flowers have 5 petals, white, deeply bilobed, each petal about 3/8" long, 5 prominently exserted styles. Calyx 1/2"-3/4" long, purple-striped, becoming inflated in later stages. Fields and roadsides. ***Bladder Campion*** (*S. vulgaris*) has much smaller calyxes. ***Night-flowering Catchfly*** (*S. noctiflora*) has 3 styles, not 5. All are native to Europe.

FIELD MORNING GLORY
FIELD BINDWEED

Convolvulus arvensis
(Morning Glory family, *Convolvulaceae*)
(Photo: Near Lake Creek, Jackson Co., late May)

Prostrate and spreading, stems up to 3' long, many-flowered. Leaves mostly arrowhead-shaped, 1"-1½" long, on petioles of about same length. Peduncles slender, 1"-4", with pair of small bracts near middle. Corollas white or pinkish, 5/8"-7/8" long. Widespread in fields and waste ground. Considered a noxious weed. Introduced from Europe. A similar plant, **Hedge Bindweed** *(Calystegia sepium*), a native, has larger flowers, and 2 broad overlapping bracts that conceal the calyx.

DWARF DOGWOOD
BUNCHBERRY

Cornus canadensis (Dogwood family, *Cornaceae*)
(Photo: Odell Lake, Klamath Co., late June)

Stems only 6" high or so, each with whorl of leaves at the top. The showy white "flowers" are actually modified leaves; the true flowers are the greenish-yellow rounded clump at the center. In fall, the plant bears clumps of showy red berries, from which it gets its name "Bunchberry." Moist shady forests at moderate altitudes, where the plants sometimes literally carpet the ground, to AK and CA.

PACIFIC DOGWOOD
WESTERN FLOWERING DOGWOOD

Cornus nuttallii (Dogwood family, *Cornaceae*)
(Photo: Mill Creek Falls Trail, Jackson Co., late May)

(Photo of berries on p. 154.) Small tree, usually less than 40'. One of the best-known trees in our western forests. At moderate elevations west of the Cascades, from BC to CA, the white flowers illuminate the woods in May. In fall, the rosy leaves do the same, when the sunlight falls on them. The true flowers are not the bright white "petals" that are so highly visible: these are modified leaves called "bracts." The flowers are the clustered yellow balls at the centers, that turn into clumps of red berries in fall.

RED OSIER DOGWOOD
CREEK DOGWOOD
AMERICAN DOGWOOD

Cornus sericea [*C. stolonifera*]
(Dogwood family, *Cornaceae*)
(Photo: Near Salt Creek Falls, Lane Co., late June)

Large shrub, to 12' tall, younger branches dark red. Leaves 2"-4" long, more or less elliptic, pointed, strongly veined. Flowers with 4 white petals about 1/8" long, narrow and pointed, in a dense somewhat flat-topped cyme. Highly variable, intergrading among subspecies. Moist ground, both sides of Cascades, to AK and CA. **Brown Dogwood** (*C. glabrata*) is similar, but has leaves about 1"-2" long.

OREGON WILD CUCUMBER
COAST MAN-ROOT
OLD-MAN-IN-THE-GROUND

Marah oreganus (Gourd family, *Cucurbitaceae*)
(Photo: Harris Beach SP, Curry Co., mid May)

Trailing stems to 30' long, from large roots (hence, "Man-Root"). Leaves 3"-6" across, lobed, resembling maple leaves. Staminate and pistillate flowers usually on same plant, small, petals united into a tube, 5-lobed, the staminate flowers whitish and the pistillate greenish. Staminate flowers are in a raceme with peduncles 4"-16" long; pistillate flowers solitary, usually arising from same axil as staminate. Fruit oval, 2"-3" long, somewhat spiny. Common, west of Cascades, to BC and CA.

PACIFIC MADRONE

Arbutus menziesii (Heath family, *Ericaceae*)
(Photo: Fish Hatchery Park, Josephine Co., early April)

Madrone trees have smooth reddish-brown branches, glossy evergreen leaves, and lovely white flowers in spring. Trees can be 30' or more tall, with spreading branches, often with the rough outer bark scaling off to show the satiny reddish skin. Leaves are 3"-5" long, thick and leathery, dark green above, lighter below. Flowers are urn-shaped, about ¼" long, white or creamy, in large clusters. In fall, the trees bear orange-red berries, eagerly sought by birds. Open woods west of the Cascades.

PACIFIC LABRADOR TEA
TRAPPER'S TEA

Ledum glandulosum (Heath family, *Ericaceae*)
(Photo: Near O'Brien, Josephine Co., late May)

Small shrub, to 3' tall, usually with leaves clustered at ends of branches. Leaves narrowly elliptic, ¾"-2¼" long, dark green above, lighter colored and somewhat scurfy-looking beneath. Flowers 3/8"-1/2" across, in more or less flat-topped clusters, 15-30 to a cluster, mostly at ends of branches, white to pinkish-white, 5 petals, 10 stamens. Leaves are **TOXIC.** Wet locations along coast and in mountains, to WA and CA.

SIERRA LAUREL
WESTERN LEUCOTHOE

Leucothoe davisiae (Heath family, *Ericaceae*)
(Photo: Near Cedar Mountain, Josephine Co., early July)

Small shrub, to 4' high. Leaves 5/8"-3" long, elliptic, stiff, entire or slightly toothed. Flowers on very short pedicels, urn-shaped, white, about ¼" long, narrowed to the opening, in showy clusters up to 6" long, densely-flowered. Damp ground at moderate elevations, southern Curry and Josephine Cos., to CA.

WHITE-VEINED WINTERGREEN
Pyrola picta (Heath family, *Ericaceae*)
(Photo: Wagner Creek Road, Jackson Co., early July)

Stems leafless, dark red, rising 6"-12". Leaves in basal rosette, spoon-shaped, 1½"-2½" long, with conspicuous white-bordered veins. Flowers about ½" across, bowl-shaped, 5 waxy petals, whitish or pink, long style, curved and bent to one side, extending beyond corolla. Dry forests at middle elevations, Canada to CA. Plants without basal leaves living off decayed vegetation have been called **Leafless Pyrola** (*P. picta* var. *aphylla*). **Pink Wintergreen** *(P. asarifolia*) taller, has pink or red flowers, lacks white veins in the leaves. In **Lesser Wintergreen** (*P. minor*), the style does not extend beyond the corolla.

MILKVETCH
ROGUE RIVER LOCOWEED
Astragalus accidens (Legume family, *Fabaceae*)
(Photo: Gin Lin Trailhead, Jackson Co., early April)

More or less bushy, to 2' high. Leaves without tendrils at the ends, pinnately compound, 15-29 leaflets, leaflets ¼" to 1" long, oblong, tip generally notched. Flower clusters on long peduncles, 7-15 flowers. Petals whitish, about 5/8" long, banner petal curved upward. Seedpods 1/2"-3/4" long, reflexed. Shrubland, open woodland, Douglas Co. to CA. **California Milkvetch** (*A. californicus*) differs in having 10-30 flowers in a cluster; seedpods are 1"-1½" long, pendulous or spreading. **Curvepod Milkvetch** (*A. curvicarpus*) has dense clusters of reflexed flowers, 13-17 leaflets, and seedpods 1"-1½" long, strongly curved, sometimes almost in a full circle.

SICKLE-KEELED LUPINE
PINE LUPINE
Lupinus albicaulis (Legume family, *Fabaceae*)
(Photo: Near Gold Ray Dam, Jackson Co., late May)

Stems clustered, stout, hairy, 20"-48". Leaflets 6-9, 1¼"-2½" long, tiny points on ends, hairy, petioles about same length as leaflets. Raceme 4"-12" long, calyx hairy. Corolla about ½" long, dirty white to bluish, banner petal narrow and sharp, keel strongly bent upward, exposed, tip not covered. Western OR to WA and CA. **Anderson Lupine** (***L.*** *andersonii*) similar, keel not as strongly bent, stems more slender. Leiberg's **Lupine** (*L. subvexus*), east of Cascades, has white or lilac flowers in distinct whorls, keel is moderately curved, and tip of keel is covered.

WHITE SWEET-CLOVER

Melilotus alba (Legume family, *Fabaceae*)
(Photo: Rogue Valley, Jackson Co., mid March)

Very leafy, with erect, branching stems, as much as 6' tall. Leaves palmate, in 3's, clover-like, each leaflet about 1" long, edges somewhat toothed. Flowers pea-like, white, in loose spike-like raceme, each corolla 1/8"-3/16" long. Sometimes abundant, in open disturbed locations. Native of Eurasia. (See also, ***Yellow Sweet-Clover***, p. 63.)

FOREST SCURFPEA
CALIFORNIA TEA

Rupertia physodes [*Psoralea physodes*]
(Legume family, *Fabaceae*)
(Photo: Briggs Valley Road, Josephine Co., late June)

Stems spreading, 12"-30" long, stout, not hairy. Leaves more or less oval, sharp pointed, 1½"-2½" long, in 3s. Flowers on long peduncles, in short dense clusters. Calyx more or less bell-shaped, 5/16" long, corolla tubular, about twice as long, yellowish-white, with small banner petal curved up. Open woods and thickets, mostly west of Cascades, to WA and CA.

WOOLLY-HEADED CLOVER

Trifolium eriocephalum (Legume family, *Fabaceae*)
(Photo: Old Siskiyou Highway, Cascade-Siskiyou NM, Jackson Co., early May)

A striking thing about this clover is the way the corollas droop downward. Stems 8"-16" high, somewhat hairy. Leaflets in 3s, up to 1½" long, narrow, slightly toothed, pointed, hairy. Calyx short, with feathery teeth; corolla dull white or yellowish, about ½" long. Moist meadows or dry, open slopes, up to 4900 feet. **King's Clover** (*T. kingii* var. *productum*) is similar, but end of flowering stem projects beyond flower head, leaves not hairy, and calyx-teeth not feathery.

WHITE CLOVER
WHITE LAWN CLOVER

Trifolium repens (Legume family, *Fabaceae*)
(Photo: Rogue Valley, Jackson Co., late March)

A familiar clover, because it invades lawns, although also found in meadows. Sprawling stems may be 15 inches long. Leaves with 3 leaflets rise on long petioles. Some leaflets have whitish patches. Many tiny white flowers, each only ½" long or so, gather in a globe-shaped head about 1" dia., borne on long stem. Flowers on lower side of head become sharply bent down with age, and the globular head lacks papery bracts below. Abundant throughout the region. Introduced from Europe.

RICHARDSON GERANIUM

Geranium richardsonii
(Geranium family, *Gerianiaceae*)
(Photo: Near Mt. Ashland, Jackson Co., early August)

Stems 16"-32" high, hairy, sticky. Leaves 3"-5" broad, deeply 5-cleft, the lobes sharply incised, petioles 4"-20". Petals 5, 1/2"-5/8" long, white with reddish veins, tapered to the base, the base hairy. Moist meadows, primarily in the Cascades, to Canada and CA.

STICKY CURRANT

Ribes viscosissimum
(Gooseberry family, *Grossulariaceae*)
(Photo: Grizzly Peak Trail, Jackson Co., mid June)

Shrub, to 5' high, no spines. Leaves 1½"-3" dia., with 3-5 wavy, toothed lobes. Leaves and petioles are hairy and sticky. Flower is also sticky, with conspicuous hollow calyx, dull white or pink-tinged, in a tube about ½" long that spreads into lobes resembling petals, about ½" across. True petals are inside the lobes of the calyx, white, about 1/8" long. Woods at middle altitudes in the Cascades, to CA. **Wax Currant** (*R. cereum*), found east of the Cascades and in the Siskiyous, has smaller leaves, is not as sticky, and has tubular flowers.

WILD MOCK ORANGE
LEWIS MOCK ORANGE

Philadelphus lewisii
(Hydrangea family, *Hydrangeaceae*)
(Photo: Gold Ray Rd., Jackson Co., late May)

Erect shrub, much branched, to 8' tall. Leaves more or less elliptic, 1½"-3" long, pointed, somewhat dentate, slightly hairy below and on edges. Flowers in loose clusters, calyx about 3/16" long, lobes pointed, petals 4 or 5, white, oblong and rounded on ends. Many stamens, well exserted. Thickets, especially near streams, east of Cascades and in southwest OR, to BC and CA.

WHIPPLEVINE
YERBA DE SELVA
MODESTY

Whipplea modesta
(Hydrangea family, *Hydrangeaceae*)
(Photo: Copeland Creek Road, Douglas Co., mid May)

Long, trailing, slender stems, somewhat woody, forming dense low mats, the flowers rising above. Leaves opposite, oval, numerous, hairy, ½"-1½" long. Flowers in small dense clusters at the tops of stems about 3" long. Petals 5, white, about 1/8" long, stamens 8-12, rising above the petals, styles 4-5. Dry open woods, western OR, to WA and CA.

YERBA SANTA

Eriodictyon californicum
(Waterleaf family, *Hydrophyllaceae*)
(Photo: Briggs Valley Rd., Josephine Co., early June)

Shrub, 3'-9' tall, leaves narrow, 1½"-6" long, entire to toothed, short-petioled, somewhat hairy, light-colored below. Flowers in open clusters, corollas cylindric, white to light bluish, with 5 spreading roundish lobes, calyxes about 1/8" long, with 5 sharp lobes. Stamens partially fused with petals. Dry fields, roadsides, woodlands, to 6000', southern Josephine and Jackson Cos., to CA.

DWARF HESPEROCHIRON

Hesperochiron pumilus
(Waterleaf family, *Hydrophyllaceae*)
(Photo: Hyatt Lake, Jackson Co., early May)

Rises only a couple of inches above the ground. The leaves are 1"-2" long, with long petioles, and are spoon-shaped. The flowers are on short stems, about 1" dia. The 5 united petals are in a "wheel-shaped" form, white or bluish, yellow centers and faint dark veins. Generally east of the Cascade crest. **California Hesperochiron** (*H. californicus*), is similar, but the flowers are bell-shaped or funnel-shaped rather than wheel-shaped, and the leaves are somewhat hairy.

FENDLER WATERLEAF

Hydrophyllum fendleri var. *albifrons*
(Waterleaf family, *Hydrophyllaceae*)
(Photo: Wrangle Camp, Jackson Co., early July)

Stems 1'-3' tall, erect, hairy. Leaves compound, 2½"-12" long, petioles to 7" long, 7-15 leaflets, deeply lobed, teeth 4-8 per side, sharp-pointed. Flowers bell-shaped, ¼"-½" long, 5-lobed, white or purplish, in loose clusters. Stamens 5, projecting far beyond petals. Moist wooded slopes, 3600 to 6600 feet elevation. **California Waterleaf** (*H. occidentale*) is similar, but the flowers are in dense clusters, and the leaflets have 2-4 teeth per side, not as sharp-pointed. **Pacific Waterleaf** (*H. tenuipes*) has 3-5 coarsely toothed leaflets, and flowers are cream, greenish, or purplish, in loose clusters.

PALE BABY BLUE-EYES

Nemophila menziesii var. *atomaria*
(Waterleaf family, *Hydrophyllaceae*)
(Photo: Bandon SP, Coos Co., late March)

Even though it is called "Baby Blue-eyes," this variety is white, and forms large patches in meadows and lawns. Stems decumbent, fleshy, and somewhat hairy. Leaves fleshy, pinnately parted, 5-9 segments, segments oblong. The flowers, rising 2"-3", are up to 1" dia., with 5 petals, slightly notched, white to bluish-tinged, spotted inside. Moist fields and open woods, west of Cascades, to CA. Flowers of the main species, *N. menziesii,* with blue petals and white centers, also occur. Three other species have flowers that are only about 5/32" long, and are difficult to separate: **Small Baby Blue Eyes** (*N. heterophylla*), **Littlefoot Nemophila** (*N. pedunculata*), and **Smallflower Nemophila** (*N. parviflora*).

MOUNTAIN PHACELIA
SILVERLEAF PHACELIA
COMPACT PHACELIA

Phacelia hastata subsp. *compacta* [*P. frigida*]
(Waterleaf family, *Hydrophyllaceae*)
(Photo: Cloudcap, Crater Lake NP, Klamath Co., mid July)

Stems 3"-8", often decumbent, strongly hairy. Leaves more or less elliptic, pointed, usually entire, ½"-1" long, hairy. Flowering head usually a rounded cluster. Corolla about 1/4" long, more or less bell-shaped, white to lavender, 5 lobes, rounded, stamens exserted, somewhat hairy, style exserted, 2-cleft. Subalpine areas in Cascades, to CA.

VARILEAF PHACELIA

Phacelia heterophylla
(Waterleaf family, *Hydrophyllaceae*)
(Photo: Lower Rogue River, Josephine Co., mid April)

Stems, fleshy and hairy, range in height from 1'-3', from a thick mass of leaves. Leaves variable, simple to compound, greenish-grayish. Compound leaves may have 3-5 leaflets, terminal leaf largest, leaflets sometimes partially uniting. The coiled clusters have many flowers, corollas white or pale lavender, 5 petals, each about 5/16" dia. Dry woods and rocky places, to WA and CA.

SLENDER-TUBED IRIS
YELLOW-LEAVED IRIS

Iris chrysophylla (Iris family, *Iridaceae*)
(Photo: Flumet Flat CG, Josephine Co., late April)

Stems to 8" high, with long slender light green basal leaves 4"-16" long. Flowers usually solitary, perianth parts 1½"-2" long, yellowish-white or whitish (sometimes pale lilac), veined reddish-brown. Floral tube 1½"-3" long above the ovary, very slender. Open woods west of Cascades, to CA.

HOWELL MARIPOSA LILY
HOWELL MARIPOSA TULIP

Calochortus howellii (Lily family, *Liliaceae*)
(Photo: Illinois River Road, Josephine Co., late June)

Stems erect, slender, 12"-18" tall. A single basal leaf, about same length as inflorescence, ¼"-½" wide, narrow bract on stem 1"-2" long. Flowers 1 or 2, on pedicels 2"-4" long. Petals 3, cream-colored or slightly greenish, large, rounded, about 1" long, with 3 sharp sepals below, about 3/4" long. Dry grassy slopes, Umpqua Valley to southern Josephine Co.

TOLMIE'S PUSSY EARS
OREGON MARIPOSA LILY

Calochortus tolmiei (Lily family, *Liliaceae*)
(Photo: Near Lost Creek Lake, Jackson Co., mid May)

Stems short, 4"-6", with 1-4 flowers. One narrow leaf, usually longer than flower stem. Flowers have 3 broad petals, creamy white to lilac, opening into a bowl, heavily fringed with hairs inside and on edges. Three sharp sepals are conspicuous, alternating with the petals. Dry grassy slopes, open woodland, at low to moderate elevations, to WA and CA. **Elegant Mariposa Lily** (*C. elegans*), is similar, but the flowers are about half as large.

QUEEN CUP
BEAD LILY

Clintonia uniflora (Lily family, *Liliaceae*)
(Photo: Odell Lake, Klamath Co., mid June)

There is hardly a more charming little flower in the forest. Two or three oblong green leaves lie at the base of a flower stalk that rises perhaps 6"- 8". Usually just 1 white flower, 1"-1½" dia. Damp shady forests at moderate altitudes, to AK and CA.

SMITH FAIRYBELL
LARGE-FLOWERED FAIRY BELLS
FAIRY LANTERNS

Disporum smithii [*Prosartes smithii*]
(Lily family, *Liliaceae*)
(Photo: Lower Rogue River near coast, Curry Co., mid May)

Stem 1'-3' long, leaves alternate, sessile, 2"-4" long, more or less oval, pointed. Flowers 2-5, white, ¾"-1" long, cylindric, perianth parts spreading slightly at tips, stamens not projecting. Moist woods along coast and west of Cascades, to BC and CA. **Hooker Fairybell** (*D. hookeri*) similar, but has smaller, bell-shaped flowers, perianth parts narrower, spreading from middle, stamens projecting.

KLAMATH FAWN LILY

Erythronium klamathense (Lily family, *Liliaceae*)
(Photo: Lily Glen, Jackson Co., early May)

Looks like a miniature version of its larger cousins such as Cream-colored Fawn Lily, which grows at lower elevations. Plants 6"-7" high, narrow leaves 4"-5" long, not mottled. Usually is only 1 flower, but may be more. Perianth parts are typically less than 1" long, narrow, the outer half (or more) white, and the basal part yellow. Anthers are yellow, and stigma is unlobed. Jackson, Klamath, and Douglas counties, to CA, at elevations generally above 4000 feet.

OREGON FAWN LILY
WHITE FAWN LILY
OREGON TROUT LILY

Erythronium oregonum (Lily family, *Liliaceae*)
(Photo: King Mountain, Josephine Co., late May)

Typically, 2 heavily mottled leaves, stem 4"-18" high, usually 1 flower, but sometimes more. Perianth parts white, strongly curved backward, yellow at the base, sometimes with a band of brownish purple. Anthers yellow, sometimes maroon, stigma deeply divided at the end into 3 lobes. Woods west of the Cascades, to WA and CA. **Cream-colored Fawn Lily** (*E. citrinum*), found in southern Josephine Co., is similar, but has a stigma that is nearly entire and only shallowly lobed.

SERPENTINE RUSH-LILY
SISKIYOU HASTINGSIA

Hastingsia serpentinicola
(Lily family, *Liliaceae*)
(Photo: 8 Dollar Road, Josephine Co., mid May)

Flowers on leafless stems 11"-20" high, basal leaves to 14" long, narrow. Whitish to greenish flowers, in terminal spikes, 6 perianth parts, less than 1/8" long, stamens projecting beyond corolla. Moist meadows, generally with serpentine, in southern Josephine Co. to CA. A similar species, **White-flowered Rush-Lily** (*H. alba*), has perianth parts about 1/4" long, and stamens do not project beyond corolla. **Large-flowered Rush-Lily** (*H. bracteosa*) has perianth parts nearly 1/2" long, and stamens are well below the corolla.

WASHINGTON LILY

Lilium washingtonium (Lily family, *Liliaceae*)
(Photo: Westside Road, Klamath Co., early July)

One of our more beautiful lilies, especially because it tends to rise from dry clumps of brush, appearing out of place. White flowers (turning purplish with age) are at the top of a stout stem up to 4'-5' high, with leaves in whorls. Sometimes may be as many as 20 flowers in a clump. Narrow flower segments are dotted with purple, and may be 3"-4" long, curving backward at the tip. Yellow anthers project prominently beyond corolla. Found on both sides of the Cascades, and in the Siskiyous, to CA.

FALSE LILY OF THE VALLEY
BEADRUBY

Maianthemum dilatatum
[*M. bifolium* var. *kamtschaticum*]
(Lily family, *Liliaceae*)
(Photo: Otter Point SP, Curry Co., mid May)

Often forms extensive ground carpets in shaded locations, the flowering stems rising to 12". Leaves generally 2, alternate, glossy, 2"-5" long, parallel-veined, triangular, heart-shaped at base, often tapering to long points. Many small white flowers on spikes 1"-2" long, perianth-parts in 4s instead of the 3s or 6s that are usually the case in the Lily family. Berries greenish with red spots, ultimately turning red. Shady moist woods at lower elevations west of Cascades, to AK and CA.

FALSE SOLOMON'S SEAL
WESTERN SOLOMON PLUME

Smilacina racemosa
[*S. amplexicaulis, Maianthemum racemosum*]
(Lily family, *Liliaceae*)
(Photo: Near Hyatt Meadows, Jackson Co., early June)

Stems rising to 3' and more. Leaves 3"-8", broad and pointed, clasping, or with very short petioles. Flowers white, in dense terminal clusters, perianth parts about 1/8" long, stamens longer than perianth parts, the filaments broad and flat. Shady woods, both sides of Cascades, to BC and CA.

FEW-FLOWERED FALSE SOLOMON'S SEAL
STARRY FALSE LILY OF THE VALLEY
STARRY SOLOMON PLUME

Smilacina stellata
[*S. sessilifolia, Maienthemum stellatum*]
(Lily family, *Liliaceae*)
(Photo: Wood River Day-Use Area, Klamath Co., late May)

Long stems, up to 2' long, often with zig-zag pattern. Leaves more or less elliptic, 2"-6" long, pointed, sessile, clasping. Small white flowers in loose racemes 1"-3" long, with 6 narrow perianth parts, each about 3/16" long. Moist shade, streambanks, open slopes, western OR, to BC and CA.

GIANT TRILLIUM
GIANT WAKE-ROBIN

Trillium albidum (Lily family, *Liliaceae*)
(Photo: Beekman Arboretum Trail, Jackson Co., late April)

Differs from Western Trillium (*T. ovatum*) primarily because the flowers in Western Trillum are on top of a fairly long stem rising above the whorl of leaves, whereas in Giant Trillium the flowers arise directly from the leaves. Petals usually light greenish yellow, although can also be reddish or nearly white. The large green leaves may have purple mottling. Damp woods west of Cascades, to WA and CA. **Giant Purple Wake-robin** (*T. kurabayashi*) occurs in Curry Co., is similar in structure, but has dark maroon-red flowers.

WESTERN TRILLIUM
WESTERN WAKE-ROBIN

Trillium ovatum (Lily family, *Liliaceae*)
(Photo: Near Fourmile Lake, Klamath Co., late June)

Stems rise 6"-18", each bearing whorl of 3 leaves at summit, and a single flower. Leaves without petioles, 3"-6" long. Flower on stem 1"-2½" long, with 3 green sepals and 3 white petals, 6 stamens. Sepals ¾"-2" in length, petals somewhat larger. Petals white or pink. (See, also, p. 100.) Moist woods at moderate elevations, to BC and CA.

BROOK TRILLIUM
BROOK WAKE-ROBIN

Trillium rivale (Lily family, *Liliaceae*)
(Photo: Illinois River Canyon, Josephine Co., early March)

Resembles Western Trillium (*T. ovatum*), but differs in being only about half the size (less than 6" tall, leaves about 2" long). Petals white, about 1" long, generally purple-spotted within. A major difference from *T. ovatum* is that the leaves have distinct petioles, whereas in *T. ovatum* the leaves generally lack petioles. Usually along rocky streambanks, in southern Josephine and Curry Cos., to CA.

HENDERSON TRITELEIA
HENDERSON STARS
HENDERSON BRODIAEA

Triteleia hendersonii [*Brodiaea hendersonii*]
(Lily family, *Liliaceae*)
(Photo: Pilot Rock Road, Cascade-Siskiyou NM, Jackson Co., early June)

Stems leafless, basal leaves 4"-20" long, narrow, stems about same length as leaves. Flowers 4-15, in umbel, with slender spreading pedicels 3/4"-1½" long. Perianth united at base, more or less bell-shaped, about 3/4" long, 6 lobes spreading, whitish or pale yellow, with violet median stripes. Stamen filaments thin, widening at base. Open slopes, from Umpqua Valley to CA. **Pretty Face** (*T. ixioides*) is similar, but has yellower flowers, and the stamens are broad, with wings that often extend past the anthers.

WHITE BRODIAEA
WHITE HYACINTH
WHITE CLUSTER-LILY
FOOL'S ONION

Triteleia hyacinthina [*Brodiaea hyacinthina*]
(Lily family, *Liliaceae*)
(Photo: Agate Desert Preserve, Jackson Co., late April)

Flowers on long leafless stalks 12"-28" high, with 2-3 narrow basal leaves to 16" long, often withering by flowering time. Many flowers in umbel-like cluster, each on stem ½"-1" long, perianth parts white, about 3/8" long, greenish midveins, shallowly bowl-shaped, 6 stamens about 1/8" long, wider at base than at top. Grassland, vernal pools, widely distributed, to BC and CA.

CALIFORNIA FALSE HELLEBORE
CALIFORNIA CORN LILY

Veratrum californicum (Lily family, *Liliaceae*)
(Photo: Near Hyatt Lake, Jackson Co., early July)

Tall and leafy, to 6', with dense, pyramidal flower spikes. Sometimes erroneously called "skunk cabbage." Leaves 10"-12" long, about 6" wide, smooth and sharp-pointed. Flower spikes 8"-20" long, flowering branches ascending, perianth parts 6, greenish-white, oval, mostly about ½" long. Wet meadows at moderate altitudes, to WA and CA. Two similar species are: **Green False Hellebore** (*V. viride*), greenish flowers, the lower flowering branches drooping; **Siskiyou False hellebore** (*V. insolitum*), perianth parts fringed. All species are **TOXIC.**

BEARGRASS
BASKET-GRASS

Xerophyllum tenax (Lily family, *Liliaceae*)
(Photo: Wagner Gap Rd., Jackson Co., early July)

Instantly recognizable, reminding some of Pampus Grass, although on a smaller scale. A given plant may not bloom every year. Stems 3'-5' high, rising from dense clumps of wiry grass-like leaves. Flower clusters may contain hundreds of small creamy white flowers. Typically grows in open woods or on bare slopes, at moderately high elevations in the Cascades and Siskiyous, to BC and CA.

MEADOW DEATH CAMAS
POISON CAMAS

Zigadenus venenosus (Lily family, *Liliaceae*)
(Photo: Shale City Road, Jackson Co., late May)

Tall, slender stems, 1'-2' high. Leaves mostly basal, about as long as stems, about ¼" wide, 1-2 smaller stem leaves. Creamy white flowers in a loose spike, pedicels typically less than 1" long. Perianth parts 6, typically oval, less than ¼" long; stamens 6, about same length as perianth parts. Both sides of Cascades, to 8000', to BC and CA. **Small-flowered Zigadenus** (*Z. micranthus*) has slightly smaller flowers, and longer pedicels. **Fremont Star Lily** (*Z. fremontii*) has larger flowers and stamens about ½ the length of the perianth parts. All are **TOXIC.**

WOOLLY MEADOWFOAM

Limnanthes floccosa
(Meadowfoam family, *Limnanthaceae*)
(Photo: Agate Desert Preserve, Jackson Co., late March)

Stems 2"-4" high, rather fleshy, leaves segmented, 1/2"-3/4" long exclusive of the long petioles, the segments linear, about 1/4" long. Flowers solitary on long peduncles, 5 petals, the petals 1/4"-5/16" long, sepals about the same. Calyx loosely woolly. Gravelly flats, Rogue Valley and southward to CA. Subspecies *L. f.* ssp. *grandiflora* (shown in photo) is **Federally classified endangered. Dwarf Woolly Meadowfoam,** *L. f.* ssp. *pumila,* found only on Table Rocks, Jackson Co., is shorter, leaves longer, and is **State classified threatened. Douglas Meadowfoam** (*L. douglasii*) occurs from the Umpqua Valley southward, is yellow at the base of the petals, and leaves have 5-9 leaflets, which are 5-9 parted.

PHANTOM ORCHID

Cephalanthera austiniae [*Eburophyton austiniae*]
(Orchid family, *Orchidaceae*)
(Photo: Near Chinquapin Mt., Jackson Co., early July)

Plant white, without chlorophyll, on slender stem 8"-20" high, becoming yellowish or brown. Leaves scale-like, 1"-2" long, Flowering spike 3"-8" long, the perianth-parts 1/2"-5/8" long, a dilated lip in the center about half as long, with a yellow spot. Shady coniferous woods at moderate altitudes, to WA and CA.

WESTERN RATTLESNAKE PLANTAIN
RATTLESNAKE ORCHID

Goodyera oblongifolia
(Orchid family, *Orchidaceae*)
(Photo: Tub Springs Wayside, Jackson Co., early August)

Stems 7"-14" high, leafless. All leaves in flat basal rosette, each 1½"-2½" long, dark green, with white mottling down the center that resembles the pattern on a rattlesnake skin. Flowers about 5/16" long, greenish-white, in a dense spike, each with white hood arching over. Shady woods, western OR to BC and CA.

ROYAL REIN-ORCHID
MOUNTAIN PIPERIA

Piperia transversa (Orchid family, *Orchidaceae*)
(Photo: Whiskey Springs CG, Jackson Co., early July)

Slender stemmed, 6"-20" high, stem leaves bract-like, basal leaves few, broad. Flower spikes may be open or dense, the sepals and lateral petals white to yellowish, lower lip white, spur 1/4"-3/8" long, more or less straight, perpendicular to stem axis. Differs from Bog-Orchids in that it is usually found in dry forests or shrub-land, rather than in boggy sites, to fairly high elevations, to BC and CA. **Alaska Rein-Orchid** (*P. unalascensis*) has green flowers, and spur is shorter. In **Elegant Rein-Orchid** (*P. elegans*) the spur is long, curved, and parallel to stem axis.

WHITE BOG-ORCHID
WHITE REIN-ORCHID
BOG-CANDLE

Platanthera dilatata [*Habenaria dilatata*]
(Orchid family, *Orchidaceae*)
(Photo: Spring Creek, Collier Memorial SP, Klamath Co., late June)

Slender stems, 1'-4' high, leaves narrow, pointed, 3"-8" long, reduced upward. Flowers in dense spikes, white, upper sepals oval, lateral petals lance-shaped, lower lip 1/4"-3/8" long, spur curved, about as long as lip. Wet places, western OR to BC and CA. **Sierra Bog-Orchid** (*P. leucostachys*) has long spur, much longer than lip. **Sparse-flowered Bog-Orchid** (*P. sparsiflora*) has a more open flowering spike, and flowers are green.

BALLHEAD IPOMOPSIS
BALLHEAD GILIA
DENSELY-FLOWERED GILIA

Ipomopsis congesta [*Gilia congesta*]
(Phlox family, *Polemoniaceae*)
(Photo: Cloudcap, Crater Lake NP, Klamath Co., mid July)

Often several stems, 4"-8" high, hairy. Leaves about ½" long, palmately parted into 3-7 linear segments. Flowers in dense clusters, calyxes about 3/16" long, pointed lobes, hairy. Corolla tubes about as long as the calyxes, 5 rounded lobes, white, about 3/32" long. Dry areas, often alpine, east of Cascades and in Siskiyous, to WA and CA.

NAVARRETIA

Navarretia sp.
(Phlox family, *Polemoniaceae*)
(Photo: Agate Desert Preserve, Jackson Co., late April)

Low-growing, stems generally spreading, flowers in terminal bunches, together with needle-like bracts. Leaves bipinnately divided, with needle-like segments. Corollas generally white, light blue, or pink, generally 5-lobed, mostly about 1/4"-3/8" long. **Mountain Navarretia** (*N. divaricata*) has branches that often are partly naked, flowers with stamens well included. **Needle-leaved Navarretia** (*N. intertexta*) has branches that are ascending to nearly erect, leaf segments sharp, flowers with stamens and style unequally exserted. **White-flower Navarretia** (*N. leucocephala*) generally has flaccid leaves, flowers with stamens and style long-exserted.

GREAT POLEMONIUM
ROYAL JACOB'S LADDER
SALMON POLEMONIUM

Polemonium carneum
(Phlox family, *Polemoniaceae*)
(Photo: Pilot Rock Road, Cascade-Siskiyou NM, Jackson Co., early June)

Stems erect, 8"-18" high. Leaves pinnately compound, 3"-5" long, 11-19 leaflets, narrow, pointed. (Called "Jacob's Ladder" because of the leaves.) Flowers in loose clusters, corollas cream-colored, pinkish, or bluish, about ¾" long, 5 petals, spreading. Stamens and style project beyond corolla. Grassy openings and moist shade in Cascades and Coast Range, to WA and CA.

NORTHERN BUCKWHEAT
ARROWLEAF ERIOGONUM

Eriogonum compositum
(Buckwheat family, *Polygonaceae*)
(Photo: Near Old Siskiyou Summit, Jackson Co., early June)

Long, stout, stems may rise 18" above basal clumps of leaves. Blades of leaves 3"-4" long, more or less arrowhead or heart-shaped, white and woolly below, slightly hairy above, petioles to 6" long. Tiny white to pale yellow flowers in dense clusters in an umbel, sometimes compound, the rays 1"-2" long, with long, narrow bracts below. Dry rocky cliffs, to WA and CA. **Tall Woolly Buckwheat** (*E. elatum*) also has large basal leaves, but the stems are repeatedly branched, with long naked branches.

COAST BUCKWHEAT
COAST ERIOGONUM

Eriogonum latifolium
(Buckwheat family, *Polygonaceae*)
(Photo: Humbug Mountain SP, Curry Co., late July)

Bare stem to 16" tall, branched, basal leaves with blades 1"-2" long, white and woolly on the undersides, petioles about same length as blades. Flowers in umbels, usually with 3 long rays, with dense globe-like clusters of small white or pink flowers at the ends. Bluffs or rocky cliffs along coast from Curry County to CA. **Barestem Buckwheat** (*E. nudum*), an inland species, is similar, but generally grows taller, has white or yellow flowers, and has leaves with longer petioles.

ALPINE BUCKWHEAT
SHASTA BUCKWHEAT
DIRTY SOCKS

Eriogonum pyrolifolium
(Buckwheat family, *Polygonaceae*)
(Photo: Rim Drive, Crater Lake NP, Klamath Co., early August)

Stems 2"-8" tall. Leaves basal, thick, oval, 1"-2" long, white-woolly below, petioles as long as the blades, hairy. Umbel has 3 short rays, with 2 small narrow bracts below. Flowers about 3/16" long, in dense clusters, white, aging reddish. Plants have an odor reminiscent of sweaty socks. High elevations in Cascades, to CA.

WHITE or CREAM
Polygonaceae

WESTERN BISTORT
AMERICAN BISTORT
MOUNTAIN MEADOW KNOTWEED

Polygonum bistortoides
(Buckwheat family, *Polygonaceae*)
(Photo: Near Mount Ashland, Jackson Co., mid July)

Stems 6"-30". Basal leaves narrowly oblong, pointed, 6"-12" long including long petioles, stem leaves smaller, without petioles. Inflorescense dense, oblong, ½"-2" long, with numerous papery brown bracts below. Flowers white to pinkish, about 1/8" long, the stamens well exserted. Common in wet meadows, to fairly high elevations, but also at coast.

BEACH KNOTWEED

Polygonum paronychia
(Buckwheat family, *Polygonaceae*)
(Photo: Near Pistol River, Curry Co., early May)

Prostrate woody stems, dark brown, 1'-3' long. Leaves 5/8"-1" long, narrow, thick, white lacerate sheathing often conspicuous. Flowers in terminal clusters, with leaves crowded close, 5 lobes, white or pinkish, 1/4"-5/16" long, greenish midribs. Beaches and dunes on coast, to BC and CA.

ALPINE KNOTWEED
JIMSON KNOTWEED
POKE KNOTWEED

Polygonum phytolaccifolium
(Buckwheat family, *Polygonaceae*)
(Photo: Near Dutchman Peak, Jackson Co., mid July)

Stems stout, erect, 2'-4' tall. Leaves oval or lance-shaped, the margins wavy and slightly hairy, blades 3"-6" long, petioles ½"-1½" long. Flowers white, about 3/32" long, unequally 5-6 cleft, usually numerous, in open spikes. Wet locations at high altitudes in Siskiyous and Cascades, to AK and CA. **Newberry Knotweed** (*P. newberryi*) and **Davis Knotweed** (*P. davisiae*), merged by some authorities into one species, *P. davisiae*, are shorter and sprawling, and have fewer flowers, in axillary clusters.

SHASTA KNOTWEED
Polygonum shastense
(Buckwheat family, *Polygonaceae*)
(Photo: Rim Drive, Crater Lake NP, Klamath Co., early August)

Shrubby, stems numerous, spreading, rising 2"-6" high. Leaves thick, narrow, ½"-¾" long. Flowers in axils, 1/4"-3/8" dia, petals 5, rounded, whitish or pinkish with green ribs, 8 stamens. Dry pumice slopes, summits, from Crater Lake to CA.

SPRING BEAUTY
LANCE-LEAVED SPRING BEAUTY
Claytonia lanceolata
(Purslane family, *Portulacaceae*)
(Photo: Near Little Hyatt Lake, Jackson Co., early May)

Flowers in racemes of 3-15 on slender stalks 6" high or less. Two basal leaves 2"-3" long, elliptic and sharp-pointed, but may be absent altogether. Pair of stem leaves half-way up the stem, sessile or nearly so, 1"-3" long, narrow, pointed. Petals 5, ¼"-½" long, not united, white or pinkish, sometimes with yellow bases, may be slightly notched at tip. More or less dry areas in woodlands and meadows, moderate to high elevations, to BC and CA.

MINER'S LETTUCE
Claytonia perfoliata [*Montia perfoliata*]
(Purslane family, *Portulacaceae*)
(Photo: Fish Hatchery Park, Josephine Co., early April)

Grows in the shade, and sometimes in sun. Leaves and fleshy stems rise in dense growth, to 15" high. Basal leaves oval to linear, blades 1" long and more, on long petioles. Two stem leaves, near top of stem, are usually united into shield-like disk, with flower stem coming from the center. Flowers are tiny, white to slightly pinkish, in small clusters on stems 1"-3" long. Moist ground, widely distributed, to BC and CA. **Narrow-leaved Miner's Lettuce** (*C. parviflora*) has basal leaves that are linear.

OPPOSITELEAF LEWISIA
Lewisia oppositifolia
(Purslane family, *Portulacaceae*)
(Photo: Near O'Brien, Josephine Co., early May)

Stems 3"-8" high, each stem with 2-5 flowers. Leaves in loose rosette, 2"-4" long, relatively narrow, tapering to slender base, 1-3 pair of stem leaves similar, opposite. Petals typically 8-11, white or pink, each 1/2"-5/8" long, tips blunt or somewhat jagged, 2 rounded sepals with jagged edges, many stamens, stigmas 3-5. Moist places in pine forests, southern Josephine Co. to CA. **Nevada Lewisia** (*L. nevadensis*) typically has 1 flower per stem, sepals are more or less acute, and leaves are thread-like. **Dwarf Lewisia** (*L. pygmaea*), is more slender than *L. nevadensis*, has rounded sepals, and grows at higher elevations.

COLUMBIA WINDFLOWER
WESTERN WHITE ANEMONE
Anemone deltoidea
(Buttercup family, *Ranunculaceae*)
(Photo: Near Prospect Ranger Station, Jackson County, early June)

Generally less than 10" tall, a single flower on a slender stem, 3 leaflets, ovate, toothed or lobed, midway on the stem. Sepals 5, petal-like, each 1" or less long, stamens clustered in center. Shaded coniferous forest, below 6000 feet, west of Cascades, to WA and CA. **Drummond Windflower** (*A. drummondii*) has parted and cleft leaflets. **Little Mountain Anemone** (*A. lyallii*), found at high altitudes, has smaller flowers.

MARSH MARIGOLD
ELK'S LIP
Caltha leptosepala [includes *C. biflora*]
(Buttercup family, *Ranunculaceae*)
(Photo: Near Mt. Ashland, Jackson Co., late June)

Stems 3"-12" tall, fleshy. Leaves mostly basal, more or less round, 1"-3½" across, scalloped edges, petioles 1"-10" long. Flowers showy, usually white, 5/8"-1½" diameter, with 5-9 petal-like sepals. Wet places at moderate to high altitudes, Cascades and Siskiyous, to AK and CA. **Two-flowered Marsh Marigold** (*C. biflora*) is included within *C. leptosepala* by many authorities.

MOUNTAIN PASQUE FLOWER
WESTERN PASQUE FLOWER
WESTERN ANEMONE

Pulsatilla occidentalis [*Anemone occidentalis*]
(Buttercup family, *Ranunculaceae*)
(Photo: Crater Lake NP, near The Watchman, Klamath Co., late June)

Flowers are among the first to appear after the snow melts. Plants 5"-10" tall, stems hairy, a single blossom on the end of each stem. Leaves lacy and fern-like, many times pinnate, with a group of leaves a short distance below the flower, and the rest basal. Flower has 5-8 creamy-white petal-like sepals, about 1" long, forming a bowl, hairy on the outside. After flowering, heads turn shaggy and mop-like. Subalpine rocky slopes in Cascades.

BUCKBRUSH
WEDGELEAF CEANOTHUS
GREASEWOOD

Ceanothus cuneatus
(Buckthorn family, *Rhamnaceae*)
(Photo: Lower Table Rock Trail, Jackson Co., late March)

Rigid, copiously-branched shrub, evergreen, 3'-12' high. Leaves 3/8"-3/4" long, more or less oblong, finely-toothed or 3-toothed at apex, strongly veined, often in clusters. Flowers small, white, 5 petals, in small rounded clusters. Dry, rocky ground, from Willamette Valley south to CA.

SNOWBRUSH
STICKY LAUREL
CINNAMON BUSH

Ceanothus velutinus
(Buckthorn family, *Rhamnaceae*)
(Photo: Natural Bridge, Jackson Co., early June)

Erect, spreading shrub, 6'-15' high. Leaves oval or elliptic, 1½"-2½" long, dark glossy green above (sticky during warm weather), paler beneath, finely toothed, spicy smelling. Flowers small, white, in dense clusters 1½"-2½" long. Dry woods and thickets, throughout western U.S. **Redstem Ceanothus** (*C. sanguineus*), sometimes called **Buckbrush,** is similar, but shrubs tend to be smaller, and the young branches are reddish.

WESTERN SERVICEBERRY
SASKATOON

Amelanchier alnifolia [*A. florida*]
(Rose family, *Rosaceae*)
(Photo: Little Hyatt Lake Road, Jackson Co. early May)

(Photo of berries on p. 156.) Large shrub or tree, to 30'. Leaves oblong or rounded, ¾"-1" long, serrate all around or only on outer half. Flowers white, 5 narrow petals, about ½" long, often twisted in appearance. Widely distributed in woods, to BC and CA. **Utah Serviceberry** (*A. utahensis*), a Great Basin species that extends to Josephine Co, is lower, and has leaves that usually are serrate at least half way around. **Pale Serviceberry** (*A. pallida*) is low-growing, and has leaves that are dentate only near the apex. The species apparently intergrade.

COAST STRAWBERRY
BEACH STRAWBERRY

Fragaria chiloensis (Rose family, *Rosaceae*)
(Photo: Harris Beach SP, Curry Co., late March)

White flowers may be up to 1¼" in dia., with numerous yellow anthers in the center. In summer, tiny red strawberries appear. Leaves are dark green, leathery, 1" or more long, more or less oval, with 7-11 coarse teeth. Widely distributed along coast, on dunes and bluffs. **Mountain Strawberry** (*F. virginiana*), found inland, is similar; also generally has 7-11 teeth, but flowers are smaller; leaves usually exceed the inflorescence. (Photo of berries on p. 156.) **Woodland Strawberry** (*F. vesca*) is similar, but teeth on the leaves generally are 12-21, and inflorescence usually exceeds the leaves.

OCEAN SPRAY

Holodiscus discolor (Rose family, *Rosaceae*)
(Photo: Butte Falls, Jackson Co., mid July)

Bush or small tree, 3'-15' high. Leaves more or less oval-shaped, rounded at apex, coarsely toothed, 1½"-2½" long, petiole about ½" long, whitish and somewhat hairy beneath. Small white flowers are in conspicuous sprays up to 10" long. Flowers are about 5/32" across, 5 petals and 5 sepals, 20 conspicuous stamens rising above petals. Stream banks and dry slopes, through most of Oregon. **Dwarf Ocean Spray** (*H. microphyllus* var. *glabrescens*), grows to about 5', has leaves ½"-¾" long.

CARROTLEAF HORKELIA
CARROTLEAF HONEYDEW

Horkelia daucifolia (Rose family, *Rosaceae*)
(Photo: Shale City Road, Jackson Co., mid June)

Plants 6"-12" high, more or less open flower clusters. Leaves with silky hairs, compound, 10-20 narrow leaflets, crowded, each ¼"-1" long. Flowers with 5 narrow bractlets alternating with 5 sharp sepals, sepals about equal to petals, petals 5, white or cream, more or less roundish, 3/16" across, tapering to base. Dry woods and slopes, southern Jackson Co. to CA. **Howell Horkelia** (*H. sericata*) has up to 30 leaflets, each 1/8"-3/8" long, flowers smaller, often pinkish, and sepals shorter than petals.

PINEWOODS HORKELIA
DUSKY HORKELIA

Horkelia fusca (Rose family, *Rosaceae*)
(Photo: Collier SP, Klamath Co., mid June)

Clustered stems 10"-24" high, somewhat hairy and glandular. Basal leaves compound, 4"-8" long, including petioles, 9-15 leaflets, roundish in outline, heavily lobed; cauline leaves few. Flowers in dense clusters; calyx purplish, hairy, glandular, sepals about 1/8" long. Petals 5, wedge-shaped, 1/8"-1/4" long, white. Stamen filaments flat, often forming a tube. Dry woods east of Cascades, to WA and CA.

WESTERN CHOKE-CHERRY

Prunus virginiana var. *demissa*
(Rose family, *Rosaceae*)
(Photo: Old Siskiyou Highway, Jackson Co., early May)

Shrub or small tree to 20' high. Leaves green and glossy above, lighter below, 2"-4" long, pointed, finely serrate. Racemes 3"-6" long, densely flowered, flowers about 3/8" across, 5 petals, white. Fruit red to purple, about 3/8" dia. Rocky slopes, oak/pine woodland, coniferous forest, at moderate elevations, western OR, to BC and CA. **Bitter Cherry** (*P. emarginata*) has short racemes with 3-12 flowers; fruit red to purple, about 3/8" dia. **Klamath Plum** (*P. subcordata*) has umbel-like flower clusters; fruit yellow to red, about 3/4" dia.

HIMALAYA BLACKBERRY

Rubus armeniacus [*R. discolor, R. procerus*]
(Rose family, *Rosaceae*)
(Photo: Harris Beach SP, Curry Co., late March)

(Photo of berries on p. 157.) Stems long, trailing, sturdy, 5-angled, sometimes purplish, armed with large spines. Even the flower stems are spiny. Leaves palmately compound, 3-5 oval leaflets, with toothed margins. Flowers white or pinkish, 5/8"-1" across, 5 petals. Fruit 5/8"-3/4" long, black. Widespread in western OR. Old World native. ***Cutleaf Blackberry*** (*R. laciniatus*), also not native, has leaflets that are variously parted and incised. **Pacific Blackberry** (*R. ursinus*), native, has long trailing stems up to 18' long, round (not 5-angled), leaves mostly with 3 leaflets, and male and female flowers on different individual plants.

BLACKCAP RASPBERRY
WESTERN BLACKCAP
WHITEBARK RASPBERRY

Rubus leucodermis (Rose family, *Rosaceae*)
(Photo: Near Onion Mt., Josephine Co., late May)

Shrub 5'-8' high, arching stems, armed with stout prickles, stems greenish or reddish, covered with whitish bloom, round in cross-section. Compound leaves, usually with 3 leaflets, each 1"-2" long, sharply toothed, white-woolly beneath, with prickly petioles. Calyx with 5 pointed lobes, each about 3/8" long, surpassing the white petals, which are about half as long. Many stamens. Many pistils, united into a thimble-like fruit. Fruit typically black, about 3/8" across. Open woods, widely distributed, to BC and CA.

THIMBLEBERRY

Rubus parviflorus (Rose family, *Rosaceae*)
(Photo: Fish Lake Trail, Jackson Co., late June)

(Photo of berry on p. 157.) Plants to 6' tall, with woody stems and virtually no prickles, often creating thickets. Flowers white, to 1½" in dia., with petals that resemble crinkled tissue paper. Leaves large, to 8" across, more or less resembling maple leaves, with 5-7 lobes, soft to the touch. Berries bright red, 1/2" dia. or more. When pulled from the vine, the berry has a shallow cup-like depression that resembles a thimble. Moist woodlands, AK to CA.

FRAGRANT BEDSTRAW
SWEET-SCENTED BEDSTRAW

Galium triflorum (Madder family, *Rubiaceae*)
(Photo: Union Creek CG, Jackson Co., late July)

Stems slender and weak, 8"-18" tall. Leaves 6 in a whorl, ¼"-1½" long, more or less oval-shaped. Flowers tiny, about 1/8" across, 4-lobed, ovary hairy, in 3-flowered cymes coming from the upper leaf axils. Widespread in woods nationwide. There are a number of similar bedstraws. Some are: **Catchweed Bedstraw** (*G. aparine*), has leaves narrower than in *G. triflorum*, hairy on the margins; **Small Bedstraw** (*G. trifidum*), generally has flowers with 3 lobes rather than 4, and ovaries without hairs; **Oregon Bedstraw** (*G. oreganum*), typically has 4 leaves in a whorl, rather than 6.

MOUNTAIN BOYKINIA
GREATER BOYKINIA

Boykinia major (Saxifrage family, *Saxifragaceae*)
(Photo: Wagner Creek Road, Jackson Co., early September)

Plants to 4' tall, robust, sticky, hairy stems. Leaves broad, hairy, to 6" across, deeply cleft and incised. Lower leaves typically have long petioles, but upper leaves may have none; petioles have leaf-like stipules at the bases. Flowers white, in rounded to flat-topped clusters, 5 petals, each petal about ¼", almost round, with a narrow claw attaching petal to base. Calyx has 5 broadly triangular lobes that are visible between the petals. Mountain meadows and wet places, Cascades and Siskiyous, to WA and CA. **Slender Boykinia** (*B. occidentalis*) has slender stems, bristle-like stipules, and smaller flowers.

SMALL-FLOWERED ALUMROOT
CREVICE ALUMROOT

Heuchera micrantha
(Saxifrage family, *Saxifragaceae*)
(Photo: Near Onion Mt., Josephine Co., late May)

Loose, open clusters of tiny white flowers on long, usually leafless, hairy stems, to 40" tall. Leaves primarily basal, more or less round, heart-shaped at base, with rounded toothed lobes, tiny point on each tooth, very long hairy petioles. Flowers on slender pedicels, with bell-shaped calyxes about 1/8" long, 5 white petals 3/32" long, spoon-shaped with narrow claws, stamens and pistil exserted. Moist rocky slopes, mostly west of Cascades, to BC and CA.

SMALLFLOWER WOODLAND STAR
PRAIRIE STAR

Lithophragma parviflorum
(Saxifrage family, *Saxifragaceae*)
(Photo: Grizzly Peak Trail, Jackson Co., mid June)

Stems slender, somewhat hairy, 8"-20" tall. Stem leaves 3-5 parted, deeply lobed, with slender petioles. Flowers white (sometimes pinkish), 5 petals, petals deeply 3-lobed, with middle lobe longest. Open areas, both sides of Cascades, to BC and CA. A similar species, **San Francisco Woodland Star** (*L. affine*) has leaves that are less deeply lobed.

HOWELL SAXIFRAGE

Saxifraga howellii (Saxifragc family, *Saxifragaceae*)
(Photo: Near Indian Mary CG, Josephine Co., late February)

Appears in early spring, and forms extensive groups on shady wet cliffs. Tiny white flowers in loose clusters on stems 3"-5" high, rising from clumps of basal leaves, each leaf 1" or so long, with long petiole, and scalloped edges. There are 5 petals; 10 tiny red anthers stick out above the petals. Lower Umpqua and Rogue Rivers, to CA. **California Saxifrage** (*S. californica*) is taller and has larger leaves. **Marshall Saxifrage** (*S. marshallii*) also has larger leaves, strongly and evenly dentate, and yellowish spots on the petals.

NORTHWESTERN SAXIFRAGE
WHOLELEAF SAXIFRAGE

Saxifraga integrifolia [*S. fragosa*]
(Saxifrage family, *Saxifragaceae*)
(Photo: Lower Table Rock, Jackson Co., mid March)

Flowering stems 6"-12" tall, slightly hairy, stems generally leafless except for a few small leaves on some plants. Basal leaves entire to slightly toothed, blades oval, ¾"-2" long, tapering to petioles ¼"-1½" long. Flowers generally in 1 head-like cluster at top of stem, stem sometimes branched into 2-3 clusters. Flowers 3/16"-5/16" diameter, 5 petals, more or less oval, white to greenish, 5 sepals, shorter than petals. Vernally moist meadows, below 3000', to BC and CA.

COOLWORT
COOLWORT FOAMFLOWER
SUGAR-SCOOP

Tiarella trifoliata var. *unifoliata*
(Saxifrage family, *Saxifragaceae*)
(Photo: Near Watson Falls, North Umpqua River Valley, Douglas Co., late June)

Tiny white flowers on long hairy stems to 16" high. Leaves maple-like, 3-5-lobed, dentate, hairy, basal leaves with long petioles and up to 2½" across. Corolla has 5 lobes, with slender stamens that project far beyond the corolla. ("Sugar-Scoop" comes from the shape of the seed capsule.) Moist woods at low elevations west of Cascades, to AK and CA. **Three-leaved Coolwort** (*T. trifoliata* var. *trifoliata*) similar, but has compound leaf with 3 leaflets.

HAIRY OWL-CLOVER
HAIRY INDIAN PAINTBRUSH

Castilleja tenuis [*Orthocarpus hispidus*]
(Figwort family, *Scrophulariaceae*)
(Photo: Shale City Road, Jackson Co., late May)

Erect stems 4"-16" high, hairy. Leaves narrow and thin, the lower entire, the upper lobed. Inflorescence loose, the greenish bracts deeply cleft into 3-7 long thin lobes, hairy. Corollas about ¾" long, white, creamy, or yellow, the lower lips with 3 pouches about 1/8" dia. Moist open places, widely distributed, to AK and CA. **Cream Sacs** (*C. rubicundula*) similar, but with pouches about 3/8" dia.

HOT ROCK PENSTEMON
SCORCHED PENSTEMON
SCABLAND PENSTEMON

Penstemon deustus
(Figwort family, *Scrophulariaceae*)
(Photo: Near Old Siskiyou Summit, Cascade-Siskiyou NM, Jackson Co., late June)

Multiple fleshy stems rise ½'-2' high from woody base. Leaves opposite, sessile, narrow, sharply serrate, ½"-1½" long. Flowers in clusters in upper axils, uppermost leaves bract-like. Calyx 3/16"- 1/4" long, segments pointed. Corolla whitish to yellowish or tinged with pink, about ½" long, lower lobes broad with thin purplish lines. Dry rocky ground mostly east of Cascades and in the southwest counties, to BC and CA.

MOUNTAIN VALERIAN
SITKA VALERIAN
MOUNTAIN HELIOTROPE
NORTHERN VALERIAN
Valeriana sitchensis
(Valerian family, *Valerianaceae*)
(Photo: Copeland Creek Road, Douglas Co., mid May)

Stem 1'-2', robust, much of stem with no leaves. Leaves to 8" long, mostly compound with 3-9 leaflets, terminal leaflet largest, leaflets usually coarsely toothed or lobed. (In some subspecies, the leaflets are less strongly lobed.) Many small flowers in terminal clusters, clusters branched, dense or open, corollas funnelform, about 5/16" long, white or pinkish, spreading into 5 lobes, stamens projecting beyond petals. Moist places in Cascades, to BC and CA.

WEDGE-LEAVED VIOLET
Viola cuneata (Violet family, *Violaceae*)
(Photo: 8 Dollar Rd., Josephine Co., early March)

Flowering stem rises 2"-6", with oval, scalloped leaves at the base, 1" long or so, tapered to long petioles, and smaller stem leaves with shorter petioles. Petals ½" long or less, mostly white with some yellow at the base, purple-red veins on lower petal, and purple spot at base of each lateral petal. Backs of petals are purplish. Open pine or oak forests, often on serpentine, Josephine and Curry Cos., to CA. **Western Heart's Ease** (*V. ocellata*) similar, but leaves are either squared off or heart-shaped at the base, rather than tapered.

Wiggins Lily

YELLOW to ORANGE FLOWERS

Yellow and orange flowers mostly don't cause a problem in deciding what color group to put them in. However, some yellow flowers may verge on whitish, and it may be a matter of interpretation to decide where to put them. This is especially the case with flowers that may show two colors, as with **California Lady's Slipper,** which is both yellow and white. In such cases, it again is a matter of interpretation, concerning where to put the flower. Also, with some yellow flowers, in which most of the subspecies indeed are yellow, there may be some subspecies that are white. Thus, it is advisable to check the "White to Cream-Colored" section, if you don't find your flower here.

SWEET FENNEL

Foeniculum vulgare (Carrot family, *Apiaceae*)
(Photo: Whalehead Beach, Curry Co., late July)

Stems 3'-6' tall, stout, waxy-blue. Leaves compound, with broad sheaths attaching to stems, the compound segments thin and wire-like, spicy smelling. Flowers in umbels, 10-30 rays, involucres lacking. Fairly common in disturbed localities in western OR, to CA. Native of Europe.

NARROW-LEAVED DESERT PARSLEY
NINELEAF BISCUITROOT
HOGFENNEL

Lomatium triternatum (Carrot family, *Apiaceae*)
(Photo: Old Siskiyou Highway (Old Highway 99), Jackson Co., early May)

Stem 1'-2' tall. Leaves compound, mostly in 3s, with final divisions consisting of long slender segments. Flowers in spreading umbel, with rounded clusters at ends of 5-20 rays 1"-4" long. Flowers tiny, yellow, densely clustered. Dry ground, both sides of Cascades, to BC and CA. **California Lomatium** (*L. californicum*) similar, but leaflets are wedge-shaped and coarsely toothed. **Barestem Lomatium** (*L. nudicaule*) has tall, glaucous, leafless stem that is conspicuously swollen at the top.

DESERT PARSLEY
COMMON LOMATIUM
FOOTHILL LOMATIUM

Lomatium utriculatum (Carrot family, *Apiaceae*)
(Photo: Lower Table Rock Trail, Jackson Co., late March)

Fleshy-stemmed, 4"-20" tall, with umbels composed of clusters of tiny bright yellow flowers. Leaves fern-like, both basal and on stems, conspicuously sheathing the stems, divided many times until the final leaflets may be only 1/8" long. Umbels with 5-20 spreading rays, each ray 1"-5" long, involucel bractlets more or less oval-shaped. Dry, grassy places throughout western Oregon, to BC and CA. **Agate Desert Parsley** (*L. cookii*), **Federally listed endangered**, is similar, but the flowers are light yellow, leaves are strictly basal, and involucel bractlets are narrow.

FOOTSTEPS-OF-SPRING
YELLOW MATS
BEACH SNAKE-ROOT

Sanicula arctopoides (Carrot family, *Apiaceae*)
(Photo: Bandon SP, Coos Co., late March)

Leaves in flat rosette 4"-12" across. Leaves yellowish green, 1"-2" long, cleft into 3 segments, the segments lobed into sharp teeth. Stems short, terminating in button-like umbels of tiny yellow 5-petaled flowers. Open bluffs along coast, to BC and CA. **Western Snake-Root** (*S. crassicaulis*) has yellow flowers in umbels and similarly-shaped leaves, but has erect stems 1'-3' high, and leaves are dark green.

YELLOW SKUNK CABBAGE

Lysichitum americanum (Arum family, *Araceae*)
(Photo: Near Gold Beach, Curry Co., late March)

The huge green leaves, massed together in a shady, moist site identify the plant. Leaves, all basal, 3'-4' long, thin, with fleshy midribs. In early spring, the odd poker-shaped flowering-bearing spadix appears, 2½" long and 1" thick, surrounded by the bright yellow leaf-shaped spathe. The spathe soon drops away, leaving the spadix alone, bearing numerous tiny yellow-green flowers on its surface. West of Cascades, mostly near coast, moist shady sites, to BC and CA.

ORANGE AGOSERIS
SLENDER AGOSERIS

Agoseris aurantiaca (Sunflower family, *Asteraceae*)
(Photo: Near Mount Ashland, Jackson Co., late August)

Slender leafless stems, 4"-20" tall, 1 flower per stem. Leaves basal, to 16" long, very narrow, entire or with a few small teeth. Head composed entirely of ray flowers, equal in length to the involucre or projecting beyond it, dull orange or reddish. Involucre somewhat hairy, ½"-1" long, composed of narrow tapered bracts. Sap milky. Mountain meadows, Siskiyous and Cascades, to BC and CA. **Pale Agoseris** (*A. glauca*) occurs in the Cascades, is somewhat similar, but has light yellow ray flowers. See, also, *Crepis,* p. 49, *Hypochaeris,* p. 52, *Leontodon,* p. 53, *Nothocalais,* p. 54, and *Taraxacum*, p. 57.

SERPENTINE ARNICA

Arnica cernua (Sunflower family, *Asteraceae*)
(Photo: Near O'Brien, Josephine Co., late April)

Flowers usually solitary, on somewhat hairy stems 4"-12" high. Leaves long-petioled, blades 1"-1½" long, more or less heart-shaped at base, toothed. Involucre ½" long, hairy, with sharp-pointed bracts. Bright yellow ray flowers 7-10, about ¾" long, fringed on ends. Southern Curry and Josephine Cos., to CA, on serpentine soils. **Heart-leaf Arnica** (*A. cordifolia*), has larger, heart-shaped leaves, and 10-15 ray flowers. **Broadleaf Arnica** *(A. latifolia)* is similar to Heart-leaf Arnica, but stem leaves lack petioles, and are sharply dentate.

DELTOID BALSAMROOT
NORTHWEST BALSAMROOT

Balsamorhiza deltoidea
(Sunflower family, *Asteraceae*)
(Photo: Little Hyatt Lake Road, Jackson Co., early May)

The large plants and bright yellow flowers often cover large sections of hillside. Flowering stems to 3' high, arrowhead-shaped basal leaves to 10" long, with long petioles; stem leaves smaller and linear. Leaves generally entire, but may be wavy-margined. Flowers 1-3 per stem, with bright yellow rays 1" or more long, dull yellow disk flowers in center. Dry open ground, to 7000 feet, mostly west of the Cascades, to BC and CA. A related species, **Silky Balsamroot** (*B. sericea*), occurs from central Josephine Co. to CA. It has leaves that are parted and divided into many segments, with silvery hairs.

YELLOW STAR THISTLE
ST. BARNABY'S THISTLE

Centaurea solstitialis
(Sunflower family, *Asteraceae*)
(Photo: Denman Wildlife Area, Jackson Co., late June)

Grows from 1'-3' high, with ridged, woolly, sprawling, dull green stems. Stem leaves small, linear, and appressed to the stems. Basal leaves deeply incised. Flowers yellow, with calyx about ½" long. Sharp spines on the calyx are yellow, up to 1" long. Fields and disturbed ground, Josephine and Jackson Cos., to CA. Native to Europe. In ***Maltese Star Thistle*** (*C. melitensis*), also non-native, the stem leaves are toothed, and the spines are purplish.

SMOOTH HAWKSBEARD

Crepis capillaris (Sunflower family, *Asteraceae*)
(Photo: Near Tiller, Douglas Co., late April.)

Dandelion-like flowers, on tall, mostly bare, slightly hairy, branching stems, to 3' high. Leaves mostly basal, 3"-10" long, deeply lacerated, smaller above, basal leaves petioled, hairy on midribs below. Inflorescence open, many flowering heads, each about 1" dia., yellow ray flowers only. Involucre about ¼" high, slightly hairy, many narrow, pointed bracts. Widespread in most of western OR, to BC and CA. Introduced from Europe. **Bristly Hawksbeard** *(C. setosa)* is similar, but has bristly hairs on the stems. See, also, *Agoseris,* p. 47, *Hypochaeris,* p. 52, *Leontodon,* p. 53, *Nothocalais,* p. 54, *Taraxacum*, p. 57.

NAKED-STEMMED HAWKSBEARD

Crepis pleurocarpa (Sunflower family, *Asteraceae*)
(Photo: Near Dutchman Peak, Jackson Co., mid July)

Stems 12"-20" high, branched, somewhat hairy. Basal leaves to 8" long, with deep, narrow, sharp lobes; stem leaves reduced and not well developed, usually not lobed. Flowering heads in the inflorescence 10-30. Involucres 5/16"-5/8" long. Ray flowers only, yellow, 5-10, about 5/16" long. Dry slopes, often on serpentine, mountains of southern Jackson and Klamath Cos., to CA. **Long-leaved Hawksbeard** (*C. acuminata*), is similar, but has much longer basal leaves, well-developed stem leaves, and 20-100 flowering heads in the inflorescence.

SPRING GOLD
GOLD-STAR

Crocidium multicaule
(Sunflower family, *Asteraceae*)
(Photo: Lower Rogue River Canyon, Josephine Co., late February)

Among the first to appear in spring; may form yellow masses in open sunny spots. Each slender stem bears 1 flower, and rises 6" or so above basal rosette of small fleshy leaves, spoon-shaped, each ¾" long or less, with thin petioles. Stem leaves without petioles, few, alternate, tiny. Ray flowers bright yellow, usually less than ½" long, generally 8-12 in number. Wet banks, to WA and CA.

GREENE GOLDENWEED
GOLDENBUSH

Ericameria greenei [*Haplopappus greenei*]
(Sunflower family, *Asteraceae*)
(Photo: Near Mount Ashland, Jackson Co., late August)

Low-growing shrubs with flowers in terminal clusters. Leaves ¾"-1½" long, narrow, somewhat sticky. Involucre ½" long, with 2-6 yellow ray flowers 3/8" long, and 7-20 yellow disk flowers. Open rocky areas at moderate elevations in Cascades and Siskiyous, to WA and CA. A related species, **Rabbitbrush Goldenweed** (*E. bloomeri*) is taller and has longer, narrower leaves. The two intergrade, and some authorities consider *E. greenei* to be a variety of *E. bloomeri.*

RUBBER RABBITBRUSH
GRAY RABBITBRUSH

Ericameria nauseosa [*Chrysothamnus nauseosus*]
(Sunflower family, *Asteraceae*)
(Photo: Dead Indian Memorial Road near Howard Prairie, Jackson Co., mid August)

Shrub, many-branched, 2'-6' high. Leaves persistent, grayish-green, ½"-2½" long, about 1/16" wide. Flowering heads in dense more or less round-topped clusters, involucres ¼"-½" high, disk flowers only, usually 5, yellow, less than ½" long. Dry areas, mainly east of Cascades, but also in southwestern OR, to WA and CA. **Green Rabbitbrush** (*E. viscidiflorus*) is similar, but has light green foliage, and is more or less sticky.

SCABLAND ERIGERON

Erigeron bloomeri (Sunflower family, *Asteraceae*)
(Photo, Airport Drive, near Rough and Ready, Josephine Co., late May)

Cluster of nearly leafless stems rising 3"-7" from crowded base of grass-like leaves 1"-3" long. Heads solitary, about 3/8" dia., yellow disk flowers only, no ray flowers, involucre about ¼" long, sometimes slightly hairy. Leaves and stems not hairy. Open areas in eastern OR and in southern Jackson and Josephine Cos., to CA. The subspecies *nudatus,* in Jackson and Josephine Cos., has been called **Waldo Daisy.**

WOOLLY SUNFLOWER
OREGON SUNSHINE

Eriophyllum lanatum
(Sunflower family, *Asteraceae*)
(Photo: Illinois River Road, Josephine Co., early May)

Height 6"-36", branched, thinly to densely hairy, with single or loosely-clustered flowers. Leaves variable, 1"-3" long, sometimes with 1-2 short narrow lobes, sometimes pinnately parted, whitish hairs below, often without hairs above. Overall dia. of flower head 5/8"-1¾", 8-13 ray flowers, disk and ray flowers yellow. Widely distributed in dry open places, to WA and CA.

COASTAL GUMWEED
OREGON GUMPLANT

Grindelia stricta [*G. arenicola*]
(Sunflower family, *Asteraceae*)
(Photo: Humbug Mountain SP, Curry Co., late July)

Plant very sticky; involucre sticky, and equipped with downward-curving spines that look sharp, but aren't. Stems spreading, up to 18" long, with flowering heads on rising stems. Leaves 1"-2" long, smaller above, narrow, serrate. Involucre typically ½" across, and the bright yellow ray flowers about ½" long. Dunes and banks along the coast, to AK and CA.

COAST SNEEZEWEED
BOLANDER SNEEZEWEED

Helenium bolanderi (Sunflower family, *Asteraceae*)
(Photo: Otter Point, Curry Co., late July)

Heads on long stems, the hemispheric central disks yellow or brownish, the yellow rays about ¾" long, deeply 3-lobed, often drooping. Stems may rise to 3', with long slender, pointed leaves that clasp the stems. Open ground, from Coos County to CA. The only differences between this and an interior species, **Tall Sneezeweed** (*H. bigelovii*), are that *H. bolanderi* has coastal distribution, and a slightly longer pappus.

FITCH SPIKEWEED
FITCH TARWEED

Hemizonia fitchii (Sunflower family, *Asteraceae*)
(Photo: Rogue Valley near White City, Jackson Co., early June)

Stems 8"-20" tall, reddish, fleshy, branching, hairy. Leaves dense, 3"-4" long, hairy, the lower usually divided into narrow sharp lobes, upper shorter, generally in clusters. Involucre about ¼" high, hairy, subtended by several conspicuous leaves extending well beyond head, with sharp points. Ray flowers yellow, less than ¼" long, bilobed. Disk flowers many, yellow. Dry fields, open woodland, Rogue Valley to CA.

GREENE HAWKWEED

Hieracium greenei (Sunflower family, *Asteraceae*)
(Photo: Mt. Ashland, Jackson Co., mid July)

Stems 8"-16" high, hairy. Leaves mainly near the base, 2"-4" long, narrow, nearly entire, very hairy, stem leaves few and bract-like. Inflorescence few-flowered, heads composed of 8-15 rays, about 1/2" long, yellow, 5-lobed on ends. Sunny slopes, summits, to fairly high elevations, to CA.

FALSE DANDELION
HAIRY CAT'S-EARS
GOSMORE

Hypochaeris radicata
(Sunflower family, *Asteraceae*)
(Photo: S. Umpqua River, near Tiller, Douglas Co., late March)

Resembles Common Dandelion, but stems are generally longer, up to 30", and are multi-branched. Leaves mostly basal, to 8" long, lobed, hairy. Involucre has many overlapping layers, outer bracts not sharply bent backward. Head showy, all yellow ray flowers. Widespread in lawns and roadsides. Introduced from Europe. ***Smooth Cat's-Ears*** (*H. glabra*), also introduced, has mostly hairless leaves and smaller flowers. See, also, *Agoseris,* p. 47, *Crepis,* p. 49, *Leontodon,* p. 53, *Nothocalais,* p. 54, *Taraxacum*, p. 57.

GOLDFIELDS
SLENDER GOLDFIELDS
CALIFORNIA GOLDFIELDS

Lasthenia californica
[*Lasthenia chrysotoma, Baeria chrysotoma*]
(Sunflower family, *Asteraceae*)
(Photo: Agate Desert Preserve, Jackson Co., late March)

Stems 5"-8" high, leaves slender, opposite, entire, 3/4"-2" long. Flower heads at ends of branches, ray flowers 6-13, yellow, about 5/16" long, involucre hairy. Often in extensive masses. Dry ground, Rogue Valley to CA. **Large-flowered Goldfields** (*L. macrantha*), found on the coast, is similar, but has ray flowers 3/8"-1/2" long. **Smooth Goldfields** (*L. glaberrima*) has very small, inconspicuous ray flowers.

HAIRY HAWKBIT

Leontodon taraxacoides
(Sunflower family, *Asteraceae*)
(Photo, Cape Blanco, Curry Co., mid May)

Resembles Common Dandelion, but outer row of bracts under the head do not turn downward. Flower stems long, decumbent or erect. Leaves variable, to 6" long, notched or lobed, in flat rosette. Ray flowers yellow, head more than 1" in dia., outer row of rays may be purplish on the back. Disturbed ground in many places. Introduced from Europe. See, also, *Agoseris,* p. 47, *Crepis,* p. 49, *Hypochaeris,* p. 52, *Nothocalais,* p. 54, *Taraxacum,* p. 57.

LEMON SCENTED MADIA
LEMON TARWEED

Madia citriodora (Sunflower family, *Asteraceae*)
(Photo: Stevenson Park, Klamath Co., early June)

Slender stems, 6"-20" tall, sticky, hairy, herbage fragrant. Leaves slender, usually not denticulate, 1"-2" long, hairy. Heads few, at the ends of stems. Involucre about 1/4" long, hairy. Ray flowers generally 5-12, 3/16"-3/8" long, 3-lobed on ends, greenish-yellow. Dry ground, southwest OR to CA. **Common Tarweed** (*M. gracilis*} is similar, but leaves tend to be longer, ray flowers are lemon yellow, and herbage is not fragrant.

COMMON MADIA
SHOWY TARWEED

Madia elegans (Sunflower family, *Asteraceae*)
(Photo: Denman WA, Jackson Co., early June)

Stems 8"-20" high, branched, hairy, sticky. Leaves narrow, entire to more or less serrate, 1"-3" long, basal leaves few or none. Ray flowers light yellow, sometimes with reddish-maroon at the base of the rays (as in photo), rays 9-15, 1/4"-3/4" long, fan-shaped, deeply lobed. Dry ground west of Cascades, to CA. **Woodland Tarweed, (*M. madiodes*)** similar, but the flowers usually smaller.

FALSE AGOSERIS
WAVYLEAF PRAIRIE DANDELION

Nothocalais troximoides [*Microseris troximoides*]
(Sunflower family, *Asteraceae*)
(Photo: Near Malone Springs, Klamath Co., late May)

Dandelion-like, but leaves are narrow and grass-like, basal, 4"-12" long, sometimes wavy-edged. Heads composed of ray flowers only, solitary on leafless stems 2"-16" high. Involucre ½"-1" long, bracts narrow and pointed, midribs purple-lined. Ray flowers much longer than involucre, numerous, bright yellow, often reddish below. Dry, open places east of Cascades, to WA and CA. **Alpine Agoseris** (*N. alpestris*), found at high elevations, similar, but involucre bracts are evenly and finely purple-dotted. Alpine Agoseris is often mistaken for Pale Agoseris (*Agoseris glauca*), see p. 47, under *A. aurantiaca*. See, also, *Crepis*, p. 49, *Hypochaeris*, p. 52, *Leontodon*, p. 53, and *Taraxacum*, p. 57.

SILKY RAILLARDELLA
SILVERY RAILLARDELLA

Raillardella argentea
(Sunflower family, *Asteraceae*)
(Photo: Rim Drive, Crater Lake NP, Klamath Co., early August)

Flowering stems 2"-3" tall, each with single head. Leaves basal, 1"-3" long, narrow, entire, petioled, very silvery-silky haired on top and bottom. Involucre 5/8" long, greenish-brownish, surrounding tightly packed yellow disk flowers, pistils exserted. No ray flowers. In high Cascades, to CA.

CALIFORNIA CONEFLOWER

Rudbeckia californica
(Sunflower family, *Asteraceae*)
(Photo: Near O'Brien, Josephine Co., mid July)

Tall, 2'-6' high, not hairy, flowers singly, on long stems. Leaves more or less oval, irregularly toothed, 6"-14" long, the lower ones with petioles. Involucre large, with many pointed leafy bracts. Flower head has prominent cone-shaped disk, 1" long and more, with many tiny yellowish-brown disk flowers. Ray flowers 10-14, bright yellow, 1¼"-2" long. Moist places, from Umpqua Valley to CA. **Western Rudbeckia** (*R. occidentalis*), in Southern Cascades and Siskiyous, is similar, but lacks ray flowers.

TALL WESTERN GROUNDSEL
TOWER BUTTERWEED
LAMBSTONGUE RAGWORT

Senecio integerrimus
(Sunflower family, *Asteraceae*)
(Photo: Cantrall-Buckley Co. Park, Jackson Co., early April)

Plants to 4' high. Stems stout, slightly hairy, with leaves 3"-6" long, oval to lance-shaped, entire, dentate, or wavy-margined, lower leaves long-petioled. Flowering cluster may be loose or compact, with numerous yellow heads ½" or more dia., each with 5-10 rays. Widely distributed, dry open woods. A similar species, **Arrowleaf groundsel** (*S. triangularis*), grows in wet places, has arrowhead-shaped leaves.

TANSY RAGWORT
TANSY BUTTERWEED

Senecio jacobaea (Sunflower family, *Asteraceae*)
(Photo: Lone Ranch Beach, Curry Co., late July)

Tall, 2'-4' high, branching toward top, often in massed clumps. Leaves 2"-8" long, sometimes longer, pinnately divided and cleft, the terminal lobe largest. Flower heads numerous, both ray and disk flowers yellow, rays 10-15, ¼"-½" long. Locally abundant along coast. Native of Europe. **TOXIC.** ***Common Tansy*** (*Tanacetum vulgare*), also a native of Europe, and also **TOXIC**, is sometimes mistaken for Tansy Ragwort, but its flowers are primarily made up of disk flowers, and the ray flowers, if present, are inconspicuous.

COMMON GROUNDSEL
COMMON BUTTERWEED

Senecio vulgaris (Sunflower family, *Asteraceae*)
(Photo: Lone Ranch Beach, Curry Co., late March)

Plants 12"-15" tall, branched, with clusters of small yellow flowers -- disk flowers only, no ray flowers. Flowers open into puffy heads ½" dia. or more, preparatory to distributing seeds. Flowers encased in cylindrical tube of bracts, 1/4"-3/8" long, with tiny, sharp, black outer bracts at the base. Leaves deeply divided. Abundant in western OR on waste and cultivated ground. Introduced from Europe.

CANADA GOLDENROD
MEADOW GOLDENROD

Solidago canadensis (Sunflower family, *Asteraceae*)
(Photo: Diamond Lake, Douglas Co., late July)

Stems 1'-3' high, often clustered. Leaves nearly sessile, numerous, variable, narrow and pointed, usually without hairs, 2½"-3½" long, nearly entire to dentate. Flowers yellow, usually in narrow, pyramidal clusters, involucres less than 1/8" high, 12-18 small ray flowers. Meadows, open woods, and roadsides, mostly west of Cascades, to BC and CA. **California Goldenrod** (*S. californica*) is similar, but the foliage has grayish hairs.

PRICKLY SOW THISTLE

Sonchus asper (Sunflower family, *Asteraceae*)
(Photo: Millicoma Marsh, Coos Co., late July)

Here is a weed that looks like a weed. Stem is robust and fleshy, to ½" thick, and 1'-6' high. Leaves large and abundant, some more than 1' long, heavily divided, toothed and spiny, clasping the stems. Flowers are yellow and dandelion-like, composed exclusively of ray flowers, ½" across and more. Bracts of involucre tightly compressed, about ½" long. Abundant west of the Cascades, in open ground. Native of Europe.

DUNE TANSY
SEASIDE TANSY
WESTERN TANSY

Tanacetum camphoratum [*T. douglasii*]
(Sunflower family, *Asteraceae*)
(Photo: Near Bandon, Coos Co., early May)

Stems and leaves hairy and mostly decumbent, with flower heads rising a few inches. Leaves lacy and fern-like, 2½"- 8" long, the final lobes tiny and fleshy. Flower heads are about ½" across, yellow, slightly concave, consisting almost entirely of disk flowers, with a few tiny ray flowers around the periphery, in a tight hemispheric involucre with overlapping bracts. Beaches and dunes along the coast. ***Common Tansy*** (*T. vulgare*), **TOXIC**, a native of Europe, is taller, and flower heads are more numerous. (See p. 55.)

COMMON DANDELION

Taraxacum officinale
(Sunflower family, *Asteraceae*)
(Photo: Tou Velle SP, Jackson Co., early April)

Homeowners detest dandelions because of their tenacity in lawns, but in the wild they can be beautiful, with their bright yellow heads lining the edges of trails and roads. Leaves all basal, bright green, sharply cut with reversed lobes. Each flower head rises on a bare stem from 2"-12" tall, and consists of densely crowded, bright yellow ray flowers. Outer bracts of involucre are sharply bent backward. Native of Europe. See, also, *Agoseris*, p. 47, *Crepis,* p.49, *Hypochaeris,* p. 52, *Leontodon,* p. 53, and *Nothocalais,* p. 54.

YELLOW SALSIFY
GOATSBEARD

Tragopogon dubius (Sunflower family, *Asteraceae*)
(Photo: Soda Mountain Rd., Jackson Co., mid June)

Resembles a glorified dandelion, except it may be 3'-4' tall, and has sharp, narrow bracts that extend well beyond the petals. Leaves long and grass-like. Flower heads, 2"-3" dia., borne singly on fleshy stems that are enlarged just below the heads, composed of bright yellow ray flowers. Later in the season the heads become large, brown puffy balls. Widespread, especially roadsides. Native of Europe. ***Meadow Salsify*** (*T. pratensis*), also native to Europe, is similar, but stem is not enlarged below the flower, and the long bracts do not extend beyond the petals.

NARROWLEAF MULE'S EARS

Wyethia angustifolia (Sunflower family, *Asteraceae*)
(Photo: Near Wolf Creek, Josephine Co., late May)

The large sunflower-type flowers are showy. Stems 1'-2' high, fleshy, each stem with 1 flower head. Basal leaves to 18" long, on short petioles; stem leaves smaller. The leaves taper to the petioles, while in a similar plant, **Deltoid Balsamroot** (*Balsamorhiza deltoidea*), p. 48, the leaves are arrowhead-shaped. Flowers yellow, 2"-3" dia. Involucre large, about 1" high, with many hairy bracts. Dry open ground, west of the Cascades, to CA.

OREGON-GRAPE
HOLLYLEAF BARBERRY

Berberis aquifolium [*Mahonia aquifolium*]
(Barberry family, *Berberidaceae*)
(Photo: Tou Velle SP, Jackson Co., early April)

(Photo of berries on p. 152.) Oregon's state flower. Shrub, to 15' tall. Tall form has been called **Tall Oregon-Grape** (*B. aquifolium* var. *aquifolium*); prostrate form has been called **Creeping Oregon-Grape** (*B. aquifolium var. repens*). Leaves compound, 5-7 leaflets (sometimes 9), 1½"-3" long, leathery, spiny. Small yellow flowers in racemes up to 4" long. Woodlands west of Cascades, to BC and CA. **Mountain Oregon-Grape** (*B. nervosa*) is not as tall, has 9-21 leaflets, and is usually found at higher elevations.

SISKIYOU INSIDE-OUT FLOWER
GOLDEN INSIDE-OUT FLOWER

Vancouveria chrysantha
(Barberry family, *Berberidaceae*)
(Photo: Near O'Brien, Josephine Co., late May)

Flowering stems leafless, rising 8"-16". Leaves rise from the base, often as high as flowering stems, compound, leaflets roundish, sometimes slightly lobed, 1"-1½" broad. Few-flowered, slender pedicels. Sepals 6, bright yellow, about 1/4" long, petals 6, bright yellow, both sepals and petals are bent backward, then arched outward. Stamens join in a point. Shady forests of western Josephine Co. and Curry Co., to CA.

FIDDLENECK
RANCHER'S FIREWEED
Amsinckia menziesii [*A. intermedia*]
(Borage family, *Boraginaceae*)
(Photo: Rogue Valley, Jackson Co., mid March)

Plants to 2' tall, fleshy, hairy stems. Leaves long and thin, hairy, generally without petioles. Flowers on outside edge of a coil. Corollas 1/4"-3/8" long, orange, tube-like, 5 lobes. Similar species of Fiddleneck are distinguished by factors such as shape and texture of the nutlets, and by presence of sac-like intrusions in the corolla throats. One species, **Small-flowered Amsinckia** *(A. micrantha)*, has flowers smaller than the others, about 3/16" long. Dry ground, open places, to CA.

WESTERN GROMWELL
WESTERN PUCCOON
WESTERN STONESEED
Lithospermum ruderale
(Borage family, *Boraginaceae*)
(Photo: Near O'Brien, Josephine Co., late April)

Stems 8"-20" tall, numerous leaves, 1½"-3" long, narrow, hairy. Flowers in dense clusters, calyxes hairy with slender lobes about 3/8" long, corollas yellow, 3/8"-5/8" long, slender-tubed, expanding into 5 rounded lobes. Dry areas, mostly east of Cascades, to BC and CA. **California Gromwell** (*L. californicum*) has fewer, broader leaves, and larger flowers.

FIELD MUSTARD
COMMON MUSTARD
Brassica rapa [*Brassica campestris*]
(Mustard family, *Brassicaeae*)
(Photo: Rogue Valley, Jackson Co., late February)

Plants 3' high or more. Lower leaves to 1' long, pinnately parted, toothed, with large terminal leaflet. Upper leaves smaller, entire, more or less arrowhead shaped. Both lower and upper leaves have bases that clasp the stems. Yellow flowers, with 4 petals. Abundant and widespread in fields. Native of Europe. Two other non-native mustards, with leaves that do not clasp the stems, are: ***Black Mustard*** (*B. nigra)*, and ***Indian Mustard*** (*B. juncea*). These are separated by their fruits: in *B. nigra* the fruits are closely appressed to the stems; in *B. juncea* the fruits are ascending, and not appressed to the stems.

MOUNTAIN TANSY-MUSTARD WESTERN TANSY-MUSTARD

Descurainia incana [*D. richardsonii*]
(Mustard family, *Brassicaeae*)
(Photo: Wood River Day-Use Area, Klamath Co., mid June)

Stems 1'-4' high, slender, branched. Leaves mostly once or twice compound, leaflets narrow to somewhat oval, upper leaves simple or compound. Flowers in clusters, 4 petals, yellow, about 1/8" long. Seedpods ¼"-1" long, very thin, straight, erect. Meadows, sagebrush, open groves east of Cascades, to BC and CA. A similar species, also called **Western Tansy-Mustard** (*D. incisa*) has seedpods that are curved, and often spreading outward.

WESTERN WALLFLOWER DOUGLAS WALLFLOWER

Erysimum capitatum [*E. asperum*]
(Mustard family, *Brassicaceae*)
(Photo: Rough and Ready, Josephine Co., early April)

Stems are 12"-20" high, rising above basal rosettes of leaves. Leaves narrow, alternate, many of them toothed, 1½"-3" long. Flowers bright yellow to orange, about ¾" dia., with 4 petals, seedpods not flattened. Dry slopes at moderate to low altitudes, mostly west of Cascades, to WA and CA. **Pale Wallflower** (*E. occidentale*), east of Cascades, is similar, has narrower leaves, pale yellow flowers, and flattened seedpods.

HEDGE MUSTARD

Sisymbrium officinale
(Mustard family, *Brassicaceae*)
(Photo: Rogue Valley, mid March)

A common weedy plant -- vigorous, sprawling, and ungainly. Stems thin and wiry, emerging from a dense clump of leaves, each stem with small group of flowers at the end, with thin seed pods about ½" long closely pressed to the stems. Leaves long, pinnately divided, leaflets dentate, with large terminal segment. Flower has 4 pale yellow petals about 3/16" long. Dry, sunny, waste places, especially west of the Cascades. Introduced from Europe. ***Tumbling Mustard*** (*S. altissimum*), also a non-native, abundant east of the Cascades, is somewhat similar, but has long, thin seedpods, 3"-4" long, and upper leaves have very thin, threadlike lobes.

SEA-CLIFF STONECROP
POWDERY LIVEFOREVER
BLUFF LETTUCE
HEN-AND-CHICKENS

Dudleya farinosa (Stonecrop family (*Crassulaceae*)
(Photo: Harris Beach SP, Curry Co., late July)

Plants often densely crowded on rocky cliffs, the flowering stems rising 4"-20". Thick leaves, 1"-2" long, more or less triangular, in basal rosettes, covered with a powdery substance that makes them appear gray. Stem leaves smaller, resembling scale-like clasping bracts. Flowers in somewhat flat-topped clusters, the petals about ½" long, pale yellow, barely spreading. Sea cliffs from Bandon south to CA.

SPREADING STONECROP
CASCADE STONECROP
PACIFIC STONECROP

Sedum divergens (Stonecrop family, *Crassulaceae*)
(Photo: Mount Ashland summit, Jackson Co., mid July)

Mat-forming, stems rising only 2"-6". Leaves mostly opposite, about ¼" long, fleshy, round or oval, widest below the middle, sessile, turning red in exposed locations. Flowering stems leafy, with clusters of bright yellow flowers, 5 distinct petals about 3/8" long, lance-shaped; 10 stamens, about ¾ as long as the petals. Rocky places, ledges, at high elevations, to BC and CA.

BROAD-LEAVED STONECROP
PACIFIC SEDUM

Sedum spathulifolium
(Stonecrop family, *Crassulaceae*)
(Photo: Shan Creek Road, Josephine Co., late May)

Fleshy stems rise to 10", from rosettes of fleshy leaves that are widest above the middle, tapering to base, usually rounded at outer edge, and sometimes notched. Rosette leaves less than 1" long, outer leaves in rosette much longer than the inner; stem leaves less than ½" long, elliptic. Five yellow petals, 1/4"-5/16" long, narrow and sharp-pointed, generally spreading, not fused at base. Rocky outcrops, west of Cascades, to BC and CA.

WORMLEAF STONECROP
NARROW-PETALED SEDUM

Sedum stenopetalum [*S. douglasii*]
Stonecrop family (*Crassulaceae*)
(Photo: Near Gold Ray Dam, Jackson Co., late May)

Stems erect, 2"-10" tall, basal leaves sometimes absent. Stem leaves ¼"-¾", very narrow, sharp. Leaf axils on flowering stems often bear short rosettes, that may drop off for propagation. Branches of the flower cluster usually less than 1" long, petals 5, yellow, narrow, about ¼" long. Rocky places, southwestern OR, to BC and CA.

SCOTCH BROOM

Cytisus scoparius (Legume family, *Fabaceae*)
(Photo: Highway 101 north of Brookings, Curry Co., late March)

Usually, the pea-like flowers of this woody shrub are entirely yellow, but occasionally plants of variety *andreanus* are found, which have crimson petals, as in the photo. Plants may grow to 10', with green branches. Leaflets generally in groups of 3, and may be only ½" long. The blossoms are considered attractive by many, but others look upon Scotch Broom as an invasive weed. It was originally introduced as an ornamental, but is now widely naturalized, especially along the coast. Native of Europe.

BIRDFOOT TREFOIL
BIRD'S FOOT LOTUS
BIRDFOOT DEERVETCH

Lotus corniculatus (Legume family, *Fabaceae*)
(Photo: Wagner Creek Road, Jackson Co. early July)

These little pea-type flowers may show up as yellow strips along the edges of roads. Stems numerous, ascending or prostrate, 1'-3' long. Leaves compound, usually with 5 leaflets 1/2" or so long, but with 2 leaflets next to the stem that resemble stipules. Flowers are in clusters of 3-8, on stems 2"-4" long, bright yellow, corolla 3/8"-1/2" long, banner petal 5/16" across. **TOXIC.** Meadows and disturbed areas at moderate elevations. **Big Trefoil** (*L. pedunculata*) is similar, but has clusters of 8-12 flowers.

BOG LOTUS
MEADOW BIRD'S-FOOT TREFOIL
BUTTER-AND-EGGS

Lotus pinnatus (Legume family, *Fabaceae*)
(Photo: Wagner Creek Road, Jackson Co., early July)

Stems ascending or partially decumbent, 8"-20" long. Leaves compound, leaflets 5-7, more or less oval, ½"-1" long. Flowers in loose umbel, 4-10 in number. Corolla 1/2"-5/8" long, banner yellow, turned sharply upward, other petals white. Wet meadows and ditches, west of Cascades to 5600', to WA and CA. **Streambank Lotus** (*L. oblongifolius*) is similar, corolla about 5/16" long.

BUTTER LUPINE

Lupinus luteolus (Legume family, *Fabaceae*)
(Photo: Near Old Siskiyou Summit, Jackson Co., early June)

Erect stems to 20" high, branched. Leaves palmate, 7-9 leaflets ½"-1¼" long, 3/16"-3/8" wide, petioles about twice as long as the leaflets. Flowers whorled, in dense racemes, with thin bracts 1/4"-3/8" long below the whorls. Corollas about ½" long, light yellow. Clearings and disturbed areas below 6000', Josephine, Jackson, and Klamath Cos., to CA. **Bush,** or **Tree Lupine** (*L. arboreus*), a California native that has been introduced on the coast for "sand-binding" purposes, also has yellow lupine flowers (sometimes blue), forms bushes to 6' tall, and has woody stems.

YELLOW SWEET-CLOVER

Melilotus officinalis (Legume family, *Fabaceae*)
(Photo: near Old Siskiyou Summit, Cascade-Siskiyou NM, Jackson Co., early June)

Erect, branching stems, 1'-4' high. Leaves palmate, in 3's, clover-like, edges somewhat toothed. Flowers pea-like, pale yellow, in narrow racemes, each flower ¼" long or less. In meadows and waste ground, especially east of the Cascades. Native of Europe. See, also, ***White Sweet-Clover*** (*M. alba*), p. 19.

FALSE LUPINE
GOLDEN PEA
Thermopsis macrophylla [*T. gracilis*]
(Legume family, *Fabaceae*)
(Photo: Galice-Agness Rd., Josephine Co., early June)

Somewhat resembles a lupine, but there are only 3 leaflets, with pairs of large leaf-like stipules at the bases of the petioles. Also, the 10 stamens are all separate, whereas in lupines they are joined. Stems 12"-30" tall, generally branched. Leaflets 1"-2½" long, entire. Flowers lupine-like, yellow, 5/8"-1" long, in terminal racemes. Regionally diverse, with several subspecies. Open dry sites, woodlands, roadsides, below 4000', west of Cascades, to CA.

GORSE
FURZE
Ulex europaeus (Legume family, *Fabaceae*)
(Photo: Harris Beach SP, Curry Co., late March)

The brilliant yellow flowers that clothe Gorse bushes in spring conceal the fact that the branches are almost all spines. Flowers pea-like, bright yellow, with a large banner petal. Branches stiff, green, arching, and woody. In some places, the plants form dense thickets over 6' high that are virtually impossible to enter. Abundant on the southern coast, and difficult to remove, once established. Most people dislike it, because of its spines and its invasive nature. Native of Europe, originally introduced as an ornamental.

KLAMATH WEED
ST. JOHN'S WORT
Hypericum perforatum
(St. John's Wort family, *Hypericaceae*)
(Photo: Near Star Flat, Josephine Co., late June)

An aggressive weed that reportedly is toxic to livestock, but has attractive yellow flowers. The multiple wiry stems may grow to 3', with paired linear leaves about 1" long. There are 5 petals, each about 3/8" long, bright yellow, often with black dots along the margins, numerous stamens. Meadows, pastures, and waste ground. Introduced from Europe.

SISKIYOU IRIS

Iris bracteata (Iris family, *Iridaceae*)
(Photo: Waldo Road, Josephine Co., mid May)

Stems clustered, 8"-12" high. Basal leaves 10"-20" long, 1/4"-3/8" wide, stiff; stem leaves bract-like. Flowers often 2 on a stem, pale yellowish, the floral tube about ¼" long, stout; sepals petal-like, 2"-2½" long, the petals narrower and shorter. Dry open forest, southern Josephine Co. to CA.

GOLDEN IRIS
DEL NORTE COUNTY IRIS

Iris innominata (Iris family, *Iridaceae*)
(Photo: Lower Rogue River, Curry Co., mid May)

Stem 8"-12" tall, with long narrow leaves about 1/8" wide, leaves sometimes longer than the stem, with two bracts about 1½" long sheathing the stem below the flowering head. Flowers, often 2, are deep, clear yellow, usually with darker, narrow veins, the outer segments 1½"-2" long. The narrow funnelform floral tube is about ¾"-1" long to the top of the ovary. Dry open woods, Josephine and Curry Cos., to CA. ***Water Iris*** (*I. pseudacorus*), an ornamental that has escaped into the wild, has large yellow flowers, grows to 3' tall, has tall stiff leaves to 1" wide, and forms large patches in water edges.

CALIFORNIA LAUREL
OREGON MYRTLE
CALIFORNIA BAY
PEPPERWOOD

Umbellularia californica (Laurel family, *Lauraceae*)
(Photo: Near O'Brien, Josephine Co., mid March)

Often a shrub, but can be a tree to 60' high, sometimes with a trunk 5'-6' dia., that divides into multiple smaller trunks. Leaves evergreen, more or less oblong, tapering to points at both ends, 2½"-4" long, short-petioled, strongly aromatic. Flowers small, clustered, about 5/16" across, with 6 yellowish-green sepals (petals lacking), 9 stamens, with 3 of the stamens in the center, each with a pair of orange glands at base. Coos and Douglas counties, to CA.

YELLOW FAWN LILY
GLACIER LILY
YELLOW LAMB'S TONGUE
YELLOW ADDER'S TONGUE
PALE DOGTOOTH VIOLET

Erythronium grandiflorum (Lily family, *Liliaceae*)
(Photo: Near Bear Camp, Curry Co., early June)

Leafless stems 4"-14" tall, 2 elliptic leaves at base, not mottled, 3"-6" long. Flowers 1-3, yellow, nodding, perianth parts lance-shaped, spreading and often turned backward. Anthers purplish, or white in local subspecies. Style 3-cleft. Woods and wet open slopes in mountains, at moderate to high elevations, to BC and CA.

YELLOW BELLS
YELLOW FRITILLARY

Fritillaria pudica (Lily family, *Liliaceae*)
(Photo: Hyatt Meadows, Jackson Co., late April)

Stems 3"-7" high, leaves 2-8, somewhat grass-like, mostly basal, 2"-5" long, with a few smaller leaves on stem. Flowers 1-2, perianth parts about 1/2"-3/4" long, deep yellow (sometimes orangish), nodding, narrowly bell-shaped. Open, more or less dry ground, mostly east of Cascades, but in southern OR extending west as far as the Rogue River Valley, to BC and CA.

VOLLMER LILY

Lilium pardalinum ssp. *vollmeri* [*L. vollmeri*]
(Lily family, *Liliaceae*)
(Photo: Wet bog near O'Brien, Josephine Co., early July)

These lovely flowers are sometimes called "Tiger Lily," or "Leopard Lily." Stems to 6' tall. Leaves typically 2"-10" long, narrow and pointed, usually in whorls, but also sometimes singly distributed. May be 1 to many flowers on a stem, perianth parts 2"-3½" long, mostly strongly curved backward, *2-toned,* inner surfaces pale orange, spotted with maroon, changing to red on outer portions. Pistil 1½"-2½" long, filaments spreading, *anthers magenta or purple,* ¼"-½" long. Bogs and springs, sw OR to CA.

WIGGINS LILY

Lilium pardalinum ssp. *wigginsii* [*L. wigginsii*]
(Lily family, *Liliaceae*)
(Photo: Wagner Creek Road, Jackson Co., early July)

Sometimes called "Tiger Lily," or "Leopard Lily." Stems to 6' tall. Leaves typically 2"-10" long, narrow and pointed, usually in whorls, but also sometimes singly distributed. May be 1 to many flowers on a stem, perianth parts 1½"-3" long, mostly strongly curved backward, *not* 2-toned, generally uniformly orange or yellow-orange, with maroon spots. Pistil 1½"-2" long, filaments spreading, *anthers pale yellow,* 3/16"-1/2" long. Wet thickets and meadows, sw OR to CA.

CALIFORNIA BOG ASPHODEL

Narthecium californicum (Lily family, *Liliaceae*)
(Photo: Near O'Brien, Josephine Co., early July)

Solitary stems 16"-20" high, with 2 or 3 very small stem leaves. Basal leaves 4"-12" long, 1/8"-1/4" wide, somewhat grass-like. Flowers in a spike 3"-6" long, 6 perianth parts, narrow, pointed, bright greenish-yellow. Wet meadows and bogs, southern Josephine Co. to CA.

YELLOW SAND VERBENA
YELLOW ABRONIA

Abronia latifolia
(Four O'Clock family, *Nyctaginaceae*)
(Photo: Humbug Mt. SP, Curry Co., late July)

The round balls of yellow flowers rise above spreading stems, which can form conspicuous mats. Leaves succulent, sticky, roundish, about 1" across. Yellow flowers, each a tube about ½" long and flaring out to ¼" dia., are in round heads about 1½" across. Beaches and dunes along the coast, to BC and CA.

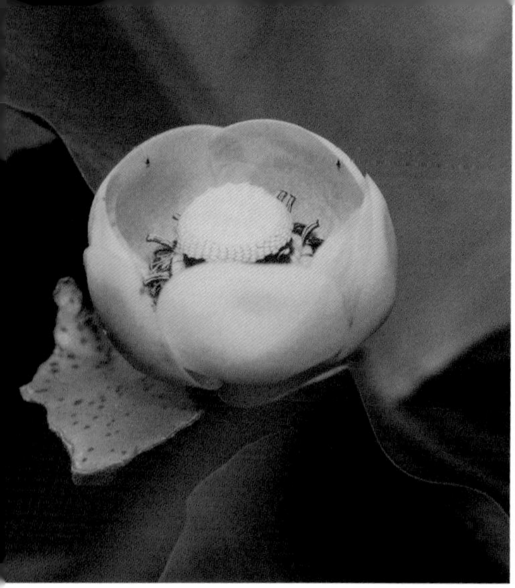

YELLOW POND-LILY
INDIAN POND-LILY
SPATTERDOCK
COW-LILY

Nuphar lutea ssp. *polysepala* [*N. polysepala*]
(Water-lily family, *Nymphaeaceae*)
(Photo: Near Bandon SP, Coos Co., mid May)

Hard to mistake for anything else, with its large bowl-shaped yellow flowers, and floating leaves. Stems are rooted in the mud, leaves large, heart-shaped, leathery, up to 18" long. Flowers are 2"-3" wide, with 7-12 sepals, the outer ones greenish, and the larger inner ones bright yellow (sometimes reddish-tinged) and petal-like. The 10-20 petals are thin and stamen-like, and the disk-like stigma is up to 1" diameter. Ponds and lakes from sea level to 8000', to AK and CA.

BEACH EVENING-PRIMROSE

Camissonia cheiranthifolia
[*Oenothera cheiranthifolia*]
(Evening primrose family, *Onagraceae*)
(Photo: Near Pistol River, Curry Co., early May)

Long, sprawling, fleshy stems, slightly hairy, 8"-20" long, radiating from rosette of basal leaves. Basal leaves narrow, fleshy, 1½"-3" long, including slender petioles. Stem leaves shorter and broader, fleshy. Flowers with 4 broad oval petals, each petal 1/4"-3/8" long, bright yellow, turning red with age. Calyx 3/16" long, with 4 narrow lobes about as long, strongly reflexed. Pistil rather globe-shaped on end. Beaches, sand dunes, sandy slopes, Coos Co. to CA.

TANSY-LEAF EVENING-PRIMROSE
TANSY-LEAF SUN CUP

Camissonia tanacetifolia [*Oenothera tanacetifolia*]
(Evening primrose family, *Onagraceae*)
(Photo: Hyatt Lake, Jackson Co., mid August)

No main stem, flowers rising on short pedicels from flat rosette of basal leaves. Leaves 3"-8" long, narrowly elliptic, deeply and irregularly lobed. Flowers yellow, turning reddish later, 4 petals, 3/8"-3/4" long, calyx with 4 narrow sharp lobes, lobes turned downward. Meadows and moist flats, widely distributed east of Cascades, to WA and CA. **Sun Cup** (*C. ovata*) is similar but has leaves that are almost entire, or are wavy-edged.

WOLF EVENING-PRIMROSE

Oenothera wolfii [*O. hookeri* ssp. *wolfii*]
(Evening Primrose family, *Onagraceae*)
(Photo: Whalehead Beach, Curry Co., late July)

The large yellow flowers are attention-grabbing, as are the reddish erect buds. Plants to 4' tall, with fleshy, hairy stems. Leaves 2"-7" long, narrow, pointed, hairy. The 4 showy yellow petals are ½"-1" long; the long, narrow sepals are hairy and hang downward. Stigma split into 4 linear lobes. **Federal species of concern.** Coastal areas, dunes, bluffs, roadsides, to CA. Two other species of ***Evening Primrose,*** *O. glazioviana* (non-native) and *O. elata* are similar, but have larger flowers.

CALIFORNIA LADY'S SLIPPER

Cypripedium californicum
(Orchid family, *Orchidaceae*)
(Photo: Near O'Brien, Josephine Co., late June)

Stems 1'-2' high, stout, leafy, hairy. Leaves lance-shaped or somewhat oval, pointed, clasping, 3"-5" long. Flowers 3-10, sepals and petals 1/2"-5/8" long, yellowish, lip oval, appearing inflated, white or pinkish, about 3/4" long. Moist places, Douglas Co. to CA. **Mountain Lady's Slipper** (*C. montanum*), found on both sides of Cascades, has narrow purplish sepals 1½"-2½" long

STREAM ORCHID
GIANT HELLEBORINE

Epipactis gigantea (Orchid family, *Orchidaceae*)
(Photo: Near O'Brien, Josephine Co., late June)

Stems 1'-2' high, stout and fleshy, not hairy. Leaves 5-7, long and narrow, clasping, 2½"-6" long. Flowers 3-12, perianth parts yellow-green, 1/2"-5/8" long, petals purple-veined, lip 1/2"-5/8" long, often bent downward. Generally along streams and lakes, to WA and CA.

YELLOW WOOD SORREL
SUKSDORF WOOD SORREL
WESTERN YELLOW OXALIS

Oxalis suksdorfii (Oxalis family, *Oxalidaceae*)
(Photo: Harris Beach SP, late July)

Stems erect, slender, 3"-10" high, somewhat hairy. Leaflets in 3s, heart-shaped, about ½" long, on petioles 1"-2½" long. Flowers 1-2 per stem, petals 5, bright yellow. Thickets west of Cascades, to WA and CA. ***Creeping Yellow Wood Sorrel*** (*O. corniculata*), non-native, often found in lawns and disturbed areas, is similar, but has smaller flowers, herbage usually is purplish, and stems are creeping and rooting.

CALIFORNIA POPPY

Escholtzia californica
(Poppy family, *Papaveraceae*)
(Photo: Rogue Valley, Jackson Co., late May)

Plants 8"-20" tall, clustered, many-flowered, flowers showy. Leaves bunched, 3-5 parted into narrow divisions, bluish-green. Flowers on long stems, buds sharply pointed, petals yellow or orange, satiny, about 1" long, more or less oval or wedge-shaped, base of flower with conspicuous collar-like rim. Roadsides and grassy open areas, sea level to 6000', west of Cascades, to WA and CA. **Slender California Poppy** (*E. caespitosa*) is similar, occurs in southern Klamath Co., but is smaller, lighter yellow, and has a relatively undeveloped collar-like rim.

CREAM CUPS

Platystemon californicus
(Poppy family, *Papaveraceae*)
(Photo: Bandon SP, Coos Co., late March)

Sometimes in masses, stems erect or decumbent, 2"-8" long, hairy; flowers solitary on peduncles 2"-10" long. Leaves hairy, narrow, ¾"-3" long, opposite or whorled, mostly near base. Flowers ½"-1" diameter, 6 petals, yellow to almost white, many stamens. Open areas, lower Rogue River Valley and along coast, from Coos Co. to CA.

GRAND COLLOMIA
LARGE-FLOWERED COLLOMIA
MOUNTAIN COLLOMIA

Collomia grandiflora
(Phlox family, *Polemoniaceae*)
(Photo: Near Lost Creek Lake, Jackson Co., late June)

Rises 1'-3', leaves alternate, mostly narrow, pointed, entire, 1"-3" long. Flowers in dense, mostly terminal clusters, bracts sticky, corollas trumpet-shaped, 5/8"-7/8" long, yellow to salmon-colored, flaring into 5 lobes. Dry open areas, moderate to high elevations, both sides of Cascades, to BC and CA. **Narrow-leaved Collomia** *(C. linearis)*, similar, but flowers are smaller, and are pink to lilac.

SULFUR FLOWER
SULFUR-FLOWER BUCKWHEAT

Eriogonum umbellatum
(Buckwheat family, *Polygonaceae*)
(Photo: Grouse Gap, Jackson Co., late August)

Plants shrubby, low-growing, flowering stems rising 4"-12". Leaves narrow, ½"-1¼" long, green above, whitish below, slender petioles. Flowers in umbels with 2-10 rays to 4" long, in globose clusters, yellow or tinged with red, each flower about ¼" long, whorls of leafy bracts below the umbels. Dry ground in Cascades and Siskiyous, to WA and CA. **Mountain Buckwheat** (*E. marifolium*), at higher elevations in Cascades, resembles a dwarf version of Sulfur Flower. **Rock Buckwheat** (*E. sphaerocephalum*), east of Cascades and in Siskiyous has cream-colored or light yellow flowers, and 2-3 rays.

SOUTHERN OREGON BUTTERCUP

Ranunculus austro-oreganus
(Buttercup family, *Ranunculaceae*)
(Photo: Upper Table Rock Trail, Jackson Co., mid March)

Found only in Jackson Co. Resembles *R. occidentalis* (see p. 72), but outsides of petals are reddish-brown. Inside, flowers are yellow. Plants 8"-16" high, sometimes branched, hairy stems. Basal leaves typically 1½" long, petioles 3"-4" long, palmate, deeply cleft into 3 leaflets, each leaflet again cleft. Sepals sharply bent backward; may drop off early. **Straightbeak Buttercup** (*R. orthorynchus*) also may be reddish-brown on the outsides of petals, but leaves are pinnate, rather than palmate.

SAGEBRUSH BUTTERCUP

Ranunculus glaberrimus
(Buttercup family, *Ranunculaceae*)
(Photo: Sprague River Day-Use Area, Klamath Co., early May)

Low-growing, to 3"-4" exclusive of flower stems. Leaves longer than broad, somewhat fleshy, typically 3-lobed, the points blunt. Flowers on long stems, 1-3 to a stem, petals broadly oval, deep yellow, ¼"-½" long. Juniper-sagebrush areas east of Cascades, to BC and CA. **Eschscholtz Buttercup** (*R. eschscholtzii*), found at high elevations in the Cascades, is somewhat similar, but is taller, with leaves broader than long, 3-parted, the divisions often cleft.

WESTERN BUTTERCUP

Ranunculus occidentalis
(Buttercup family, *Ranunculaceae*)
(Photo: Little Hyatt Lake Road, early May)

Stems 8"-20" high, branching, usually hairy. Basal leaves roundish in outline, on petioles 2½"-6" long, 3-parted or cleft, the divisions again cleft, the divisions 1"-1½" long, either pointed or rounded, stem leaves few. Flowering stems widely branched, with long slender stems. Petals usually 5 or 6, but may be more, about 3/8"-1/2" long, bright yellow, both inside and outside (see *R. austro-oreganus,* p. 71). Open ground, mostly west of Cascades, to BC and CA.

MOUNTAIN BUTTERCUP

Ranunculus populago
(Buttercup family, *Ranunculaceae*)
(Photo: Near Mount Ashland, Jackson Co., late June)

Stems 4"-8" long, usually erect and few-branched. Leaves oval to heart-shaped, usually entire, blades ½"-1½" long with petioles 1"-3" long, sheathing the stems. Flowers yellow, mostly 5-petaled, petals oval, 3/16"-1/4" long. Wet meadows and pond edges at moderately high elevations in Cascades and Siskiyous, to WA and CA. Other somewhat similar species: **Creeping Spearwort** (*R. flammula*) has long runners, rooting at the nodes; **Plantain-leaved Buttercup** (*R. alismifolius*) has narrow leaves.

CREEPING BUTTERCUP

Ranunculus repens
(Buttercup family, *Ranunculaceae*)
(Photo: Lone Ranch Beach, Curry Co., late March)

Flowers often solitary and showy. Stems long, fleshy, and somewhat hairy. Leaves large, often with long petioles, up to 4 inches long, deeply lobed into 3 parts, the parts further lobed and cleft. Flowers bright yellow, glossy, up to 1" dia. Moist ground, sometimes in lawns, widespread, plentiful along the coast. Introduced from Europe.

PACIFIC SILVERWEED

Argentina egedii [*Potentilla pacifica*]
(Rose family, *Rosaceae*)
(Photo: Near Bandon, Coos Co., early May)

Low, creeping plant that likes the sand. Leaves compound, to 12" long, with 13-17 leaflets, principal leaflets 1"-2" long, heavily dentate, silvery-white below, with much smaller leaflets interspersed along the stem. Flowers about 1" across, borne singly on slender stems, 5 bright yellow petals. On immediate coast, from AK to CA. **Silverweed Cinquefoil** (*A. anserina* [*Potentilla anserina*]), with smaller leaves and flowers, is found inland.

STICKY CINQUEFOIL

Potentilla glandulosa (Rose family, *Rosaceae*)
(Photo: Cloudcap, Crater Lake NP, Klamath Co., mid July)

Highly variable, with many subspecies. Stems may rise 6"-36", hairy, often sticky. Leaves compound, generally 2"-8" long, pinnate, leaflets more or less oval, hairy, deeply toothed, 3-5 per side. Petals yellow or cream-colored, usually 5, about ¼" long, widely oblong. Stamens numerous, about 25, short. Common, in wide variety of habitats, from moist, shady locations to open rocky places, from moderate to high altitudes, throughout the west.

SLENDER CINQUEFOIL
NORTHWEST CINQUEFOIL
FIVEFINGER CINQUEFOIL

Potentilla gracilis (Rose family, *Rosaceae*)
(Photo, near Hyatt Meadows, Jackson Co., early June)

Stems erect, 12"-28" high, hairy. Leaves palmate, whitish below, long-petioled, the petioles hairy, 5-7 leaflets 1½"-3" long, the leaflets deeply cleft into many segments. Inflorescence branched, flowers few to many, petals 5, yellow, broadly oval, 3/16"-3/8" long. Widespread in meadows, mostly west of Cascades, to AK and CA. Highly variable, with many varieties. **Shrubby Cinquefoil** (*Dasiphora floribunda* [*Potentilla fruticosa*]) found east of Cascades and in the Siskiyous, has similar flowers, but is shrubby, and has pinnate, rather than palmate, leaves.

ANTELOPE BITTERBRUSH

Purshia tridentata (Rose family, *Rosaceae*)
(Photo: Westside Road, Klamath Co., late May)

Shrub to small tree, to 8' high, spreading branches. Leaves numerous, ½"-1" long, wedge-shaped, typically 3-lobed, whitish below. Flowers solitary on short twigs, calyx about ¼" long with spreading rounded lobes, 5 petals, about ¼" long, tapering to long claws, pale yellow, stamens 15-25. Dry areas east of Cascades, sagebrush scrub, coniferous forest, to WA and CA.

CALIFORNIA PITCHER-PLANT
COBRA LILY

Darlingtonia californica
(Pitcher-plant family, *Sarraceniaceae*)
(Photo: 8 Dollar Road, Josephine Co., early May)

Many people have seen pitcher-plants, at locations such as the Darlingtonia Wayside on the Oregon coast. But not as many have seen the flowers, which bloom before the usual tourist season. The leaves are the most remarkable part of the plant, because they rise 2' and more, to form cobra-like greenish-brown hoods that trap insects. But the flowers are remarkable, too. They stand on stems to 3' tall, rising separately from the leaves, the heads nodding. Sepals are conspicuous, yellowish-green, to 2" long. Petals are somewhat concealed by the sepals, purplish, shorter than the sepals. Wet places, sometimes on flats, but also in flowing springs on hillsides, on the coast and southern Curry and Josephine Cos., to CA.

COBWEBBY PAINTBRUSH
COTTON PAINTBRUSH

Castilleja arachnoidea
(Figwort family, *Scrophulariaceae*)
(Photo: Near Siskiyou Peak, Jackson Co., late June)

Stems 3"-8" high, with dense floral spikes, hairy. Leaves narrowly linear, 3/4"-2" long, generally with 1 or 2 pairs of very narrow lobes. Bracts of the inflorescence ½"-1" long, dull yellow or rusty red, hairy, lobed. Corolla hairy above, about 3/4" long, green. Calyx hairy, almost as long as corolla. Sisikiyous and east of Cascades.

DALMATIAN TOADFLAX

Linaria genistifolia ssp. *dalmatica* [*L. dalmatica*]
(Figwort family, *Scrophulariaceae*)
(Photo: Shale City Road, Jackson Co., mid June)

Tall, erect stems, to 48" high, branched, with yellow flowers in spikes. Leaves crowded, mostly oval, generally 1"-2" long, pointed, more or less clasping. Flowers 3/4"-2" long, snapdragonlike, with long pointed spurs, lower lips whitish or orange-hairy. Widely naturalized, considered a noxious weed. Native of Europe. ***Butter-and-Eggs*** (*L. vulgaris*), also non-native, is similar, but has smaller flowers and long narrow leaves.

BUSH MONKEYFLOWER

Mimulus aurantiacus
(Figwort family, *Scrophulariaceae*)
(Photo: Whalehead Beach, Curry Co., late July)

Mostly a California species. Plants are bushy, grow to 4' tall. Leaves 1"-2" long, narrow, often somewhat dentate, sticky, the latter characteristic causing some people to call this plant "Sticky-monkey." Flowers large and showy, deep yellow-orange, funnel-form, almost 2" long, spreading out into 5 unequal lobes. Open slopes on the coast, southern Curry Co., to CA.

COMMON MONKEYFLOWER
SEEP-SPRING MONKEYFLOWER

Mimulus guttatus
(Figwort family, *Scrophulariaceae*)
(Photo: Humbug Mt. SP, Curry Co., mid May)

Highly variable, often occurring as small, tightly packed plants in wet places, but also may be 3' high. Stems may be stout or slender, often somewhat hairy. Leaves oval shaped, shallowly to deeply dentate, ¾"-2" long. Calyx less than half as long as corolla, bell-shaped, lobes pointed, upper lobe longer than the others. Corolla bright yellow, ¾" to nearly 1½" long, lower lip larger than the upper, throat hairy and more or less red-spotted. Moist places from the coast to moderate elevations, to BC and CA. **Larger Mountain Monkeyflower** (*M. tilingii*) at moderately high elevations, is similar, has fewer but larger flowers. **Chickweed Monkeyflower** (*M. alsinoides*), in the Cascades and eastward, has smaller flowers, each with a large maroon spot on the throat.

YELLOW GLANDWEED
EYEBRIGHT

Parentucellia viscosa
(Figwort family, *Scrophulariaceae*)
(Photo: Whalehead Beach, Curry Co., late July)

Plants grow to 3' tall, stout hairy stems and numerous leaves, the leaves 1"-2½" long, narrow, sharp-pointed, dentate, sessile, hairy, and sticky. Flowers yellow, funnel-shaped, with a hooded upper lip, and a 3-lobed lower lip, in a leafy-bracted spike. There are 4 stamens, with hairy anthers. Moist ground west of Cascades. Native of Europe.

JOHNNY-TUCK
BUTTER-AND-EGGS

Triphysaria eriantha [*Orthocarpus erianthus*]
(Figwort family, *Scrophulariaceae*)
(Photo: Near White City, Jackson Co., early April)

Plants 4"-14" high, leaves ½"-2" long, fairly broad at base, cleft 5-7 times with filiform lobes, upper bracts smaller, dense, lobed, purple tipped. Inflorescence 1"-6" long, dense, numerous flowers. Calyx with sharp points, less than half as long as corolla, corolla ½"-1" long, slender-tubed, whitish, lower lip with 3 yellow pouches about 1/8" deep, purple beak extending slightly above pouches. Grassland, foothills, southwest OR to CA.

MOTH MULLEIN

Verbascum blattaria
(Figwort family, *Scrophulariaceae*)
(Photo: Butte Creek Falls, Jackson Co., early July)

Tall stems, sometimes branched, 1'-4' tall. Leaves more or less oval, 2½"-4" long, toothed, upper leaves smaller and clasping. Flowers in a tall spike, sticky, yellow or white, about 1" diameter, 5-lobed, saucer-shaped, stamen filaments purple. Disturbed places. Introduced from Europe.

WOOLLY MULLEIN
COMMON MULLEIN

Verbascum thapsus
(Figwort family, *Scrophulariaceae*)
(Photo: Wagner Creek Road, Jackson Co., early September)

Instantly recognizable, stout, tall, up to 6'. Stems and leaves densely woolly, stems spire-like, unbranched except at top. Lower leaves up to 18" long and 5" wide, the upper smaller and clasping. Flowers about 5/8" across, 5 petals, yellow, densely packed in a spike 1'-3' long. Common along roadsides and in waste places. Introduced from Europe.

BAKER VIOLET

Viola bakeri (Violet family, *Violaceae*)
(Photo: Little Hyatt Lake Road, Jackson Co., early May)

The plants are low, the flowers about even with the leaves. Leaves mostly rise from the base, 3"-5" long, lanceolate, tapering to long petioles. Flowers yellow, lower 3 petals with brownish veins, on stems 1"-3" long. Open coniferous forests above 4000 feet, to WA and CA.

STREAM VIOLET
YELLOW WOOD VIOLET
SMOOTH WOODLAND VIOLET

Viola glabella (Violet family, *Violaceae*)
(Photo: Little Applegate Valley, Jackson Co., late April)

Stems 2"-12" high, leaves mostly near the top. Leaves more or less heart-shaped, 1"-2½" long, scalloped, pointed, the basal leaves with long petioles. Petals bright yellow, each about ½" long, the lower 3 with purple veins, the lateral pair bearded. Widely distributed in moist woods, from low to moderate elevations, to AK and CA. **Pine Violet** (*V. lobata*), in southern Josephine Co., is similar, but the leaves are broader than long, up to 2" across, with 3-9 broad fingerlike lobes.

EVERGREEN VIOLET
REDWOOD VIOLET

Viola sempervirens (Violet family, *Violaceae*)
(Photo: Floras Lake, Curry Co., late March)

Flowering stems and leaf stems rise from decumbent runners that root at the nodes. Leaves are leathery, with petioles from ½"-6", blades from ½"-1½", usually more or less round, scalloped on the edges, sometimes finely brown-dotted beneath. Flowering stems rise 2"-4", with lemon-yellow flowers, the lower 3 petals purple-veined. West of cascades, especially on the coast, in shady woods, to BC and CA. **Darkwoods Violet** (*V. orbiculata*), found at higher elevations in Cascades, is similar, but lacks the rooting runners, and the leaves are not finely brown-dotted beneath.

SHELTON VIOLET

Viola sheltonii (Violet family, *Violaceae*)
(Photo: Colestin Road, Jackson Co., mid April)

Flowers rise above the leaves, on stems 1"-2" high. Leaves in overall outline are broader than long, are palmately divided, with the segments further parted and cleft into oblong rounded lobes. Petals are light yellow, about ½" long, purple tinged on the backs, relatively narrow, with dark streaks on the lower 3. Open woods, west of the Cascades, to WA and CA. A similar species, **Douglas Violet** (*V. douglasii*) is found in Josephine and Jackson Cos. to CA, in which the petals are somewhat larger and less narrow, and the leaves, though deeply lobed and parted, are typically longer than broad, the segments linear.

Checkermallow

RED to PINK FLOWERS

ed and pink flowers clearly belong here, but flowers merging into the violet can be a problem, and ight wind up either in this section or the next one, "Blue to Violet." Also, white flowers sometimes n be pink, and then it becomes a matter of choice whether to include them here on in the "White to ream" section.

VINE MAPLE

Acer circinatum (Maple family, *Aceraceae*)
(Photo: Near Salt Creek Falls, Lane Co., mid June)

Vine maples generally aren't thought of in terms of their flowers, but mostly because of their spectacular yellow, orange, and red leaves in autumn. But they do have attractive little flowers, in clusters, with 5 red sepals, about 3/16" long, sharp-pointed, and 5 white petals, about half as long. The tree-like shrubs are often multiple-branched, 3'-18' tall. Leaves are opposite, more or less round in outline, usually 7-lobed, 2"-4" across. The winged fruits stick out almost 180 degrees apart, resembling an airplane propeller. Damp woods, from BC to CA.

SEA FIG
FIG MARIGOLD

Carpobrotus chilensis
[*Mesembryanthemum chilensis*]
(Fig-Marigold family, *Aizoaceae*)
(Photo: Harris Beach SP, Curry Co., mid May)

This species and its relatives are often broadly lumped as "ice-plant." Stems stout, prostrate, to 5' long, rooting at the nodes. Leaves fleshy, triangular in cross-section, 1"-2" long. Flowers showy, 1½"-2" dia., with many rose-purple petals, yellow centers. Coast, from Cape Blanco to CA. Native of South Africa.

SPREADING DOGBANE
BITTER DOGBANE

Apocynum androsaemifolium
[*A. medium, A. pumilum*]
(Dogbane family, *Apocynaceae*)
(Photo: Near Mount Peavine, Josephine Co., early June)

Low-growing, 12" tall or less, diffusely branched. Leaves opposite, 1½"-2½" long, somewhat heart-shaped, drooping to spreading, dark green above, paler below, short-petioled. Corolla bell-shaped, less than ½" long, generally pink, to purplish or white, sometimes pink-striped, lobes spreading or recurved. Open dry slopes, coniferous forest or chaparral, to Canada and CA. **Indian Hemp** (*A. cannabinum*) is taller, with narrow ascending leaves, and smaller greenish or white flowers.

SHOWY MILKWEED

Asclepias speciosa
(Milkweed family, *Asclepiadaceae*)
(Photo: Near Howard Prairie Lake, Jackson Co., mid August)

Milkweeds are hosts for monarch butterflies, but are toxic to livestock. Plant to 3' high, stout stem, somewhat woolly, large fleshy opposite leaves 3"-6" long. There are 5 reflexed corolla lobes, pinkish, ovate, about ½" long. The 5 hoods are petal-like, narrow, pointed, yellowish to pinkish, each with a small horn that curves toward central column. Dry ground, both sides of Cascades, to CA. A somewhat similar species, **Narrow-leaved Milkweed** (*A. fascicularis*), has narrow leaves 2"-4" long, in whorls.

CANADA THISTLE

Cirsium arvense (Sunflower family, *Asteraceae*)
(Photo: Lone Ranch Beach, Curry Co., late July)

Many spiny thistles have lovely flowers, as in this case. Plants grow to 6' high, with long, deeply lobed leaves, the lobes armed with sharp spines. Flower heads are lavender or pink, less than 1" in dia., with large bell-shaped involucres ½"-¾" long, the bracts in many tightly overlapping layers, some with tiny prickles. Male and female flowers are on separate plants. Widely distributed, and considered to be a troublesome weed. Introduced from Europe, originally in Canada.

BULL THISTLE
COMMON THISTLE

Cirsium vulgare (Sunflower family, *Asteraceae*)
(Photo: Hyatt Lake, Cascade-Siskiyou NM, Jackson Co., late August)

Tall, robust, unmistakable, spiny, ugly, and beautiful. Grows to 5' tall, with large, deeply lobed leaves to 12" long, tipped with spines. Flowering heads with large involucres, 1"-1½" in diameter, the bracts with spines. Disk flowers only, reddish purple, showy. Abundant almost throughout state in disturbed places. Introduced from Europe. **Snowy Thistle** (*C. pastoris*) a native plant, is somewhat similar, but the flowers are bright crimson, and the foliage is covered with dense white hairs.

EASTWOOD DAISY
ALICE'S FLEABANE

Erigeron aliceae (Sunflower family, *Asteraceae*)
(Photo: Near Hyatt Lake, Cascade-Siskiyou NM, Jackson Co., early July)

A lovely daisy, 2' tall and more, with clustered hairy stems. Leaves hairy, slender, pointed, lower ones to 11" long including the long slender petioles, upper ones sessile. Flower heads large and showy, about 1½" in dia., the bright yellow disk ½" across, and the pink or lilac-colored (sometimes white) ray flowers numbering 40-80. Involucre hemispheric, with slender pointed bracts, hairy. Widespread in open woods in the Cascades and Siskiyous, to WA and CA. **Subalpine Daisy** (*E. peregrinus*) is similar, but the lower leaves often are spoon-shaped and ciliate, and the involucre bracts are broader.

WALDO ROCK CRESS

Arabis aculeolata (Mustard family, *Brassicaceae*)
(Photo: Rough and Ready, Josephine Co., late March)

The flowers shine like beacons in the dry areas where these plants live. Hairy stems rise 6"-8" above tight rosettes of small leaves, few flowers to a cluster, with some small linear stem leaves. Basal leaves oval or spatulate, somewhat ciliate, tapering to short petioles, ½"-1" long including petioles. Calyx deep purple, about 3/16" long. There are 4 petals, deep pink to magenta, about 1/2" long. Dry ground, southern Josephine and Curry Cos., to CA. **Oregon Rock Cress** (*A. oregana*) is similar, but leaves mostly are larger. **Rogue River Rock Cress** (*A. modesta*), is similar, also has mostly larger leaves than Waldo Rock Cress, but hairiness is much less.

SEA ROCKET

Cakile maritima (Mustard family, *Brassicaceae*)
(Photo: Humbug Mountain SP, Curry Co., late March)

Sprawling plant with fleshy stems to 2' long. Leaves also are fleshy, 2"-3" long, deeply divided into leaflets ½" long. Flowers clustered at ends of stems, light pink to white, 4 petals, about ½" across, with short petioles. Ocean beaches and dunes. Native of Europe. ***American Sea Rocket*** (*C. edentula*), a native of eastern North America, is similar, but has wavy-edged and lobed leaves, rather than deeply divided, and petals are narrower.

PALMATE TOOTHWORT
NUTTALL TOOTHWORT
SLENDER DENTARIA

Cardamine nuttallii [*Dentaria tenella*]
(Mustard family, *Brassicaceae*)
(Photo: Near O'Brien, Josephine Co., late March)

Low-growing, 4"-10" tall, variable. Basal leaves typically with long petioles, roundish, scalloped edges, occasionally lobed, bases often heart-shaped. Stem leaves few, compound, parted in 3-5 (sometimes 7) narrow leaflets ½"-1½" long. Flowers few, in clusters, 4 petals, about 3/8" long, usually pink, sometimes white. Wooded, generally moist sites, to WA and CA.

DAGGER-POD

Phoenicaulis cheiranthoides
(Mustard family, *Brassicaceae*)
(Photo: Near Hyatt Lake, Cascade-Siskiyou NM, Jackson Co., mid May)

Stems erect or decumbent, 3"-8" high. Basal leaves narrowly oval, with fine dense woolly surfaces, entire, 2"-3½" long, stem leaves smaller. Flower clusters dense, petals 4, about 3/8" long, reddish-purple to pink. Seedpods long and slender (hence, the name "Dagger-Pod"), up to 3" long, spreading. Dry areas east of Cascades, to WA and CA.

WILD RADISH

Raphanus sativus (Mustard family, *Brassicaceae*)
(Photo: Highway 101 north of Brookings, Curry Co., late March)

A widespread weed, native to the Mediterranean region, superficially resembling mustard. There are 4 petals, each about ½" long, arranged in a cross, varying in color from purplish, to pink, to white. Plants to 3' tall, with stout stems. Leaves pinnately lobed or compound, toothed, with leaflets increasing in size to terminal leaflet, which is very large. ***Jointed Charlock*** (*R. raphanistrum*), also non-native, is similar, but usually has yellowish petals, and seedpods are more deeply constricted between the seeds than in *R. sativus.*

TWINFLOWER
AMERICAN TWINFLOWER

Linnaea borealis
(Honeysuckle family, *Caprifoliaceae*)
(Photo: Union Creek CG, Jackson Co., early July)

These tiny flowers always appear in pairs, the blossoms dangling at the ends of V-shaped, erect stems that are 2"-4" high. Stems rise from slender, evergreen, trailing, woody vines, with small, somewhat leathery, partially toothed leaves. Corolla is funnelform, about ½" long, pink or white, with 5 lobes. Shady moist woods, throughout most of western North America.

ORANGE HONEYSUCKLE
WESTERN TRUMPET HONEYSUCKLE

Lonicera ciliosa
(Honeysuckle family, *Caprifoliaceae*)
(Photo: Fish Lake Trail, Jackson Co., late June)

Stems woody, climbing, to 18' high. Leaves elliptic, 2½"-4" long, upper pairs joined, with flower stalk penetrating. Flowers in dense clusters, corollas tubular, about 1" long, orange-red to red. Woods on both sides of Cascades, to WA and CA. Two other climbing honeysuckles are: **Hairy Honeysuckle** (*L. hispidula*), with yellowish, pink, or purplish-red flowers; **Chaparral Honeysuckle** (*L. interrupta*), with small cream-colored flowers.

GRASS PINK
DEPTFORD PINK

Dianthus armeria (Pink family, *Caryophyllaceae*)
(Photo: Near Butte Falls, Jackson Co., early July)

Slender stems, 8"-20" high, often with closely ascending branches; leaves mostly very slender, 1½"-2½" long. Flowers in terminal clusters; calyxes narrow, about 3/4" long; petals 5, deep rose color, flecked with whitish dots, slightly toothed on ends, flaring into wheel-shape about 1/2" dia. Fields and waste ground, in scattered locations through much of North America. Native of Europe.

COMMON CATCHFLY
SMALL-FLOWERED CATCHFLY
WINDMILL PINK

Silene gallica (Pink family, *Caryophyllaceae*)
(Photo: Lone Ranch, Curry Co., mid May)

Plants 12"-20" tall, hairy, sticky. Leaves narrow, ¾"-2" long. Flowers in narrow, usually one-sided racemes. Calyxes generally less than ½" long, cylindric, inflated in fruit, hairy, with dark longitudinal stripes. Flowers said to resemble windmills, with 5 petals, white to dark red, long-clawed, each less than ¼" long, entire or slightly notched, 2 small appendages at bases of petals. Common in waste ground in western OR, especially along coast, to BC and CA. Native of Europe.

HOOKER INDIAN PINK
HOOKER SILENE
STRINGFLOWER

Silene hookeri (Pink family, *Caryophyllaceae*)
(Photo: Flumet Flat CG, Jackson Co., late April)

Variable; the name "stringflower" best applies to variety with white petals and stringlike lobes. Stems 2"-8", hairy, often decumbent, leaves narrow, petioled, sharp-pointed. Flowers generally solitary, calyx about ¾" long, faintly veined, becoming distended in fruit. Petals 5, bright pink to white, about 5/8" long, each tapered to a broad claw, petals lobed with 4 linear lobes with the middle pair longer, the lobes sometimes string-like. Dry forest and open areas, west of Cascades to moderate elevations, to CA.

SCOULER CATCHFLY

Silene scouleri (Pink family, *Caryophyllaceae*)
(Photo: Near White City, Jackson Co., late April)

Height from 6" to more than 2', stem hairy; narrow stem leaves only 1"-2" long, the upper ones almost without petioles. Lower leaves larger, may be somewhat spoon-shaped, and are long-petioled. Petals white or rose-colored, each deeply bilobed, narrow at the base. Calyx ½"-1" long, 10 prominent longitudinal veins, cylindrical at first, later becoming swollen. Dry, open areas, at lower elevations, to BC and CA.

BEACH MORNING-GLORY

Calystegia soldanella [*Convolvulus soldanella*]
(Morning-Glory family, *Convolvulaceae*)
(Photo: Humbug Mt. SP, mid May)

This gorgeous morning-glory far outshines its familiar relative with the undignified name of "Bind-weed" (see p. 15). Vines spreading, with almost round fleshy leaves 1"-2" in dia. Flowers trumpet-shaped, pink to purplish, to 2" long. Sandy ocean beaches to WA and CA.

SUGAR STICK
CANDY STICK
BARBERPOLE

Allotropa virgata (Heath family, *Ericaceae*)
(Photo: Near Mill Creek CG, Jackson Co., late June)

Single stout stem, 8"-20" high, a non-green plant, obtaining its nutrition from decaying vegetable matter. Stem white with red stripes, hence the common names. Leaves scale-like. Flowers crowded in a long spike, short pedicels, corollas cup-shaped, 5 white petals, 10 stamens projecting beyond corollas, dark purplish anthers, ovaries brown, with disk-like stigmas. Shady coniferous or mixed forests, at low or moderate elevations, in Coast Range or Cascades, to WA and CA.

GREEN-LEAF MANZANITA

Arctostaphylos patula (Heath family *Ericaceae*)
(Photo: Near Collier SP, Klamath Co., early May)

Manzanitas have leathery green leaves and reddish-brown smooth bark. There are 8 species of shrub-like species in Southern Oregon, many showing only small differences. Two widespread shrubs are **Green-leaf Manzanita** (*A. patula*), mostly in the Cascades, and **White-leaf Manzanita** (*A. viscida*), in Jackson and Josephine Cos. Both have leaves about 1"-2" long. In "Green-leaf" the leaves are bright green; in "White-leaf" the leaves are pale green. Flowers are in clusters, urn-shaped and pink or whitish, but the flower clusters are sticky in "White-leaf."

KINNIKINNICK
BEARBERRY

Arctostaphylos uva-ursi (Heath family *Ericaceae*)
(Photo: Near Pistol River, Curry Co., early May)

Stems are up to 1½' long and trailing, forming dense mats. Leaves about 5/8"-1" long, mostly rounded on the ends. Flowers in clusters, urn-shaped and pinkish or white, about ¼" long. Along the coast and in the mountains, to AK and CA. **Pinemat Manzanita** (*A. nevadensis*) has decumbent stems, resembles Kinnikinnick, but stems are more rigid, and they form dense low cushions, rather than mats. Leaves are 1" long or less, oval, mostly with distinct sharp points on the ends.

PRINCE'S PINE
PIPSISSEWA

Chimaphila umbellata (Heath family, *Ericaceae*)
(Photo: Wagner Creek Rd., Jackson Co., early July)

Flowers are on a stem that rises 8"-12" above the leaves, and hang facing downward. Leaves dark green, 1½"-3" long, leathery, toothed on the margins, arranged more or less in whorls on woody stem. Typically 3-8 flowers, less than ½" in dia., 5 pink to red waxy-looking petals, large green pistil in center, surrounded by 10 short pink stamens in a crown-like circle. Dry conifer woods at moderate elevations, to CA. **Little Prince's Pine** (*C. menziesii*) is 3"-4" high, typically with leaves 1"-1½" long, and 1-3 white to pinkish flowers.

SALAL

Gaultheria shallon (Heath family, *Ericaceae*)
(Photo: Floras Lake, Curry Co., late March)

Shrubs to 8' high, often forming dense thickets. Leaves 2"-3" long, shiny green above, slightly toothed. Flowers urn-shaped, 1/4"-3/8" long, pink or white, up to 15 of them hanging in a row. Red to black berries 3/8" dia. appear in late summer. West of the Cascades, especially along coast, to BC and CA. Some related plants are: **Alpine Wintergreen** (*G. humifusa*), matted, branches rooting, with tiny white flowers, and leaves ¾" long or less; **Slender Wintergreen** (*G. ovatifolia*), prostrate branches, non-rooting, tiny white flowers, and leaves ¾"-1¼" long.

KALMIOPSIS

Kalmiopsis leachiana (Heath family, *Ericaceae*)
(Photo: Jack Creek Rd., near North Umpqua River, Douglas Co., mid May)

Evergreen shrub, many-branched, to 12" high, leaves thick, dark green, more or less oval, 5/16"-1/2" long. Flowers in clusters of 5-10, corollas deep rose, 5 spreading lobes, 1/2"-5/8" broad. Stamens and pistil project beyond corolla. Dry rocky slopes, in southern Curry Co. and in the North Umpqua River drainage, in Douglas Co. The North Umpqua population has been proposed to be a separate species, on the basis of pistil and stamen structure, and fragrance.

PINE DROPS

Pterospora andromedea (Heath family, *Ericaceae*)
(Photo: Near Mill Creek CG, Jackson Co., late June)

A mycotroph, living off decaying organic matter. Erect, fleshy stem, 1'-3' high, sticky, hairy, yellowish to reddish brown, emerging from dry forest floor. Leaves scale-like, brownish, ½"-1" long. Flowers numerous, in a long spike, drooping on slender curved stems, whitish, urn-shaped, about ¼" long, sticky. Widely distributed in dry woods, to BC and CA.

WESTERN RHODODENRON
CALIFORNIA ROSE-BAY

Rhododendron macrophyllum
(Heath family, *Ericaceae*)
(Photo: Lake in the Woods, Douglas Co., mid June)

One of the most delightful flowers in the forest. Shrubs, to 12' high, or occasionally small trees. Leaves leathery, evergreen, dark green on top, 3"-6", elliptic-oblong. Flowers in erect clusters, corollas bell-shaped, pink to deep rose, lobes wavy, spreading to 1½" across. Moist coniferous forests, from the coast to moderate elevations in the Cascades, to BC and CA.

WESTERN AZALEA

Rhododendron occidentale
(Heath family, *Ericaceae*)
(Photo: Azalea Park, Brookings, Curry Co., mid May)

Shrub, but can be 10' tall; deciduous. Flowers in showy clusters, with musky, sweet smell, pink or white, with yellow areas in the throat, each flower up to 2" across, with 5 stamens projecting conspicuously. Found primarily along streams from the Umpqua Valley south along coast, to CA. A city park in Brookings, called Azalea Park, is devoted to these plants. **White-flowered Rhododendron** (*R. albifrons*), grows at fairly high elevations in the Cascades, has smaller, creamy-white flowers, 1-3 in a cluster, located in the axils.

SNOW PLANT

Sarcodes sanguinea (Heath family, *Ericaceae*)
(Photo: Copeland Creek Road, Douglas Co., mid May)

A *mycotroph,* living off decaying organic matter. Snow plants emerge shortly after the snow melts, poking their bright red spikes up through the forest duff, 6"-16" tall, with red urn-shaped flowers about ½" long on the upper parts. Entire plant red, with sharp-pointed overlapping bracts on stem up to 2" long. Moderately high altitudes in the Siskiyous and southern Cascades, in shady woods with deep humus, to CA.

EVERGREEN HUCKLEBERRY
CALIFORNIA HUCKLEBERRY

Vaccinium ovatum (Heath family, *Ericaceae*)
(Photo: Harris Beach SP, Curry Co., late March)

(Photo of berries on p. 155.) Forms much of the undergrowth in woods along the coast. Evergreen plant to 10' tall, many-branched, thickly foliaged. Leaves small, dark glossy green above, paler below, thick and leathery, more or less oval shaped, finely serrate on edges. Flowers urn-shaped, pinkish, about 3/16" long, in clusters. Berries round, abundant, black, or bluish with glaucous film, to almost 3/16" dia. In the words of some, the glossy black berries sometimes look like "black widow bodies."

PERENNIAL SWEET PEA

Lathyrus latifolius (Legume family, *Fabaceae*)
(Photo: Port Orford, Curry Co., early August)

In midsummer, these flowers make a gorgeous display of color along our roadsides. Stems stout, strongly winged (i.e., flat-stemmed), long and trailing, fastening themselves with tendrils to anything available. Leaves on broadly winged petioles, the 2 leaflets narrow and pointed, up to 4" long, with a pair of sharply pointed stipules at the base of each petiole. Flowers large and showy, pink, pink-purple, or red, petals up to 1" long. Inner margin of style bearded, and no ring of hairs below stigma. Disturbed areas, especially roadsides. Native of Europe.

BIG DEERVETCH
THICK-LEAVED LOTUS
BUCK LOTUS

Lotus crassifolius (Legume family, *Fabaceae*)
(Photo: Near Hyatt Meadow, Jackson County, early June)

Stems 2'-4' high, stout and fleshy, herbage glaucous. Leaves compound, leaflets 9-20, oval, with small points at ends, ¾"-1¼" long. Flowers, 6-30, in dense clusters, peduncles shorter than the leaves, corollas about ½" long, greenish, tinged with dark purplish red, pea-flower shape, with narrow upturned banner petals. Woods on lower slopes of Cascades, to WA and CA. **Thicket Lotus** (*L. aboriginus*) is similar, but not as tall, herbage only slightly glaucous, peduncles usually equal to or longer than the leaves.

SOUR CLOVER
BULL CLOVER

Trifolium fucatum (Legume family, *Fabaceae*)
(Photo: Pistol River SP, Curry Co., mid May)

Flowers start out yellow, but then turn bright rose. Plants usually short, but may be 2' high. Leaves in 3s, to 1" long, oval, slightly toothed. Heads have long stems and are showy, with sharp-pointed involucres. Corollas light yellow, ½"-¾" long, turning bright rose, becoming inflated. Moist places along coast and in Rogue Valley, to CA. **Poverty Clover** (*T. depauperatum*), somewhat similar, but usually shorter, with smaller leaves and smaller flowers, the corollas pink-purple and white-tipped, involucre inconspicuous.

RED CLOVER
Trifolium pratense (Legume family, *Fabaceae*)
(Photo: Port Orford, Curry Co., early May)

Stems may be very long, 8"-40", erect or sprawling. Leaflets in 3s, more or less oblong, sometimes very large, 1½"-2½" long, generally with a whitish chevron in the center. Flower heads globular, on fairly short stems, 1"-1½" dia., densely packed with purplish-red flowers, each corolla about 5/8" long. Widespread. Introduced from Europe. **Long-stalked Clover** (*T. longipes*) may also have pink flowers, but flowers often are white to yellowish, has very long flower stalks and pointed, somewhat serrate leaves.

SPRINGBANK CLOVER
MARSH CLOVER
COW CLOVER
Trifolium wormskjoldii [*T. wildenovii*]
(Legume family, *Fabaceae*)
(Photo: Cape Blanco SP, Curry Co., mid May)

Mostly decumbent stems to 2' long, flower heads rising on short peduncles. Leaflets in 3s, oval, slightly dentate, about 3/8"-1½" long. Involucre large, often as broad as the head, toothed. Corollas about ½" long, reddish-purple, often white-tipped. Wet locations, especially on coast, to WA and CA. **Chilean Clover** (*T. macraei*) similar, found from OR to S. America, has smaller leaves and flowers, involucre inconspicuous.

AMERICAN VETCH
Vicia americana (Legume family, *Fabaceae*)
(Photo: near Cantrall-Buckley Co. Park, Jackson Co., early April)

(Peas have tiny hairs down one side of the style; vetches have tiny hairs around the top of the style just below the stigma.) Trailing and/or climbing stems, 2'-3' long. Leaves pinnately compound, with tendrils. Leaflets 8-16, more or less oblong, 3/8"- 1½" long, often with a little sharp point at the end of each leaflet. Flower clusters have 2-10 flowers. Corolla violet, lavender, or purple, 5/8"-1" long, with large banner petal. Widespread. Open woods and meadows.

GIANT VETCH

Vicia nigricans [*V. gigantea*]
(Legume family, *Fabaceae*)
(Photo: Lone Ranch Beach, Curry Co., mid May)

Sprawling or climbing stems, robust, to 6' long. Leaflets 16-24, ½"-1½" long, oblong or elliptic, tips rounded or pointed. Flowers 6-15, generally on one side of stem, crowded, corollas about ½" long, red-purple to pale yellow. Tiny hairs around the top of the style just below the stigma. Seedpods ¾"-1¾" long and ½" wide, not hairy. Beaches and bluffs along the coast, woods, roadsides, at low elevations, to AK and CA.

COMMON VETCH
SPRING VETCH

Vicia sativa [*V. angustifolia*]
(Legume family, *Fabaceae*)
(Photo: Harris Beach SP, Curry Co., mid May)

Stems sprawling or climbing, leaves pinnately compound, 8-14 leaflets, 5/8"-1¼" long, narrow to wedge-shaped, sometimes notched, often with a small tooth on the end. Flowers red-purple, ½"-1¼" long, sessile or with very short stems, located near the bases of the leaf stems, 1-4 in a bunch. Tiny hairs around the top of the style just below the stigma. Disturbed areas and fields, native of Europe. Sometimes planted as a winter cover-crop.

HAIRY VETCH
WINTER VETCH

Vicia villosa (Legume family, *Fabaceae*)
(Photo: Dead Indian Memorial Road, Jackson Co., late May)

In places, in spring, this vetch can cover the hillsides with great patches of magenta. Close up, the plants are a tangle of stems, leaves, and flowers. Stems somewhat hairy, to 6' long, climbing. Leaves compound, tendrils at the ends, 10-20 leaflets, each ¾"-1" long, narrow, often with a tiny point at the tip. Flowers are in dense, 1-sided raceme, 10 to many, each about ¾" long, mostly reddish-purple, sometimes white, lateral petals whitish. Tiny hairs around the top of the style just below the stigma. Widespread in grassy places. Native of Europe.

CENTAURY
EUROPEAN CENTAURY

Centaurium erythraea [*C. umbellatum*]
(Gentian family, *Gentianaceae*)
(Photo: Near Susan Creek Falls, Douglas Co., late June)

Plants 8"-24" tall, with distinct small rosettes of basal leaves. Stem leaves opposite, somewhat clasping, 1" long or less. Corolla pink, in slender tube with spreading lobes, 5-lobed, lobes about ¼" long, stamens projecting beyond corolla. Resembles *Phlox*, but *Phlox* has 3-lobed style; in *Centaurium*, style ends with a small knob or 2 short branches. Fields and roadsides at lower elevations. Native of Europe. **Muehlenberg Centaury** (*C. muehlenbergii*), native, similar, but lacks basal rosette, and lobes on corolla are 3/32"-3/16" long.

FILAREE
REDSTEM STORKSBILL

Erodium cicutarium
(Geranium family, *Gerianiaceae*)
(Photo: Rogue Valley, Jackson Co., late February)

In early spring, little geranium-like flowers appear, rose-purple, rising from rosettes of lacy leaves. Stems often reddish. Flowers have 5 petals, each petal less than ½" long. Leaves to 6" long or more, compound, leaflets arranged along the stem like a feather, each leaflet deeply toothed. Needle-shaped fruits can be as much as two inches long. Introduced from Europe. ***Musk Filaree*** (*E. moschatum*), non-native, is similar, but the leaflets are less deeply cleft. ***Long-beaked Storksbill*** (*E. botrys*), non-native, has lobed leaves, but they are not compound.

CUT-LEAVED GERANIUM

Geranium dissectum
(Geranium family, *Gerianiaceae*)
(Photo: S. Umpqua River, Douglas Co., late April)

Up to 20" high, stems hairy. Leaves on long petioles, deeply 5-parted, divisions again parted into narrow sharp-pointed lobes. Flowers with 5 petals, each about ¼" long, rose-purple, sepals with tail-like appendages. Widely distributed in fields and roadsides. From Europe. **Carolina Gernanium** (*G. carolinianum*) similar, flowers are pale pink or nearly white, leaf-lobes are rounded. ***Dove's Foot Geranium*** (*G. molle*), non-native, similar, but sepals do not have tail-like appendages, leaf-lobes rounded.

OREGON GERANIUM
WESTERN GERANIUM

Geranium oreganum
(Geranium family, *Gerianiaceae*)
(Photo: Crystal Springs, Klamath Co., early July)

Stems 1'-2' high, branched, fleshy, hairy. Leaves 2½"-6" broad, 5-7 deeply parted, with the divisions many-lobed. Basal leaves have very long petioles, 12" and longer. Calyx lobes about ½" long, sharp-pointed. Petals 5, rose-purple, to 1" long, not conspicuously dark-veined. Shady woods and meadow openings, both sides of the Cascades, to CA. **Sticky Geranium** (*G. viscosissimum*) similar, sticky, very hairy, flowers smaller, with dark veins.

SHINY-LEAVED GOOSEBERRY
SIERRA GOOSEBERRY

Ribes cruentum [*R. roezlii* var. *cruentum*]
(Gooseberry family, *Grossulariaceae*)
(Photo: Grizzly Peak Trail, Jackson Co., mid June)

(Photo of berries on page 155). Shrub, 2'-4' high, with thorns. Leaves rounded, ½"-1" dia., 3-5 lobed, scalloped, dentate. Flower has conspicuous reddish-purple calyx with lobes that resemble petals, in tube about ½" long that spreads into the lobes. Petals white, about ½" long. Style deeply cleft, extends beyond the petals. Berries about ½" dia., with dense spines. Open woods, from Douglas County to CA. **Gummy Gooseberry** (*R. lobbii*) is similar, but leaves, young shoots, and berries are glandular and sticky.

RED-FLOWERING CURRANT
OREGON CURRANT

Ribes sanguineum
(Gooseberry family, *Grossulariaceae*)
(Photo: Bandon SP, Coos Co., late March)

In spring, a small tree that explodes into gorgeous pink flowers. Grows to 12' tall, many-branched, smaller stems reddish, without prickles. Leaves generally 3-lobed, slightly hairy, up to 2" across, often wider than long, with small teeth. Flower clusters can be large and dense, the tubular flowers with 5 petals, deep pink, about ½" long. Thickets west of the Cascades, especially near the coast, to BC and CA.

CROCOSMIA

Crocosmia x *crocosmiiflora* (Iris family, *Iridaceae*)
(Photo: Port Orford Wetlands, Curry Co., late July)

This ornamental flower is a hybrid between 2 South African species. Stems to 3' high, with long narrow leaves to 18" long. Flowers typically in a triangular cluster, with blooming proceeding outward toward tip. Perianth is funnel-form, bright red-orange with some yellow, 1"-2" long, with stamens and pistil projecting beyond the petals. Plants have escaped from cultivation and become established in the wild, especially along the coast.

PURPLE-EYED GRASS
SATIN-FLOWER
GRASS WIDOWS

Olsynium douglasii [*Sisyrinchium douglasii*]
(Iris family, *Iridaceae*)
(Photo: Rough & Ready, Josephine Co., late March)

One of the delights of early spring. Flowers on round stems 6"-12" high, generally overtopped by long thin leaves, round in cross-section. Perianth parts 6, about ¾" long, usually purplish-red, sometimes white. Stigma projects beyond petals, 3-lobed. Widespread, usually on dry ground, to CA.

NETTLELEAF HORSEMINT
NETTLE-LEAVED GIANT HYSSOP

Agastache urticifolia (Mint family, *Lamiaceae*)
(Photo: Soda Mountain Road, Cascade-Siskiyou NM, Jackson Co., early July)

Stems 4- angled, rising to 4' high, aromatic, topped by dense spike-like flower clusters 4"-5" long. Leaves opposite, more or less triangular, heavily serrate, 1½"-3" long. Calyx funnel-like, about 3/8" long, 5 sharply pointed lobes, rose to rose-purple. Corolla pale purplish to nearly white, longer than the calyx. Common in woodlands and open slopes, east of Cascades and southwestern OR, to BC and CA.

PURPLE DEAD NETTLE
RED HENBIT

Lamium purpureum (Mint family, *Lamiaceae*)
(Photo: Lynn Newbry Park, Jackson Co., mid April)

Occurs in masses. First impression is that the purple color is from the flowers, but these are the leaves. The flowers are the little pink tubes peeking from the leaf clusters. Plants usually under 10" high, leaves clustered at the top. Leaves heart-shaped, scalloped, mostly reddish-purple. Corollas about ½" long, pale pink, with broad upper lip and smaller lower lobes. Fields and waste ground at lower elevations. Native of Europe.

GREAT HEDGE-NETTLE
SWAMP BETONY

Stachys chamissonis var. *cooleyae*
[*S. cooleyae*] [*S. ciliata*]
(Mint family, *Lamiaceae*)
(Photo: Odell Lake, Klamath Co., mid August)

Stems bristly, 2'-3' tall, and higher. Leaves hairy, 2"-6" long, more or less oval, pointed, coarsely crenate, petioles ½"-1½" long. Flowers showy, in whorls in loose spike-like formation. Calyxes about 3/8" long, with sharp teeth. Corollas deep red or magenta, the tubes about 5/8"-1" long, lower lips often white-spotted. Moist areas, from east slope of Cascades to coast, to BC. **Rigid Hedge-Nettle** (*Stachys ajudgoides* var. *rigida*) has smaller, paler flowers, petioles on upper leaves are shorter or absent.

NARROW-LEAVED ONION
PAPER ONION

Allium amplectens (Lily family, *Liliaceae*)
(Photo: Limpy Creek Botanical Area, Josephine Co., late May)

Leafless stems 8"-16" high, thin basal leaves, usually shorter than the stems, withering early. Broad bracts below the umbel, 2-3, pointed. Perianth segments light rose to white, about ¼" long, narrow and pointed, becoming papery. Stamens about as long as the perianth segments. Open ground on both sides of Cascades, to WA and CA.

SICKLE-LEAVED ONION

Allium falcifolium (Lily family, *Liliaceae*)
(Photo: 8 Dollar Road, Josephine Co., mid May)

A showy little plant, usually growing in the open on bare ground. Overall height 2"-8", on a stem that is flattened and winged, about 3/16" wide. Leaves 2-3 times as long as stem, fleshy, 1/4"-3/8" wide, sickle-shaped. Flowers in showy umbels, on pedicels ¾" long. Corolla rich rose-purple, 1/2"-5/8" long, with the perianth parts close together for about half that length, then flaring into thin spreading segments. Serpentine soils, southern Josephine Co., to CA.

SISKIYOU ONION

Allium siskiyouense (Lily family, *Liliaceae*)
(Photo: Shale City Road, Jackson Co., early July)

Low-growing, about 2"-3" high. Leaves 2, about twice as long as stem, flat, sickle-shaped. Flowers 10-35, in compact umbels, pedicels 1/4-5/8" long. Perianth parts about 3/8" long, pink, narrow and pointed, often with darker midveins. Open rocky slopes in southwestern OR, to CA.

SWAMP ONION
TALL MOUNTAIN ONION

Allium validum (Lily family, *Liliaceae*)
(Photo: Wagner Creek Road, Jackson Co., early July)

Grows 2'-3' tall, with a pink ball of flowers on a leafless stem, stem somewhat flat and angled. Leaves, all basal, about ½" wide, may be as long as the stem. Flowers in dense umbel, 15-40 individual flowers, rose-purple, perianth parts about 3/8" long, erect, and lance-like. Stamens project well beyond the petals. Wet meadows and bogs above 4000 feet in Cascades and Siskiyous, to WA and CA.

GREENE MARIPOSA LILY

Calochortus greenei (Lily family, *Liliaceae*)
(Photo: Near Old Siskiyou Summit, Cascade-Siskiyou NM, Jackson Co., early July)

Stems about 12" high, with small thin leaves on stems, 1-5 erect flowers. Basal leaf about 8" long, withering early. Sepals 3, about 1" long, sharp pointed, purplish. Petals 3, 1" or more long, more or less oval, rose-purple to purple, yellow at base, hairy inside. Dry shrubby hillsides, southern Jackson Co., to CA. **Federal species of concern.**

PINK STAR TULIP
SHORT-STEMMED MARIPOSA LILY

Calochortus uniflorus (Lily family, *Liliaceae*)
(Photo: 8 Dollar Road, Josephine Co., early May)

Easily overlooked. Low-growing in moist grassy areas, sometimes with only one flower. Overall height 4"-7", 1-5 flowers, basal leaves 6" long or more, stems leaves smaller, often with 1 or more bulblets at points where leaves join the stem. Perianth pink to lavender, sharp-pointed sepals, petals 5/8"-1" long. Petals plain and mostly not hairy, except for slight hairiness deep inside the petals. Moist meadows, at lower elevations, southwest OR, to CA.

HENDERSON FAWN LILY

Erythronium hendersonii (Lily family, *Liliaceae*)
(Photo: Touvelle SP, Jackson Co., mid March)

One of the loveliest of fawn lilies, and the most common one in Jackson and Josephine Counties. It is an early spring bloomer (March and April at the lower elevations). Leaves usually mottled, stem 8"-20" tall, with 1-6 flowers per stem. Petals are bright lilac with purple at the base, and they have "auricles" (swollen areas) at their bases. Anthers are yellow to dark red, and stigma is slightly 3-lobed. Oak woodlands, southwest OR, slightly into CA.

GENTNER FRITILLARY

Fritillaria gentneri (Lily family, *Liliaceae*)
(Photo: Beekman Trail, Jacksonville, Jackson Co., late April)

This beautiful lily rises 2'-3' in the shady forest. Leaves narrow, 3"-6" long, mostly in whorls, well-spaced on the stem. Flowers 1½"-2" long, purplish-red, bell-shaped, yellowish-spotted, tips somewhat flared out but not curved backward. Dry open woods, in isolated populations in southern Josephine, Jackson, and Curry Cos. **Federally endangered species.**

SCARLET FRITILLARY

Fritillaria recurva (Lily family, *Liliaceae*)
(Photo: Lower Table Rock Trail, Jackson Co., late March)

Resembles Gentner Fritillary (see above), but darker red. Leaves 2"-4", mostly in a couple of whorls. Flowers a little over 1" long, red, bell-shaped, yellow-spotted inside, tips strongly bent backward. Dry open woods, from Douglas Co. to CA.

BOLANDER LILY

Lilium bolanderi (Lily family, *Liliaceae*)
(Photo: Forest Road 4402, Josephine Co., early July)

Stems to 2' tall. Leaves more or less oval, sharp-pointed, thick, 1¼"-2" long, in whorls. Flowers 2 to several at tops of stems, funnelform, sometimes nodding, perianth parts 1¼"-1½" long, sharply-pointed, not strongly recurved, bright red to red-purple, yellowish in throat with dark spots. Dry ground, southern Josephine Co. to CA.

WESTERN TRILLIUM
WESTERN WAKE-ROBIN

Trillium ovatum (Lily family, *Liliaceae*)
(Photo: Near Little Hyatt Lake, Jackson Co., early May.)

Stems rise 6"-18", each bearing whorl of 3 leaves at summit, and a single flower. Leaves without petioles, 3"-6" long. Flower on stem 1"-2½" long, with 3 green sepals and 3 petals, 6 stamens. Sepals ¾"-2" in length, petals somewhat larger. Petals white or reddish. (See, also, p. 28.) Moist woods at moderate elevations, to BC and CA.

PURPLE LOOSESTRIFE

Lythrum salicaria (Loosestrife family, *Lythraceae*)
(Photo: Millicoma Marsh, Coos Co., late July)

Stems are tall, up to 6 feet, with dense red-purple spikes at the ends. Leaves are generally opposite, sometimes whorled, up to 5" long, narrow and pointed. Flowers, to 1" across, are in whorls, rich reddish-purple, 6 petals, generally with a wrinkled appearance. Marshes, ponds, ditches. Worldwide, native of Europe. Often planted as an ornamental, but considered a noxious weed in the wild.

COMMON MALLOW
ROUND-LEAVED MALLOW
CHEESE-WEED

Malva neglecta [*M. rotundifolia*]
(Mallow family, *Malvaceae*)
(Photo: Lone Ranch Beach, Curry Co., late July)

Stems generally decumbent, hairy, to 3' long. Leaves roughly circular in outline, 1¼"-2" diameter, shallowly lobed, petioles 2"-6" long. Flowers 1-3 in axils, calyxes about ¼" long, 5-lobed, lobes pointed, subtended by 3 bractlets. Petals 5, 3/8"-5/8" long, whitish to pink, veined, clawed, claws slightly hairy. Fruits resemble tiny green cheeses. Widespread in disturbed areas. Native of Europe. A similar plant, also called ***Cheese-Weed*** (*M. parviflora*), nonnative, has smaller flowers.

CHECKERMALLOW
CHECKERBLOOM

Sidalcea malviflora (Mallow family, *Malvaceae*)
(Photo: Near Susan Creek Falls, Douglas Co., mid June)

Plants rise 12"-28", on slender branching stems. Leaves have long petioles, are deeply cleft on the lower stem, and are parted into linear leaflets on the upper stem. Flowers in sparsely-flowered racemes, on short pedicels, with sharp-pointed calyxes, and 5 light rose-purple petals nearly 1" long. Dry open ground west of the Cascades, from Douglas County south to CA.

OREGON SIDALCEA
OREGON CHECKERBLOOM

Sidalcea oregana (Mallow family, *Malvaceae*)
(Photo: Wagner Creek Road, Jackson Co., early July)

Stems rise to 2½', hairy, with flowers in dense spikes resembling hollyhocks. Leaves deeply lobed. Flowers more or less cone-shaped or spreading, to ¾" long, 5 petals, rose-pink, calyxes densely hairy. Moist ground east of Cascades, and in Josephine and Jackson Cos., to CA.

PINK SAND VERBENA
BEACH SAND VERBENA
ROSE-PURPLE ABRONIA

Abronia umbellata
(Four O'Clock family, *Nyctaginaceae*)
(Photo: Port Orford, Curry Co., early May)

Prostrate, succulent stems, 8"-48" long. Succulent leaves, more or less oval, 1"-1½" long, the petioles as long or longer than the blades. Flowers in dense globe-like head, with cup-like involucre. Perianth of the individual flower in a tube, with colored calyx, petal-like, about ¼" long, spreading into 4 or 5 lobes, mostly pink, with some white. Beaches and dunes along the coast, to WA and CA.

FIREWEED
ROSEBAY WILLOW-HERB
BLOOMING SALLY
Chamerion angustifolium [*Epilobium angustifolium*]
(Evening Primrose family, *Onagraceae*)
(Photo: Mount Ashland Road, Jackson Co., mid July)

Instantly recognizable, often occurring in large patches, plants 2'-6' tall, topped with brilliant many-flowered spikes. Leaves alternate, 2"-3" long, narrow, dark green above, paler beneath, generally slightly toothed. Petals 4, spreading, rose-purple, 1/3"-1" long, broadly oval. Roadsides and open areas, often on logged or burned lands, widespread in North America.

FAREWELL-TO-SPRING
HERALD-OF-SUMMER
Clarkia amoena [*Godetia amoena*]
(Evening Primrose family, *Onagraceae*)
(Photo: Near Susan Creek Falls, North Umpqua River Valley, Douglas Co., late June)

Often in masses on rocky, open hillsides. May be 1'-3' high, stems branched, many-flowered. Leaves numerous, ¾"-2½" long, narrowly oblong. Petals 4, rose-colored, ½"-2" long, usually with red spot near middle of each petal. Calyx lobes united above and turned to one side. Fields and roadsides, Willamette Valley to CA. **Purple Godetia** (*C. purpurea*) similar, with or without petal-spots, calyx lobes reflexed.

SLENDER CLARKIA
Clarkia gracilis
(Evening Primrose family, *Onagraceae*)
(Photo: Near Lost Creek Reservoir, Jackson Co., early May)

Stems erect, slender, generally hairy, 1'-3' tall. Leaves 3/4"-2" long, very narrow. Axis of the inflorescence recurved when in bud, buds nodding. Petals 4, more or less fan-shaped, pinkish lavender, sometimes lighter at base, 5/16"-1½" long. Dry open ground west of Cascades, to WA and CA. **Lassen Clarkia** (*C. lassenensis*) is similar; primary difference is in the number of grooves on the ovary.

HUMMINGBIRD TRUMPET
CALIFORNIA FUSCHIA
ZAUSCHNERIA

Epilobium canum
[*Zauschneria californica, Z. latifolia*]
(Evening Primrose family, *Onagraceae*)
(Photo: Near Fiddler Mt., Josephine Co., early August)

Stems numerous, hairy, sticky, sprawling. Leaves numerous, sessile, 1"-1½" long, more or less oval, sometimes toothed. Perianth bright red, trumpet-shaped, 3/4"-1" long, sepals about as long as the petals, petals 2-cleft at apex, stamens and pistil exserted, pistil more so than stamens, stigma 4-cleft. Dry slopes, Curry and Josephine Cos, to CA.

GLAUCOUS WILLOW-HERB
SMOOTH WILLOW-HERB
SMOOTHSTEM FIREWEED

Epilobium glaberrimum
(Evening Primrose family, *Onagraceae*)
(Photo: Near Thousand Springs, Jackson Co., late June)

Variable. Stems 4"-30" high, hairless, usually unbranched. Leaves opposite, ¾"-2" long, narrowly oval, pointed, mostly sessile, often toothed. Calyx about ¼" long, points often visible between petals. Petals 4, about ¼" long, notched, pink, sometimes white. Streambanks, roadsides, middle altitudes in Cascades and Siskiyous. **Tall Annual Willow-Herb** (*E. brachycarpum*) similar, but hairy above, has narrower leaves. **Fringed Willow-Herb** (*E. ciliatum*) has leaves to 6" long.

SISKIYOU WILLOW-HERB
SISKIYOU FIREWEED
ROSE WILLOW-HERB

Epilobium siskiyouense
(Evening Primrose family, *Onagraceae*)
(Photo: Near Observation Peak, Jackson Co., early August)

Almost shrubby, 4"-10" high. Leaves opposite, sessile, ½"-1" long, more or less oval. Petals 4, ½"-¾" long, notched, pink to rose-purple, 8 stamens at 2 levels, stigma 4-lobed, projecting beyond stamens. Dry rocky areas, at high elevations, southwest OR to CA. **Stiff Willow-Herb** (*E. rigidum*) similar, grows larger, has stiff shoots, and has larger, petioled leaves. **Rock Fringe** (*E. obcordatum*), of eastern OR, similar, has smaller leaves.

CALYPSO ORCHID
FAIRY SLIPPER

Calypso bulbosa Orchid family, *Orchidaceae*)
(Photo: Near Little Hyatt Lake, Jackson Co., late May)

This exquisite little orchid hides amid the forest litter in the deep shade, and is often overlooked. The stems are only 5"-6" high, with no leaves except for the single oval leaf at the base. Floral parts rose-colored except for the lip petal, which is mottled with maroon and white. Woods, mostly west of the Cascades, to AK and CA.

WESTERN CORAL-ROOT
MERTEN CORAL-ROOT

Corallorrhiza mertensiana
(Orchid family, *Orchidaceae*)
(Photo: Thousand Springs, Crater Lake NP, Jackson Co., late June)

The reddish stems rise 6"-20" above the litter of the forest floor, often in groups. The tiny leaves are few and scale-like, sheathing the stem. Sepals are petal-like, arching over the column, which is composed of the stamen and style fused together. Lateral petals narrow and spreading, broad lower lip more or less purplish with reddish lines, generally not spotted (sometimes 1 or 2). There is a short spur at the base of the lower petal. Coniferous forests at middle elevations in Cascades, to AK and CA. **Spotted Coral-Root** (*C. maculata*) similar, but has 4 or more red or purple spots on the lower lip.

STRIPED CORAL-ROOT
HOODED CORAL-ROOT

Corallorrhiza striata (Orchid family, *Orchidaceae*)
(Photo: Near Little Hyatt Lake Road, Jackson Co., early June)

Stems 6"-20" high, red-brown to purplish, sometimes yellowish. Leaves bract-like, more or less sheathing. Sepals and petals similar to those on *C. mertensiana* (see above), yellowish-pink to pale brown, but have conspicuous longitudinal reddish to purplish stripes, and there is no spur. Coniferous woods at moderate elevations in western OR, to BC and CA.

REDWOOD SORREL
OREGON OXALIS
WOOD SORREL

Oxalis oregana (Oxalis family, *Oxalidaceae*)
(Photo: Rainie Falls Trail, Josephine Co., late March)

Leaf stems and flower stems rise directly 2"-6" from the root nodes, often forming extensive carpets on the forest floor. Leaflets in 3s, clover-like, heart-shaped and notched at the ends, 5/8"-1¼" long. They droop in direct sunlight. Flowers solitary on leafless stems, 5 petals, pink to white, distinctly veined, 3/8"-3/4" long. West of Cascades and along the coast, to WA and CA. **Great Oxalis** (*O. trilliifolia*), similar, but the stems have 4-15 flowers, and petals are slightly notched, white to pinkish.

WESTERN PEONY

Paeonia brownii (Peony family, *Paeoniaceae*)
(Photo: Shale City Road, Jackson Co., late May)

Dense rounded clumps, 12"-20" high, leaves 2"-3" long, fleshy, divided and lobed many times, lower ones long-petioled. Flowers on fleshy stems, nodding, with more or less leaf-like bracts. Sepals rounded, green, about 3/4" long. Petals 5-10, rounded, shorter than sepals, dark red, many stamens. Woods and open areas, east of Cascades; also from Josephine Co. eastward, and to CA.

BLEEDING HEARTS

Dicentra formosa (Poppy family, *Papaveraceae*)
(Photo: Upper Rogue River, Jackson Co., early June)

There is hardly any flower more appropriately named, because of its instantly recognizable heart shape. Flowers are in nodding clusters, and fleshy stalks rise to 20" high, usually well above the leaves. Leaves lacy and fern-like, ample, basal, long petioles, divided into 3, and then divided again, variously toothed. Corollas about 5/8" long, usually rose-purple, sometimes yellowish. Widespread west of Cascades, in woods at low and middle altitudes, to BC and CA.

SHORE PINE
COAST PINE
LODGEPOLE PINE

Pinus contorta (Pine family, *Pinaceae*)
(Photo: Coquille Point, Bandon, Coos Co., early May)

One would not normally think of a pine tree as a wildflower, but the bright red staminate (male) cones of the Shore Pine, about 3/8" long, are as showy and attractive as many conventional flowers. Shore pines typically are low and contorted, but can grow taller and straighter in protected locations. Two needles to a bundle; female cones relatively small, 1½"-2½" long. Along coast, from AK to CA. A variety of this species, called **Lodgepole Pine,** forms dense stands of tall, straight trees in the Siskiyous and Cascades.

SEA-THRIFT
SEA-PINK
THRIFT

Armeria maritima
(Leadwort family, *Plumbaginaceae*)
(Photo: Otter Point, Curry Co., early May)

Flowers in round balls at tops of leafless stems 4"-12" high, with dense basal tufts of grass-like leaves, 1½"-2½" long. Brown thin bracts, forming an involucre under the head. Flowers densely packed in head, each with 5 rose-pink petals, about ¼" long. Bluffs above the sea, to AK and CA.

VARI-LEAVED COLLOMIA

Collomia heterophylla
(Phlox family, *Polemoniaceae*)
(Photo: Shan Creek Road, Josephine Co., late May)

Stems erect or spreading, 3"-10" tall. Leaves variable, to 1½" long, from entire, to toothed, to pinnately compound with 3-7 segments. Flowers in terminal bracted clusters, corollas pink to lavender, occasionally white, tubular, 1/2"-5/8" long, opening up into 5 lobes, 1/4"-5/16" broad, yellow center. Open woods, from BC to CA.

SCARLET GILIA
SKYROCKET
DESERT TRUMPETS
Ipomopsis aggregata [*Gilia aggregata*]
(Phlox family, *Polemoniaceae*)
(Photo: Near Kimball SP, Klamath Co., late June)

Stems erect, 1'-3' high, sometimes branched, flowers in one-sided clusters at ends of branches. Leaves numerous, reduced upward, parted into 9-13 linear segments. Calyx about ¼" long, sharp-pointed, slightly sticky. Corolla about 1" long, trumpet-shaped, flaring into 5 sharp lobes, scarlet or salmon-colored, sometimes white, finely flecked with white or yellow. Dry slopes or woodland openings, moderate to high elevations, east side of Cascades, and in Josephine and Jackson Cos., to WA and CA.

WOODLAND PHLOX
NORTHERN PHLOX
TRAILING PHLOX
Phlox adsurgens (Phlox family, *Polemoniaceae*)
(Photo: Grayback CG, Josephine Co., late May)

Stems slender, often decumbent, 8"-20" long. Leaves narrowly elliptic to oval, ½"-1¼" long, somewhat leathery. Corolla bright pink, with tube about ½"-¾" long, flaring into a more or less flat plane ½"-¾" across, with 5 petals. Inflorescence open, few-flowered. Dry forests at moderate altitudes in southwestern OR, to CA.

SPREADING PHLOX
Phlox diffusa (Phlox family, *Polemoniaceae*)
(Photo: Near Fourmile Lake, Klamath Co., late June)

One of the delights of high elevation country is the presence of Spreading Phlox, that sometimes forms mats literally covered with little pink (or lilac, or white) flowers. The stems, with sharp needle-like leaves, spread from a woody base. The 5 petals of the flower are united at the base into a short tube, and then spread out flat to a diameter of about ½". Dry, open slopes at moderate to high elevations in the Cascades and Siskiyous, to BC and CA.

SLENDER PHLOX
PINK ANNUAL PHLOX

Phlox gracilis [*Microsteris gracilis*]
(Phlox family, *Polemoniaceae*)
(Photo: Whitehorse Park, Josephine Co., mid March)

The tiny pink flowers are almost lost in the grassy, open areas where they occur. Stems are erect, often hairy, 3"-8" tall, with clusters of flowers at the tops. Leaves are small, narrow, about 1" long, opposite below and alternate above, generally sessile. Flower is in a narrow tube, with a long calyx, expanding to about ¼" dia., with 5 pink lobes and a yellow center. Moist places, both sides of Cascades, to BC and CA.

SHOWY PHLOX

Phlox speciosa (Phlox family, *Polemoniaceae*)
(Photo: Near O'Brien, Josephine Co., late April.)

Rises 6"-12" on multiple, erect, slender stems, from a woody base. Leaves narrow, 1"-2" long, rough-edged. Corolla bright pink, sometimes white, with tube about ½" long, flaring into a more or less flat plane about ¾" dia., with 5 petals, usually deeply bilobed. Flowers may appear singly, or in clusters. Rocky areas, forests, and brushy flats in southwestern OR, to WA and CA.

CALIFORNIA MILKWORT

Polygala californica
(Milkwort family, *Polygalaceae*
(Photo: Near O'Brien, Josephine Co., mid June)

Stems 4"-10", slender, often decumbent, somewhat hairy. Leaves ½"-1½" long, more or less oblong, rounded or acutish, firm, dull green. Flowers rose-color, about ½" long, the sepals oblong, the dorsal petals narrowed toward the ends and curved. Dry thickets, Curry and western Josephine Cos., to CA.

CUSHION BUCKWHEAT
OVAL-LEAVED ERIOGONUM

Eriogonum ovalifolium
(Buckwheat family, *Polygonaceae*)
(Photo: Cloudcap, Crater Lake NP, Klamath Co., early August)

Leaves mat-forming, mats 2"-16" dia, with leafless flowering stems 2"-4" long. Leaves ¼"-½" long, oval or round, densely white top and bottom, with petioles as long or longer than the leaf blades. Flowers in globe-shaped heads, corollas about 1/8" long, pink or cream-color. Dry slopes at moderate to high altitudes, east of Cascades and in Siskiyous, to BC and CA.

WICKER BUCKWHEAT
WIRE-STEMMED ERIOGONUM

Eriogonum vimineum
(Buckwheat family, *Polygonaceae*)
(Photo: Near Star Flat, Josephine Co., late June)

Many slender branches, hairless (at least on upper stems), 4"-18" high. Leaves generally all basal, the blades more or less round, ½"-1" dia., with slender petioles about 1" long. Many small flowers, distributed on the branches and in the forks. Perianth parts 6, about 1/8" long, pink or white (sometimes yellow), each with dark stripe. Dry ground, Josephine Co. eastward, to WA and CA. **Bailey Eriogonom** (*E. baileyi*), east of the Cascades, is similar, but has flowers about half as large.

MOUNTAIN SORREL

Oxyria digyma (Buckwheat family, *Polygonaceae*)
(Photo: Cloudcap, Crater Lake NP, Klamath Co., mid July)

Low-growing, 4"-8" high, leaves basal, hairless, long-petioled, bright green, often with purplish edges, somewhat succulent, rounded, ½"-1" dia. Inflorescence spike-like, narrow and dense, 1"-8" long. Small scale-like flowers, reddish to greenish, with 4 perianth parts. Widespread in alpine areas in North America, and extending to the Old World.

WATER SMARTWEED
WATER LADY'S THUMB
Polygonum amphibium [*Polygonum natans*]
(Buckwheat family, *Polygonaceae*)
(Photo: Hyatt Lake, Jackson Co., mid August)

Floating on shallow ponds, or on wet earth nearby. Stems prostrate, rooting at nodes. Leaves more or less oblong, 2"-4" long, fleshy, short-petioled. Flowers pink, in erect dense spikes, from ½" to 1½" long. Widespread throughout North America. Some varieties may be taller, with longer flower spikes.

SLENDER MEADOW DOCK
ALPINE SHEEP SORREL
Rumex paucifolius
(Buckwheat family, *Polygonaceae*)
(Photo: Klamath Marsh Prairie, Klamath Co., mid June)

Slender stemmed, to 16" tall. Leaves 1"-4" long, narrow, pointed, with long petioles, the petioles sheathing the stem. Flowers small, about 1/8" long, bell-shaped, 6 perianth-parts, red, the 3 outer ones relatively inconspicuous, the inner ones larger. Wet meadows, mostly east of Cascades. ***Sheep Sorrel*** (*R. acetosella*), non-native, is similar, but leaves are arrowhead-shaped. ***Curly Dock*** (*R. crispus*), non-native, is taller, has larger leaves with curled edges, and green flowering heads than turn brown in seed.

RED MAIDS
ROSE CALANDRINIA
Calandrinia ciliata
(Purslane family, *Portulacaceae*)
(Photo: Whitehorse Park, Josephine Co., mid March)

Here is another lovely little flower that you have to get down on your knees to enjoy. Several stout, fleshy stems, each perhaps only 2"-3" long, sprawl from a central point. Basal leaves spoon-shaped, tapering to long petioles, 1"-2" long including petiole. Leaves on the stems are linear, with short petioles or none. Flowers are 3/8"-1/2" dia., 5 bright rose petals, whitish at the center. Open grassy places, widespread, to WA and S. America.

PUSSYPAWS
Cistanthe umbellata
[*Calyptridium umbellatum, Spraguea umbellata*]
(Purslane family, *Portulacaceae*)
(Photo: Cascade Mountain Pass, near Crater Lake NP, Klamath Co., late June)

Flowering stems often prostrate, radiating from basal rosette of spoon-shaped leaves. Leaves fleshy, 1"-3" long, petioled. Peduncles to 8" long, with dense clusters of tiny flowers on ends, rose to white in color. Dry ground at high altitudes in Cascades and Siskiyous, to BC and CA. Some authorities consider plants with a single flowering stem per rosette to be a separate species, *C. monosperma*, but others believe so much intergrading occurs that the two are effectively inseparable.

WESTERN SPRING BEAUTY
CANDY FLOWER
Claytonia sibirica [*Montia sibirica*]
(Purslane family, *Portulacaceae*)
(Photo: Lone Ranch Beach, Curry Co., late March)

Stems 6"-15" high, mostly leafless except for pair of broad leaves 2"-3" below the flower, opposite, 1"-2" long, pointed, without petioles, not united at the base. Basal leaves have similar shape, but have petioles to 4" long. Petals more or less oblong, about ½" long, notched, pinkish, with dark pink stripes. Moist locations west of Cascades, to AK and CA. **Streambank Spring Beauty** (*Montia parvifolia*) is similar, flowers slightly smaller, stem leaves numerous, alternate.

SCARLET PIMPERNEL
POOR MAN'S WEATHERGLASS
Anagallis arvensis (Primrose family, *Primulaceae*)
(Photo: Pistol River SP, Curry Co., mid May)

An old saying about this plant is, *"if the floures be shut close up, it betokeneth raine and foul weather"*; hence, one of the common names. Sprawling, fleshy stems up to 16" long, leaves oval, ¼"-¾" long, sessile, opposite or in whorls. Corolla flat and wheel-shaped, about 3/8" across, 5 petals, nearly scarlet (sometimes blue), solitary in the axils between stems and leaves. Disturbed places, especially along the coast. **TOXIC.** Introduced from Europe.

HENDERSON SHOOTING STAR
MOSQUITO BILLS

Dodecatheon hendersonii
(Primrose family, *Primulaceae*)
(Photo: Rainie Falls Trail, Josephine Co., late March)

Stems rise 8"-12" from basal rosettes of oval leaves. Leaves 1"-2½" long, tapering to broad petioles. Flowers deep rose-purple, 5 petals about 5/8" long, turned backward. Filaments of the stamens partially fused into dark-colored tube, stigma tip pointed, not enlarged. There is a yellow band between the petals and the dark tube. Dry open woods west of the Cascades, to WA and CA. **Few-flowered Shooting Star** [*D. pulchellum*] similar, but prefers wet ground, and usually has a yellowish filament tube. **Alpine Shooting Star** [*D. alpinum*], at high elevations in the Cascades and Siskiyous, has narrow leaves, and tip of stigma is enlarged.

WESTERN STARFLOWER
BROAD-LEAVED STARFLOWER
INDIAN POTATO

Trientalis borealis ssp. *latifolia* [*T. latifolia*]
(Primrose family, *Primulaceae*)
(Photo: Mill Creek Falls Trail, Jackson Co., mid May)

Stems 2"-8" high. Leaves 1½"-3" long, pointed, all crowded at the summit of the stem. One to several flowers, on slender filaments, each less than ½" dia., pink to nearly white, 6-8 lobes, star-shaped. Shady woods, western OR, to BC and CA. **Northern Starflower** (*T. europaea*) occurs in bogs along the coast, is shorter, has leaves along the stem, and has larger, white flowers.

OREGON ANEMONE

Anemone oregana
(Buttercup family, *Ranunculaceae*)
(Photo: King Mountain, Josephine Co., late May)

Small, slender-stemmed. Overall height 4"-10", with a single flower about 1" dia., consisting of 5-6 sepals that look like petals, pink, blue-purple, or nearly white. Below, on the otherwise leafless stem, are sets of 3 leaflets, each leaflet 1"-2" long, broadly lanceolate, nearly entire or few-cleft. May be a single basal leaf, that usually withers by flowering-time. Woods at moderate altitudes in the Coast Mountains and Cascades, to WA.

RED COLUMBINE
WESTERN COLUMBINE

Aquilegia formosa
(Buttercup family, *Ranunculaceae*)
(Photo: Near Golden and Silver Falls SNA, Coos Co., mid May)

Unmistakable. Stems 1½'-4' tall, flowers in open clusters, nodding. Basal leaves long-petioled, 3-lobed, the lobes again 3-lobed, leaflets 1"-2" long. Flowers scarlet, with 5 petal-like sepals, and 5 petals with long spurs, dilated at ends, the blades of the petals yellow. Open woods, widely distributed, to AK and CA.

RED LARKSPUR
CANYON DELPHINIUM

Delphinium nudicaule
(Buttercup family, *Ranunculaceae*)
(Photo: Lower Rogue River Canyon, below Grave Creek, Josephine County, mid April)

These brilliant red flowers brighten the canyon walls where they dwell. Plants rise 1'-2' or more, flowers spread out in open formation, with leaves mostly crowded at the base. Leaves 2"-3" broad, with long petioles, palmate, the lobes parted again 3-4 times. Flowers scarlet, about 5/8" across, each with a stout spur 1" and more long, on 2" pedicels. Open woods and rocky slopes, southern Curry, Josephine, and Jackson Cos., to CA.

OLD MAN'S WHISKERS
PRAIRIE SMOKE
PURPLE AVENS

Geum triflorum [*G. ciliatum*]
(Rose family, *Rosaceae*)
(Photo: Near Little Hyatt Lake Road, Jackson Co., early June)

Stems 8"-20" high, somewhat hairy, leaves mostly basal. Leaves (including petioles) 4"-8" long, pinnately divided into many segments, deeply cleft and parted, stem leaves 1 or 2. Typically, stem has 1-3 flowers, more or less cup-shaped, frequently nodding. Sepals reddish, 3/8"-1/2" long, sharp-pointed, petals same length, cream or pink-tinged. Dry meadows, open pine forest, east of Cascade crest, to BC and CA.

HENDERSON HORKELIA
HENDERSON HONEYDEW

Horkelia hendersonii (Rose family, *Rosaceae*)
(Photo: Summit of Mount Ashland, Jackson Co., mid July)

Stems 4"-6" high rise from thick clumps of basal leaves, stems hairy and leaves silky-hairy. Compound leaves to 3" long, with 5-10 small leaflets per side, 3-5 cleft. Flowers in dense clusters, each about ½" dia., 5 sharp-pointed sepals, 5 pink or white petals less than or equal to length of sepals, and 10 stamens. **Federal species of concern.** Summits of Siskiyous, Jackson Co.

DOG ROSE

Rosa canina (Rose family, *Rosaceae*)
(Photo: Old Siskiyou Highway, Cascade-Siskiyou NM, Jackson Co., early June)

Long stout stems up to 9' long, reclining or ascending, with large curved spines. Leaves compound, 5-7 oval leaflets, sharply serrate, not glandular above or below. Flowers relatively large, solitary or in close clusters, sepals persistent in fruit, about ¾" inch long, many with long thin lobes; petals up to 1" long, pink, with whitish areas. Fruits ovoid, ½"-¾" long. Dry open areas, to about 3000' elevations. Naturalized, native of Europe. **California Wild Rose** (*R. californica*) is similar, but the leaves are somewhat glandular, spines and flowers are smaller. **Cluster Rose** (*R. pisocarpa*) lacks glands, and has sparingly distributed slender straight spines. ***White Rose*** (*R. multiflora*), from Asia, is occasionally found in wild locations.

NOOTKA ROSE
COMMON WILD ROSE

Rosa nutkana (Rose family, *Rosaceae*)
(Photo: Shale City Road, Jackson Co., mid June)

Ranges from 18" to 6' tall, prickles more or less straight, few to many. Leaves compound, 5-9 leaflets, oval, toothed. Flowers large, mostly solitary (rarely in 2s or 3s), deep pink, each petal ¾"-1" long, calyx lobes sharp-pointed, persistent in fruit. Woods west of Cascades, to AK and CA. **Wood Rose** (*R. gymnocarpa*) has smaller flowers, abundant slender straight prickles, and calyx lobes that drop off early in fruit. **Ground Rose** (*R. spithamea*) is usually less than 12" high, flowers generally solitary, petals less than ½" long.

SALMONBERRY

Rubus spectabilis (Rose family, *Rosaceae*)
(Photo: Harris Beach SP, Curry Co., late March)

A shrub that sometimes forms thickets. It has prickles, but not as formidable as in Himalaya Blackberry. Leaves in 3s, doubly dentate, somewhat hairy beneath. Flowers appear in early spring, deep rose color, 5 petals, each about ¾" long. Fruit may be yellow, red, or salmon color. From coast to west of the Cascades, usually along streams, to AK and CA.

SUBALPINE SPIRAEA
MOUNTAIN SPIRAEA

Spiraea densiflora [*S. splendens*]
(Rose family, *Rosaceae*)
(Photo: Headquarters, Crater Lake NP, Klamath Co., late July)

Shrub, to 3' high. Leaves ¾"-1½" long, more or less oval, sometimes pointed, serrate. Inflorescence dense, rounded or somewhat flat-topped, up to 2" across. Flowers tiny, bright rose color. Moist places at fairly high altitudes in Cascades, to BC and CA.

DOUGLAS SPIRAEA
HARDHACK

Spiraea douglasii (Rose family, *Rosaceae*)
(Photo: Daley Creek CG, Jackson Co., late August)

A shrub to 6' high, leaves 1½"-4" long, whitish underneath, somewhat dentate. Flowers in dense fuzzy-looking spikes 3"-8" long, with leaves interspersed, at ends of branches. Individual flowers pink, tiny, with stamens projecting. West of Cascades, often on creek banks, to BC and CA.

FRINGECUPS

Tellima grandiflora [includes *T. odorata*]
(Saxifrage family, *Saxifragaceae*)
(Photo: Lobster Creek CG, Curry Co., mid May)

Slender stems 20"-40" high, hairy, flowers in long, narrow, more or less one-sided spikes. Leaves mostly on long petioles, broadly circular, 1½"-4" broad, lobed and somewhat dentate, hairy on both faces; stem leaves few, and much smaller. Calyx about ¼" long, petals also about ¼" long, whitish, soon turning red, deeply cut into thin lobes. Moist woods west of Cascades, to AK and CA.

PACIFIC PAINTBRUSH
OREGON COAST PAINTBRUSH

Castilleja affinis ssp. *litoralis* [*C. litoralis*]
(Figwort family, *Scrophulariaceae*)
(Photo: Otter Point, Curry Co., mid May)

Bright orange-red and hairy, 6"-24" tall, few-branched. Lower leaves green, 1½"-3" long, generally linear and unlobed. Bracts of inflorescence about 1" long or less, broad and obtuse, or with 2-4 short lateral lobes, bright red to orange-red tipped. Corolla 1"-1½" long, hairy, margins reddish or yellowish, calyx hairy. Coastal dunes and bluffs, to CA.

APPLEGATE PAINTBRUSH
WAVY-LEAVED PAINTBRUSH

Castilleja applegatei
(Figwort family, *Scrophulariaceae*)
(Photo: King Mountain, Josephine Co., late May)

There are at least 5 bright-red species of paintbrush in southern Oregon that resemble each other; *C. applegatei* is representative. Erect stems 4"-24" high, hairy, very sticky. Leaves narrow and thin, 1"-2" long, hairy, wavy-margined, usually entire, sometimes with narrow lobes. Bracts of head with 0-7 lobes, terminal portions bright red to yellowish. Corolla 1"-1½" long, margins reddish, stigma well exserted. calyx lobes acute. Dry woods, east of Cascades, generally above 1000' elevation, extending west in Southern Oregon as far as Josephine Co., and to CA. **Short-lobed Indian Paintbrush** (*C. hispida ssp. brevilobata*), in southern Josephine Co., is similar, but is not sticky, leaves are not wavy-margined, and calyx lobes are obtuse.

SISKIYOU PAINTBRUSH
SLENDER PAINTBRUSH

Castilleja miniata ssp. *elata* [*C. elata*]
(Figwort family, *Scrophulariaceae*)
(Photo: 8 Dollar Road, Josephine Co., early May)

This slender plant, usually solitary-stemmed, 12"-18" tall, has a compact rose-purple bloom on top. Slender pointed leaves, 1"-1½" long, are distributed down the stem. Rose-purple bracts are about 1" long, many of them 3-cleft, lateral lobes narrow and pointed, grading into those that are partially green on the bottom half. Corolla is partly enclosed in a sharp-pointed calyx. Wet places, southern Josephine Co., to CA.

SPLIT-HAIR INDIAN PAINTBRUSH

Castilleja schizotricha
(Figwort family, *Scrophulariaceae*)
(Photo: Near Dutchman Peak, Jackson Co., mid July)

Plants 3"-6" high, white-woolly, the hairs branched. Lower leaves linear, 1/4"-3/4" long, some lobed, some not. Inflorescence 1½"-3" long, bracts ½"-¾" long, purplish-red, rounded, 3-lobed. Corollas about ¾" long, hairy, the upper half purplish-red. Open places at fairly high elevations, southwest OR to northwest CA.

FOXGLOVE

Digitalis purpurea
(Figwort family, *Scrophulariaceae*)
(Photo: Harris Beach SP, Curry Co., mid May)

Striking tall racemes of vividly colored flowers, up to 6' high. Leaves oval, margins toothed, 4"-12" long, long petioles, upper leaves smaller. Racemes long, somewhat one-sided, flowers nodding, corollas pink, white, or purple, with lower part of throat whitish and purple-spotted, 1½"-2½" long, bell-shaped, inflated, lips lobed. Local, west of Cascades, especially near the coast. Introduced from Europe. **TOXIC;** has caused fatalities in humans.

CARDINAL MONKEYFLOWER
SCARLET MONKEYFLOWER
Mimulus cardinalis
(Figwort family, *Scrophulariaceae*)
(Photo: Near Fiddler Mt., Josephine Co., early August)

Stems to 2' tall, stout, hairy, sticky, branching. Leaves 2"-3" long, somewhat oval, pointed, toothed. Calyx funnelform or tubular, about 1" long, sharp pointed lobes, hairy. Corolla about 1½" long, bright scarlet, tinged with yellow, the upper petal erect, the lateral petals reflexed. Damp places, southwest OR to CA.

LEWIS MONKEYFLOWER
GREAT PURPLE MONKEYFLOWER
Mimulus lewisii (Figwort family, *Scrophulariaceae*)
(Photo: Near Sun Notch, Crater Lake NP, Klamath Co., mid July)

Plants rise 10"-30". Leaves narrow, pointed, 1½"-3" long, sessile, slightly hairy, finely dentate. Flower stalks 1¼"-3", calyx 5/8"-1" long, sharp points, hairy. Corolla rose, lavender, or purple, the tube 1¼"-2" long, lobes spreading, the throat paler within and hairy. Widely distributed, seeps and banks of streams at higher altitudes, to BC and CA. There are other species of *Mimulus* with reddish-purple or lavender flowers, but most are very small plants, and all except *M. lewisii* have flower stalks less than ¼" long.

DWARF PURPLE MONKEYFLOWER
Mimulus nanus (Figwort family, *Scrophulariaceae*)
(Photo: Near Odell Lake, Klamath Co., mid June)

Extremely short, sometimes forming dense mats of pink flowers, stems hairy, 1"-4" tall. Leaves narrow, ¼"-1" long, mostly entire. Calyx about ¼" long, bracts with sharp points. Corolla deep rose to purplish red, about ¾" long, lobes spreading, the throat hairy, with two yellow, red-dotted stripes. Dry open areas east of Cascades, to WA and CA. **Douglas Monkeyflower** (*M. douglasii*), in Jackson and Josephine Cos. is similar in color and dwarf stature, but lower lip of corolla is very small, almost absent.

WOODLAND PENSTEMON
TURTLE-HEAD
WOODLAND BEARDTONGUE

Nothochelone nemorosa [*Penstemon nemorosus*]
(Figwort family, *Schrophulariaceae*)
(Photo: Siskiyou Crest Road, Jackson Co., early September.)

Up to 3' high, leaves 2"-5" long, opposite, short-petioled, pointed, edges toothed. Corollas about 1¼" long, pink to maroon, hairy outside, but not inside. Anthers densely woolly, the single staminode (infertile stamen), about ½ as long as the fertile stamens, has hairs along its length. Once considered part of the *Penstemon* genus. Mixed evergreen forest at middle altitudes in Cascades and Siskiyous, to BC and CA.

ROSY OWL-CLOVER
BRACTED ORTHOCARPUS

Orthocarpus bracteosus
(Figwort family, *Scrophulariaceae*)
(Photo: Illinois River Road, Josephine Co., late June)

Stems 4"-20" high. Leaves narrow, pointed, 3/4"-2" long, lower ones entire, upper ones with a pair of very narrow lobes. Leaves grade into floral bracts that are not highly contrasted. (In *O. cuspidatus*, below, leaves change abruptly to highly contrasted bracts.) Corolla bright rose-purple, ½"- ¾" long, the lower lip broad and pouch-like. Meadows west of Cascades, to BC and CA.

COPELAND OWL-CLOVER
SISKIYOU MTNS. ORTHOCARPUS

Orthocarpus cuspidatus [*O. copelandii*]
(Figwort family, *Scrophulariaceae*)
(Photo: Near Mount Ashland, Jackson Co., late August)

Overall height 4"-16", leaves 1"-2" long, some with long slender lobes, abruptly changing to dense oval-shaped bracts, each with two small basal lobes, the ones at top becoming purplish pink on their upper edges, with pointed tips. Corolla ½"-1" long, lips purplish pink, upper lip sticking straight out, lower lip with conspicuous white pouch. Open slopes in the Siskiyous, to CA.

MOUNTAIN OWL-CLOVER
MOUNTAIN ORTHOCARPUS

Orthocarpus imbricatus
(Figwort family, *Scrophulariaceae*)
(Photo: Grouse Gap, Jackson Co., mid August)

Plants 4"-12" high, sometimes branched, with a short (1"-3") inflorescence, the narrow green leaves below changing abruptly into the colored bracts at the top. Bracts rounded, rose-purple on the upper third, each with 2 small lateral lobes near the base. Flowers, about ½" long, are nearly hidden by the bracts, with the upper lip rose-purple and hooked at the end, the lower lip slightly pouched and whitish-yellow. Mountain meadows in the Cascades and Siskiyous, at moderate altitudes, to WA and CA.

INDIAN WARRIOR

Pedicularis densiflora
(Figwort family, *Scrophulariaceae*)
(Photo: Johns Peak Road, Jackson Co., late March)

Thick, reddish flowering stems, to 12" high, often in clumps, with doubly pinnate leaves that appear feathery. Top of each stem is covered by dense purplish-red bracts, from which the wine-red tubular flowers stick out like feathers in an Indian war bonnet. Corollas are more than 1" long, with sharp little beaks on the overhanging upper lips, and tiny lobes at about the half-way point on the undersides of the corolla tubes. Dry woods, southern Josephine and Jackson Cos., to CA.

ELEPHANT'S HEAD
PINK ELEPHANTS

Pedicularis groenlandica
(Figwort family, *Scrophulariaceae*)
(Photo: Castle Crest Wildflower Garden, Crater Lake NP, Klamath Co., mid July)

Stems erect, 4"-30" tall. Leaves basal, deeply lobed, 2"-10" long, 25-50 segments, segments toothed. Flowers in dense spikes to 12" long, corollas pink to reddish purple, about ½" long, with trunk-like beak ¼"-½" long, curved upward, lateral lobes resembling elephant ears. Wet meadows and streamsides, moderate to high elevations in Cascades, to AK and CA. **Little Elephant's Head** (*P. attollens*) is similar, but is densely hairy on the inflorescence, and corolla has a shorter beak.

SICKLETOP LOUSEWORT
LEAFY LOUSEWORT
PARROTS BEAK

Pedicularis racemosa
(Figwort family, *Scrophulariaceae*)
(Photo: Near Big Elk Meadow, Jackson Co., late August)

These small flowers have been called "remarkably twisted," and "strangely disorganized." They aren't very tall, 8"-18", with serrate, pointed leaves 1"-3" long. The pink flowers have a sickle-shaped upper lip that has been compared to a parrot's beak or to a bird's claw, strongly deflected off-center. Broad lower lip is shallowly lobed. Shady woods at moderate elevations in Cascades, to BC and CA.

DAVIDSON PENSTEMON
CREEPING PENSTEMON

Penstemon davidsonii [*P. menziesii*]
(Figwort family, *Scrophulariaceae*)
(Photo: Crater Rim, Crater Lake NP, Klamath Co., late July)

Flowering stems rise 1"-3" above matted foliage. Leaves less than ½" long, not hairy, without serrations. (A more northerly subspecies has fine serrations.) Flowers a little over 1" long, rose-purple or bluish-lavender, with bearded folds running down interior of lower lobe. Fertile stamens have hairy anthers; sterile stamen, shorter than the fertile stamens, is densely hairy. Dry cliffs and rocky places at high altitudes, primarily in Cascades, to WA and CA. (See, also, **Rock Penstemon**, below.)

ROCK PENSTEMON
CLIFF PENSTEMON

Penstemon rupicola
(Figwort family, *Scrophulariaceae*)
(Photo: Near Odell Lake, Klamath Co., late June)

Cliff faces and rock slides are brightened with these large rose-purple blooms. Stems prostrate and creeping, forming mats, with numerous small fleshy leaves about ½" long and almost round, generally with fine hairs. Corollas rise above the mats, erect, 1"- 1½" long, bright rose-purple, with sparse hairs inside throat on the lower lobe, sterile stamen not hairy or sparsely so. Dry cliffs in central Cascades, to CA. **Cardwell Penstemon** (*P. cardwellii*), found in southern Josephine Co., similar, but grows taller, and leaves are about 1½" long, narrow.

ROSY PLECTRITIS
SHORTSPUR SEA BLUSH

Plectritis congesta
(Valerian family, *Valerianaceae*)
(Photo: Grizzly Peak, Jackson Co., late May)

Stems 4"-20" high, simple or branched. Leaves opposite, narrowly oblong to more or less oval, ¾"-2" long, rounded at apex. Flowers in dense headlike clusters of small flowers, bright rose, corollas about ¼" long, 2-lipped, lips lobed, usually with short spur below. Moist banks west of Cascades, to BC and CA. **Longhorn Plectritis** (*P. macrocera*), found east of Cascades, is similar, but flowers smaller, pale pink or white, and spur is longer.

WESTERN VERVAIN
WESTERN VERBENA

Verbena lasiostachys (Vervain family, *Verbenaceae*)
(Photo: Near Limpy Botanical Trail, Josephine Co., late May)

Multiple stems from a woody base, 15"-30" tall, branching, with 1-3 flowering spikes per branch, hairy. Leaves 1½"-3" long, often 3-cleft, irregularly incised. Small flowers opening from bottom of spike, with corollas about ¼" long, pink, blue, lavender, or white, and hairy calyx, the corollas much longer than the surrounding bracts. Dry open ground, south from Umpqua Valley to CA. **Bracted Verbena** (*V. bracteata*), east of Cascades, is similar, but flowers are smaller, and the bracts are much longer than the flowers.

Seaside Daisy

BLUE to VIOLET FLOWERS

lowers in this color category can be a real problem, because many of them show reddish tints which ight cause them to be included in the "Red and Pink" section, especially for flowers that are lavender violet. An additional problem is that flowers within the same species many sometimes be violet, blue, ink, or white, so inclusion within a particular color section becomes largely arbitrary. It is always a ood idea, if your flower is not here, to check the "Red to Pink" section.

COMMON PERIWINKLE

Vinca major (Dogbane family, *Apocynaceae*)
(Photo: Lone Ranch Beach, Curry Co., late March)

Vinca was originally planted and cultivated as a ground cover, but has become naturalized over time, usually forming large mats. Often found where buildings once stood, even though the buildings may be gone. Stems trailing, evergreen, leaves opposite, about 2" long, heart-shaped and short-petioled. Flowers blue, 5 petals that are joined at the base into a tube about ¾" long, and then expanded abruptly into a limb as much as 2" dia. Found in localized situations in western OR. Native of Europe.

CASCADE ASTER

Aster ledophyllus [*Eucephalus ledophyllus]*
(Sunflower family, *Asteraceae*)
(Photo: Near Headquarters, Crater Lake NP, Klamath Co., early August)

Stems 12"-30" tall, slender, erect, more or less hairy. Leaves oblong-linear, 1"-2½" long, sessile, entire, somewhat hairy below, not hairy above. Heads 1 to 15, size variable. Involucre about 3/8" long, many layers, bracts pointed, hairy. Rays generally 8, but may be more, up to 21, about 5/8" long, narrow, lavender to purple. Roadsides, meadows, open forest., Cascades, to BC and CA.

WESTERN MOUNTAIN ASTER

Aster occidentalis [*Symphotrichum spatulatum*]
(Sunflower family, *Asteracae*)
(Photo: Daley Creek CG, Jackson Co., late August)

Stems 8"-32" high, more or less hairy. Leaves usually entire, 2"-4" long, narrowly elliptic, pointed, somewhat hairy on edges, reduced in size upward. Involucre about ¼" high, bracts loosely appressed in several series, not entirely green. Ray flowers light purplish, blue, or violet, 3/8"-1/2" long. Damp meadows at moderate altitudes, mainly east of Cascades, to WA and CA. **Leafybract Aster** (*A. foliaceous*), **Great Northern Aster** (*A. modestus*), and **Douglas Aster** (*C. subspicatus*) similar, but have larger, clasping leaves, with technical differences in involucre bracts.

BACHELOR'S BUTTON
CORNFLOWER

Centaurea cyanis (Sunflower family, *Asteraceae*)
(Photo: Near Old Siskiyou Summit, Jackson Co., early July)

Erect stems 12"-24" high, generally branched, sometimes hairy. Leaves 1½"-4" long, lower ones often toothed or lobed, others linear and entire. Heads terminal on long stems, involucres oval-shaped, about 5/8" long, bracts unequal, fringed, with dark margins. Flowers blue, purple, pink, or white, the outer corollas nearly 3/4" long, much longer than the inner, the inner often with different color. Common in fields and on roadsides, escaped from cultivation. Native of Europe.

MEADOW KNAPWEED

Centaurea pratensis (Sunflower family, *Asteraceae*)
(Photo: Susan Creek CG, Douglas Co., late June)

Stems erect, to 3' tall, hairy. Leaves 3"-4" long, elliptic, mostly entire, with petioles, smaller above, sessile. Heads 1"-2" dia., rosy-lavender, disk flowers only, outer flowers elongated, involucre segments brown. Roadsides, waste places. Introduced from Europe. ***Spotted Knapweed*** (*C. stoebe*) is similar, but leaves are deeply parted into narrow segments. Meadow Knapweed (often shown as *C.* **x** *pratensis*) is a cross between Black Knapweed and Brown Knapweed. In ***Black Knapweed*** (*C. nigra*) involucre segments are nearly black, and outer flowers are not elongated. ***Brown Knapweed*** (*C. jacea*) and Meadow Knapweed differ in the regularity of the fringes on the involucre segments.

CHICORY
BLUE SAILORS

Cichorium intybus (Sunflower family, *Asteraceae*)
(Photo: Near Galice, Josephine Co., early June)

Tall, rangy stems, branched, 1'-5' tall. Basal leaves 3"-6" long, more or less in a rosette, somewhat dandelion-like, petioled; cauline leaves smaller, usually entire, clasping, with ears. Flowers numerous, 1"-1½" diameter, composed of ray flowers only, usually bright blue but sometimes white, 5-toothed on ends. Roadsides and fields, widespread in North America below 4900'. Introduced from Europe.

VOLCANIC DAISY
BLUE DWARF FLEABANE

Erigeron elegantulus (Sunflower family, *Asteraceae*)
(Photo: Cloudcap, Crater Lake NP, Klamath Co., mid July)

Foliage almost mat-like from a woody base, flowering stems rising 1½"-6". Leaves linear, ¾"-2" long, dense, hard and shiny. Solitary flower head on each stem, 15-20 ray flowers, each 1/4"-3/8" long, blue or pink. Dry rocky ground, from moderate to high elevations, east side of Cascades, to CA. **Threadleaf Fleabane** (*E. filifolius*) similar, but 6"-20" tall, slender leaves to 3" long, usually with several flower heads to a stem, violet or white, 30-50 rays. **Leafy Daisy** (*E. foliosus*) is usually under 16" tall, generally has one flower head per stem, pink to pale blue, 15-60 rays, and many crowded grass-like leaves about 1" long.

SEASIDE DAISY
BEACH FLEABANE

Erigeron glaucus (Sunflower family, *Asteraceae*)
(Photo: Otter Point SRS, Curry Co., late July)

A striking thing about this lovely daisy is the large number of lavender-colored rays, nearly 100, crowding the margins of the head. Overall height of stems 2"-12", with leaves that are thick, about 1" long, more or less spoon-shaped, often crowded below. Overall dia. of the head may be more than 1½ inches, with large central yellow disk, and an involucre consisting of many layers of small, hairy bracts. Coastal bluffs, to CA.

PROSTRATE BEACH ASTER
CALIFORNIA SANDASTER

Lessingia filaginifolia var. *californica*
[*Corethrogyne californica*]
(Sunflower family, *Asteraceae*)
(Photo: Bandon State Beach, Coos Co., late July)

This tiny aster grows on sprawling, woolly, grayish-green stems. Leaves are typically wedge-shaped, less than 1" long, smaller above, toothed on the outer edges. Each flower head rises a few inches on its own stem, with many layers of bracts just below the head that curl backwards at maturity. Rays 10-40, about 5/16" long, purple, pink, or white. The yellow disk flowers in the center project upward in a tight circle. Coastal scrub, dunes, and grasslands, to CA.

AMERICAN SAWWORT

Saussurea americana
(Sunflower family, *Asteraceae*)
(Photo: Near Mount Ashland, Jackson Co., late August)

Plants to 6' tall, very leafy, with stout stems. Leaves 3"-5" long, narrow, pointed, somewhat dentate with tiny points, upper ones sessile, lower ones with petioles that cling to the stem. Flowers in clusters at the tops of the stems, with involucres about ½" long, the bracts in layers, closely overlapping. Corollas are entirely disk-type, purple or blue, pointed, projecting above involucres ½" or so. Moist slopes at relatively high altitudes, Cascades and Siskiyous, to WA and CA.

MILK THISTLE
BLESSED MILKTHISTLE

Silybum marianum (Sunflower family, *Asteraceae*)
(Photo: Harris Beach SP, Curry Co., mid May)

Plants can be enormous, to 8' high. Leaves large, to 16" long, clasping, heavily lacerated, white-marbled, armed with large yellow spines on the margins. Flower heads borne singly on branches, disk flowers only, reddish-purple, 1"-2" diameter, involucre with many spines about 1½" long. Along the coast, to BC and CA. Native of Europe.

PURPLE SALSIFY
OYSTER PLANT

Tragopogon porrifolius
(Sunflower family, *Asteraceae*)
(Photo: Rogue Valley, Jackson Co., late May)

Purple Salsify resembles its relative, Yellow Salsify (*T. dubius*) (p. 57), except for its vivid purple color. It may grow 3'-4' feet tall, sparingly branched. Flowers have sharp, narrow bracts that extend well beyond the petals. Leaves are long and grass-like, the lower ones to 16" long. Flower heads, composed exclusively of ray flowers, are borne singly on tall fleshy stems that are enlarged just below the heads. Late in the season, the heads become large, brown puffy balls. Widespread west of Cascades, roadsides and other disturbed places. Native of Europe.

GREAT HOUND'S TONGUE

Cynoglossum grande (Borage family, *Boraginaceae*)
(Photo: Beekman Arboretum, Jackson Co., late March)

(See, also, **Western Hound's Tongue,** p. 148.) Leaves resemble a dog's tongue. Stems clustered, stout, not hairy, 1'-2' high. Lower leaves numerous, broadly oval, somewhat hairy, pointed, to 5" long, long petioles, base of leaf more or less heart-shaped. Upper leaves smaller, with short petioles. Flowers are in loose clusters. Corollas about ½" dia., 5 petals, bright blue (sometimes magenta), with inner circle of small white crests. Shady woods, west of Cascades, to WA and CA.

BLUE STICKSEED
JESSICA'S STICKSEED

Hackelia micrantha [*H. jessicae*]
(Borage family, *Boraginaceae*)
(Photo: Grizzly Peak Trail, Jackson County, mid June)

Resembles Forget-Me-Not (see p. 129), but Stickseed has hooked spines on its seeds, and Forget-Me-Not does not. Plants 2'-3' tall, with somewhat hairy, fleshy stems. Basal leaves numerous, fairly narrow, to 10"-12" long, about half that length taken up by flat petioles. Stem leaves 3"-6" long, narrow, without petioles. Flowers in loose clusters, ¼" dia. or less, 5 petals, light blue, with small white crests in a circle in the center. Meadows and open forests in the Cascades and Siskiyous, to CA. **Many-flowered Stickseed** (*H. floribunda*) is similar, the two species differing primarily in the prickliness of the seeds. **Bristly Stickseed** (*H. setosa*) has very hairy lower leaves, and larger flowers.

TALL BLUEBELLS
TALL LUNGWORT

Mertensia paniculata
(Borage family, *Boraginaceae*)
(Photo: Near Rabbit Ears, Douglas Co., early July)

Stems rise to 30" high. Leaves more or less oval pointed, basal 4"-8" long with petioles, upper leaves smaller, almost sessile. Flowers in open clusters corollas about 1/2" long, blue or pinkish, tube narrow and then enlarging abruptly, with 5 shallow lobes calyx about 3/16" long, with sharp narrow lobes Moist woods and meadows to fairly high altitudes west slope of Cascades, to BC. **Broadleaf Bluebell** (*M. platyphylla*), has rounded calyx-lobes. **Beautiful Bluebells** (*M. bella*) has a corolla that tapers evenly.

COMMON FORGET-ME-NOT

Myosotis scorpiodes (Borage family, *Boraginaceae*)
(Photo: Bandon SP, Coos Co., late March)

Flowers in coiled clusters at the tops of stems 1' or more high, the coils unrolling during flowering. Leaves 1"-3" long, more or less elliptic. Flowers blue, corolla in a slender tube, with 5 lobes that spread out flat, about ½" dia., with small white crests in a circle in the center. Wet ground, drainage ditches. Native to Europe.

KOEHLER ROCK CRESS
SHRUBBY ROCK CRESS

Arabis koehleri (Mustard family, *Brassicaceae*)
(Photo: Near O'Brien, Josephine Co., mid March)

Plant is a dwarf shrub, 3"-8" high, woody at the base, with hairless flowering stems rising 3"-6". Stems crowded with leaves, the lower ones slightly hairy, narrow, up to 1" long, the upper ones hairless, shorter, tightly clasping the stems with ears. Flowers in clusters, bright reddish purple, 3/8"-1/2" long, 4 petals, with long pedicels. Rocky ground, southern Josephine, Jackson, and Curry Cos.

LYALL ROCK CRESS

Arabis lyallii (Mustard family, *Brassicaceae*)
(Photo: Cloudcap, Crater Lake NP, Klamath Co., mid July)

Very short, 6" high or less. Basal leaves ½"-1" long; stem leaves few, sessile, well spaced, about ½" long. Petals 4, about ¼" long, rose to purplish. Seedpods erect to spreading, 1"-2" long, about 1/16" dia. Slopes and ridges at fairly high elevations in Cascades, to Canada and CA. **Lemmon Rock Cress** (*A. lemmonii*) similar, but stem leaves are clasping with ears, and seed pods are pendulous to spreading.

SCOULER HAREBELL
PALE BELLFLOWER
SCOULER BLUEBELL

Campanula scouleri
(Bellflower family, *Campanulaceae*)
(Photo: Near Swiftwater Falls, North Umpqua River, Douglas Co., late June)

Plants 4"-12", often reclining. Leaves serrate, blades about 1" long, petioles ½"-1". Flower bell-shaped, with sharp slender calyx lobes. Corolla pale blue to white, pointed lobes sharply curved backward. Stigma projects from flower tube about ½", bluish. Dry shady woods west of Cascades, to WA and CA. **California Harebell** (*Asyneuma prenanthoides* [*C. prenanthoides*]) similar, but generally taller, erect, and leaves are sessile or nearly so.

BACH DOWNINGIA
CALICO-FLOWER

Downingia bacigalupi
(Bellflower family, *Campanulaceae*)
(Photo: Near Hyatt Lake, Jackson Co., early July)

Rises 2"-6", with tiny leaves closely appressed to stem. Two narrow upper petals, blue, about ½" long; broad lower petal with 3 lobes, blue, 2 yellow-orange spots in white field. Horn-like anther column, anthers bent sharply down about 90 degrees from filaments. Meadows, damp places, southwestern Oregon, to CA. **Elegant Downingia** (*D. elegans*) similar, but lacks yellow-orange spots. **Cascade Downingia** (*D. yina*) similar, but lacks prominent horn-like anther column.

WILD TEASEL

Dipsacus fullonum [*D. sylvestris*]
(Teasel family, *Dipsacaceae*)
(Photo: Denman WA, Jackson Co., late June)

Stems to 6' high, stout, very spiny. Leaves 12" and more long, toothed, spiny, stem leaves united at base, forming cups that collect water around stem. Flower heads to 4" long, cylindric, with long sharp involucral bracts that curve upward, some as long as the head. Flowers dense, lavender colored, sometimes white, each with stiff spine, blooming in bands around the heads. Widespread in waste places, fields, mostly below 3000'. Native of Europe. ***Fuller's Teasel*** (*D. sativus*), also non-native, is similar, but the involucral bracts spread outward.

BEACH PEA

Lathyrus japonicus (Legume family, *Fabaceae*)
(Photo: Bandon SP, Coos Co., mid May)

(Peas have tiny hairs down one side of the style; vetches have tiny hairs around the top of the style just below the stigma.) The sprawling stems of this pea may be tangled in other vegetation. Compound leaves about 6" long, 6-10 leaflets, mostly alternate, ovate, each leaflet 1"-1½" long. Stipules almost as large as the leaflets. Flowers, each about 1" long, 4-12 in number, violet to blue-purple, sometimes 2-colored, on stems 5"-6" long. Beaches, to AK and CA. **Silky Beach Pea** (*L. littoralis*), also found along the beaches, has densely soft-hairy foliage, vestigial or non-functional tendrils, and 2-colored flowers, pink-purple and white.

NEVADA PEA
THICK-LEAVED PEA

Lathyrus lanszwertii (Legume family, *Fabaceae*)
(Photo: Trapper Creek CG, Odell Lake, Klamath Co., late June)

Stems erect, slender, 1'-2' high. Leaves compound, usually with 1 simple tendril, with 4-12 elliptic or linear leaflets 1"-2" long, stipules small and narrow. Flowers 3-8 in clusters at the ends of long peduncles, corollas generally purple to lavender, 5/16"-1/2" long. Inner margin of style with tiny hairs. Open woods east of the Cascades, to WA and CA. **Sierra Pea** (*L. nevadensis*) similar, flowers larger, 2-5 in a cluster, leaflets broader.

WHITE-LEAVED LUPINE

Lupinus albifrons (Legume family, *Fabaceae*)
(Photo: Near Applegate Lake, Jackson Co., early April.

Usually shrubby at the base, many-branched, with stems rising to 20". Foliage has silvery appearance, compound leaves, palmate, 6-10 leaflets, petioles generally longer than leaflets, each leaflet about 1"-1½" long, somewhat hairy. Calyx hairy, lower point longer than upper. Corolla about ½" long, petals mostly blue, sides of banner petal folded back, back of banner slightly hairy, middle of banner yellow or white, lateral petals strongly folded around keel, keel slightly hairy. Open sandy or rocky ground, west of Cascades, to CA.

MINIATURE LUPINE
BICOLORED LUPINE

Lupinus bicolor (Legume family, *Fabaceae*)
(Photo: Agate Desert Preserve, Jackson Co., late March)

Grows 4"-24" high, hairy throughout, with 5-8 palmate leaflets ½"-¾" long, petioles 2-3 times as long. Flowers in whorls, on racemes 1"-2½" long, pedicels about 1/8" long. Corolla about 5/16" long, banner petal roundish, strongly turned upward, the middle white, changing to purple, sometimes with black dots. Open ground, mostly west of Cascades, to CA. **Small-flowered Lupine** (*L. micranthus*) has a banner petal that is wedge-shaped, and the sides are not strongly turned upward.

DWARF LUPINE
PRAIRIE LUPINE
LOW MOUNTAIN LUPINE

Lupinus lepidus [*L. lyalli,* in part]
(Legume family, *Fabaceae*)
Photo: Near Crescent, Klamath Co., late June)

Highly variable, with many varieties, some with white or yellow banner patches, some without. The variety in the photo, **Prairie Lupine** (var. *sellulus*) occurs at moderate elevations, grows to 5"-14" high, with 5-8 palmate leaflets 1/2" long or less, and has blue petals with a white patch or yellow patch on the banner petal. **Low Mountain Lupine** (var. *lobbii*) is similar, but is shorter, and occurs at higher elevations. Mostly in the mountains, dry rocky areas, meadows, open woodlands, roadsides to WA and CA.

SEASHORE LUPINE

Lupinus littoralis (Legume family, *Fabaceae*)
(Photo: Otter Point, Curry Co., mid May)

Stems mostly prostrate, up to 2 ft. long, hairy, often with long hairs. Leaflets 5-9, ½"-1½" long, more or less hairy, petioles 1"-2½" long. Racemes short, flowers more or less in whorls. Pedicels about 1/8"-1/4" long. Flowers 3/8"-1/2" long, blue to lavender and white, banner petal strongly bent upward. Seedpods about 1½" long, hairy. Beaches and sandy ledges along the coast, to WA and CA.

BIGLEAF LUPINE
MANY-LEAVED LUPINE

Lupinus polyphyllus (Legume family, *Fabaceae*)
(Photo: Wood River Valley, Klamath Co., late June)

One of our largest lupines. Very tall, to 4' high, stems stout and succulent. Palmate leaves with 9-16 leaflets, leaflets 2"-6" long, petioles to 12" long and more. Flowers in long compact to open racemes, corollas about ½" long, bluish-purple, pink-lavender, or white. Dry or wet meadows, moist woods or bogs, from east base of Cascades to coast, to BC and CA.

ALFALFA
LUCERNE

Medicago sativa (Legume family, *Fabaceae*)
(Photo: Near Old Siskiyou Summit, Cascade-Siskiyou NM, Jackson Co., early July)

Stems 8"-32" long, decumbent to erect. Leaflets in 3s, narrowly oval, about ½" long, with small stipules at base of petiole. Inflorescence with 8-25 flowers, corollas about 3/8" long, purple, or sometimes multi-colored with violet or greenish-yellow. Escaped from cultivation and widely established in disturbed areas throughout most of U.S. Native of Eurasia.

MENDOCINO GENTIAN
ELEGANT GENTIAN
WALDO GENTIAN

Gentiana setigera [*G. bisetaea*]
Gentian family, *Gentianaceae*
(Photo: Near O'Brien, Josephine Co., late July)

Stems 6"-14" tall. Leaves 1'-1½" long, narrow, crowded toward base, opposite, sessile, thickish. Flowers usually single and terminal, but sometimes with 1-3 in axils, calyx lobes 5, sharp-pointed, narrowed at base, almost as long as the corolla tube. Corolla tubular, 1½"-2" long, deep blue, greenish on outside, 5-lobed, lobes sharp-pointed. Wet meadows, southern Josephine Co. to CA.

WHITE-STEMMED SWERTIA
WHITESTEM FRASERA
WHITESTEM GENTIAN

Swertia albicaulis [*Frasera albicaulis*]
(Gentian family, *Gentianaceae*)
(Photo: Near Old Siskyou Summit, Jackson Co., early June)

Stems 1 to a few, to 26" high, leaves in whorls close to ground, becoming opposite higher, narrow, 2"-9" long. Flowers in dense clusters, corollas about 3/4" long, 4-lobed, each lobe elliptic, sharp-pointed, greenish white to pale blue, with a narrowly oblong "nectary pit," about 1/8" long, near the base. Dry areas east of Cascades, to WA and CA. **Clustered Green-Gentian** (*S. fastigiata*) is similar, but has wider leaves, pale yellowish-green flowers, and a roundish nectary pit.

DWARF WATERLEAF
BALLHEAD WATERLEAF

Hydrophyllum capitatum
(Waterleaf family, *Hydrophyllaceae*)
(Photo: near Hyatt Lake, Cascade-Siskiyou NM, Jackson Co., mid May)

At first, the flowers might escape notice, because they are hidden at the base of the leaves, next to the ground. Overall height of plant to about 10", the leaves rising on petioles 2"-6" long, the blades somewhat shorter, heavily lobed and divided. Flowers pale blue to lavender, with 5 petals about ¼" long, on short stems, in tight clusters. Moist slopes, meadows, 3000' to 5000', east of the Cascade crest, to WA and CA.

THREADLEAF PHACELIA
NARROWLEAF PHACELIA

Phacelia linearis
(Waterleaf family, *Hydrophyllaceae*)
(Photo: Near Gerber Reservoir, Klamath Co., early June)

Plants erect, 4"-16" high, hairy. Leaves mostly linear, 1½"-3" long, hairy on edges, sometimes with narrow lobes. Racemes numerous, from axils, flowers scorpiod. Calyx lobes narrow, about ¼" long, hairy and bristly. Corollas bowl-shaped, 3/8"-1/2" across, 5 rounded petals, blue or lilac, sometimes whitish. Stamens 5, spreading, style 2-cleft. Dry open ground, Umpqua Valley to CA, and east of the Cascades. **Bolander Phacelia** (*P. bolanderi*) has similar flowers, but leaves are heavily dentate, hairy, with long petioles.

DOUGLAS IRIS

Iris douglasiana (Iris family, *Iridaceae*)
(Photo: Cape Blanco SP, Curry Co., mid May)

This coastal iris in spring sometimes covers acres of pastureland with its showy clumps. Stems rise 6"-30" above clumps of leaves, 1-3 flowers per stem. Leaves 12"-24" long, 3/4" wide or less. Flowers vary from blue, to purplish, to nearly white, dark veined, with sepals and petals 2"-3" long. Length of tube between perianth and top of the ovary is ½"-1"; ovary is ridged. Common in meadows along coast, from Coos Co. to CA. A similar iris of the interior, from Douglas Co. northward, **Oregon Iris** (*I. tenax*), has perianth tube less than ¼" long, and tough, narrow grass-like leaves, 1/8"-3/16" wide. **Rocky Mountain Iris** (*I. missouriensis*), east of Cascades, is generally pale blue, perianth tube is ¼"-½" long, stem may have a single leaf.

WESTERN BLUE-EYED GRASS

Sisyrinchium bellum (Iris family, *Iridaceae*)
(Photo: Shale City Road, Jackson Co., mid June)

Slender stems 8"-16" high, generally branched, flowers subtended by 2 bracts (called a *spathe*). Leaves about 1/8" wide, not as long as the stem. Perianth parts 6 in number, blue or bluish-purple, yellowish at base, each segment less than ½" long, often notched at apex, with a small sharp point. Open, moist places, to WA and CA. A similar species, **Idaho Blue-eyed Grass** (*S. idahoense*), has lighter blue flowers and unbranched stems.

COMMON DEAD NETTLE
HENBIT

Lamium amplexicaule (Mint family, *Lamiaceae*)
(Photo: Rogue Valley, Jackson Co., mid March)

Only 12" high or so, and easily overlooked. Stems 4-angled, leaves crowded toward top. Flowers emerge from points where leaf stems join the main stems. Leaves generally heart-shaped, scalloped, about ¾" across, lower ones with long petioles, upper ones without. Corollas deep rose-purple, about ¾" long, tube-shaped, with arched upper lip, two smaller lobes below. Frequent in waste ground. Introduced from Europe.

PENNYROYAL
Mentha pulegium
(Mint family, *Lamiaceae*)
(Photo: Lone Ranch Beach, Curry Co., late July)

The most distinctive thing about this plant is the tightly packed little clumps of flowers spaced along the stem, each subtended by leaves. Height 4"-24", stem square, leaves generally less than 1" long, reduced upward. Flowers tiny, tightly packed, violet-colored, stamens sticking out past the ends of the corollas. Occasionally found west of the Cascades, in wet places, to CA. Native of Europe. A similar species, **Field Mint** (*M arvensis*), native, is widely distributed, has larger, generally serrate, leaves.

MOUNTAIN MONARDELLA
WESTERN BALM
COYOTE MINT
Monardella odoratissima (Mint family, *Lamiaceae*)
(Photo: Near Hyatt Lake, Jackson Co., early July)

Stems 8"-16" high, flowers in dense head-like clusters. Leaves narrow, about 1" long, dull green above. Bracts below flowering heads more or less oval, sharp-pointed, not particularly leaf-like, often purplish. Corollas rose-purple, about 1/2" long, twice as long as the calyxes. Dry ground, Southern Josephine, Jackson, and Klamath Cos., to high elevations, to CA. A related species *(M. villosa)* is also called **Coyote Mint;** it differs by having bracts below the inflorescence that are green and leaf-like. **Siskiyou Monardella** (*M. purpurea*), in Curry Co. and southern Josephine Co., is similar, corolla bright rose-purple, leaves shining green above.

SELF-HEAL
HEAL-ALL
Prunella vulgaris (Mint family, *Lamiaceae*)
(Photo: Near Susan Creek Falls, Douglas Co., late June)

Stems 4"-20" tall, each with short, thick, flower-spike. Leaves 1"-3" long, more or less oval, somewhat toothed, lower ones with petioles, upper ones without. Spikes dense, 1"-3" long, with semicircular bracts that are usually purple-tinged. Calyx about 3/8" long, corolla about ½" long, bluish violet, sometimes pink or white, 2-lipped, upper lip entire, hood-like, lower lip 3-lobed and fringed. Widespread in much of the world in moist areas, including lawns, up to moderate elevations.

SNAPDRAGRON SKULLCAP
NOSE SKULLCAP

Scutellaria antirrhinoides (Mint family, *Lamiaceae*)
(Photo: Near Star Flat, Josephine Co., late June)

Slender stems 6"-12" long, erect or decumbent. Leaves narrowly oval, 1/2"-7/8", opposite, on short petioles, the lower leaves somewhat serrate, the upper reduced and entire. Flowers in axils, 1/2"-7/8" long, tubular, violet-blue, upper lip arched, lower lip spreading and with lighter spots, calyx with a noticeable crest on top (the "cap" on the "skull"). Moist ground, Willamette Valley to CA, and eastward. **Narrowleaf Skullcap** (*S. angustifolia*) is similar, but has narrower leaves and larger flowers.

ELEGANT BRODIAEA
HARVEST BRODIAEA
ELEGANT CLUSTER-LILY

Brodiaea elegans (Lily family, *Liliaceae*)
(Photo: Soda Mountain Road, Jackson Co., early July)

Stems 6"-20" high, basal leaves withering by time of flowering. Flowers 3-10, in umbel, pedicels 1"-3" long. Perianth funnelform, deep bluish-purple, 1"-1½" long, the 6 lobes spreading. Fertile stamens 3, staminodes (infertile stamens) 3, staminodes flat, white, bending away from stamens. Dry open ground, west of Cascades to fairly high elevations, to CA. **Crown Brodiaea** (*B. coronaria*)**,** similar, but staminodes bend in toward the stamens, are sharp on the ends, with margins inrolled. **California Brodiaea** (*B. californica*) similar, but staminodes are rounded or notched on the ends.

GREAT CAMAS

Camassia leichtlinii (Lily family, *Liliaceae*)
(Photo: Lower Table Rock Trail, Jackson Co., late April)

Flowers clustered at top of stout stem 2' and more high, many basal leaves 18" inches and longer. Perianth parts purplish-blue (a white form is found in the Umpqua Valley), 1" or more long, spread evenly. Unopened buds cluster tightly at top of stem. Perianth parts twist tightly together after flowering, an important distinction from *C. quamash* (see next page). Western OR, to CA. **Howell Camas** (*C. howellii*), found in northern Josephine and Jackson Cos., is similar, but has smaller flowers

COMMON CAMAS

Camassia quamash (Lily family, *Liliaceae*)
(Photo: Great Meadow, Klamath Co., late June)

Upon occasion, Common Camas can be so dense in a mountain meadow as to resemble a blue lake. It is somewhat smaller than its relative, **Great Camas** (*C. leichtlinii*), on previous page. Flowers are distributed along upper part of a relatively slender stem that may be 2' high. Buds at the top tend to be more separated, and less tightly clustered than in *C. leichtlinii*. Narrow leaves are clustered at the base. Perianth parts range from dark to light blue, each segment usually less than 1" long. The perianth parts do not twist tightly together after flowering, but wither separately -- an important distinction from *C. leichtlinii*. Widely distributed in OR, to CA.

BLUE DICKS
COMMON BRODIAEA

Dichelostemma capitatum [*Brodiaea capitata*] [*Brodiaea pulchella*] (Lily family, *Liliaceae*)
(Photo: Briggs Valley Road, Josephine Co., mid April)

Leafless stem to 2' high. Long, thin basal leaves. Flowers, 4-15, in dense ball-like head. Large pointed bracts, usually dark purple, at base of head. Flowers pink-purple, blue to white, 6 perianth parts, in short bell-shaped tube 3/4"-1" long. (In Roundtooth Ookow, below, tube is narrowed above ovary.) Pointed white stamen filaments next to anthers. Open ground, Josephine and Jackson Cos., to CA.

ROUNDTOOTH OOKOW
ROUNDTOOTH SNAKE-LILY
WILD HYACINTH

Dichelostemma multiflorum [*Brodiaea multiflora*] (Lily family, *Liliaceae*)
(Photo: Rough and Ready, Josephine Co., mid May)

Stems 12"-28" high, leaves usually 2, 12"-20" long, about 3/16" wide. Flowers in dense umbel-like clusters, bluish-purple (sometimes pink), perianth tube-like, strongly narrowed above ovary, about 3/4" long, 6 lobes, stamen filaments fused into crown-like tube, segments white or pale purple, ends rounded. Grasslands, open woodland, Rogue River Valley to CA. **Forktooth Ookow** (*D. congestum*) similar, but crown segments are forked.

LARGE-FLOWERED BRODIAEA
HOWELL TRITELEIA

Triteleia grandiflora var. *howellii*
[*Brodiaea howellii*] (Lily family, *Liliaceae*)
(Photo: Wood River Day-Use Area, Klamath Co., late June)

Stems 1'-2' high, slender basal leaves 12"-20" long. Flowers 8-16, in an umbel, on pedicels ¾"-1" long. Perianth parts bright blue, tubular, ¾"-1" long, flaring into lobes, base of tube rounded, not strongly narrowed at base. Anthers on broadly winged filaments. Moist slopes, from southwestern OR, eastward, to WA and CA. **Douglas Triteleia** (*Triteleia grandiflora* var. *grandiflora*) has perianth lobes that are strongly wavy on the margins, and the anthers are on narrow filaments. **Wally Basket** (*Triteleia laxa*) is similar to Douglas Triteleia, but floral tube is strongly narrowed at base, not rounded.

WILD BLUE FLAX
WESTERN BLUE FLAX
PRAIRIE FLAX

Linum lewisii [*L. perenne var. lewisii*]
(Flax family, *Linaceae*)
(Photo: Rocky Point, Klamath Co., late May)

Perennial, to 2' tall, slender stems, from a woody base. Leaves numerous, ½"-2" long, narrow and pointed. Flowers bright blue, 5 petals, petals 1/2"-1" long. Dry areas east of Cascades and in Siskiyous to southern Jackson Co. ***Pale Flax*** (*L. bienne*) and ***Common Flax*** (*L. usitatissimum*), both of them annuals and natives of Europe, are similar, but have smaller flowers, petals about ¼" long in Pale Flax, and about ½" long in Common Flax.

NAKED BROOMRAPE
ONE-FLOWER BROOMRAPE

Orobanche uniflora
(Broomrape family, *Orobanchaceae*)
(Photo: Near Lost Creek Lake, Jackson Co., early May)

Easily missed -- only a few inches high, no visible leaves, and usually only 1 flower, sometimes more. The bare stem bends over and supports a purplish or light violet flower 1-1½" long, corolla strongly curved, 2 lobes above, 3 below, with hairy 5-pointed calyx. A root parasite, in open woods on both sides of the Cascades, to BC and CA. **Clustered Broomrape** (*O. fasciculata*) sends up 2-10 flowering stems, flowers light yellow to light purple.

MOUNT MAZAMA COLLOMIA MOUNT MAZAMA MOUNTAINTRUMPET

Collomia mazama (Phlox family, *Polemoniaceae*)
(Photo: Hershberger Meadows, Douglas Co., mid July)

Clustered stems, erect, 6"-12" tall, with flowers in congested clusters at ends of stems. Leaves more or less lance-shaped, 1"-2" long, mostly sessile, the upper leaves entire, the lower ones sharply lobed on the ends. Corolla trumpet-shaped, about 5/8" long, 5 spreading lobes, blue-violet to pinkish, stamens and style exserted. Dry woods and meadows in southern Cascades, from 4800'-6300', especially in region around Crater Lake and Mount McLaughlin. **Federal species of concern.**

BLUEHEAD GILIA BLUE FIELD GILIA GLOBE GILIA FIELD GILLY-FLOWER

Gilia capitata (Phlox family, *Polemoniaceae*)
(Photo: Grizzly Peak, Jackson Co., mid June)

The multiple stems ascend 1'-3', with leaves 2"-4" long, divided into linear segments. Tiny flowers, tubular, with 5 lobes, light blue or white, packed into a dense round ball. Open ground, mostly west of the Cascades, to AK and CA.

WESTERN POLEMONIUM TALL JACOB'S LADDER

Polemonium occidentale
(Phlox family, *Polemoniaceae*)
(Photo: Spring Creek Day-Use Area, Collier Memorial SP, Klamath Co., late June)

Slender stem, 16"-32" tall, erect, hairy, sticky. Leaves compound, the lower ones with long petioles, 13-19 narrow leaflets,. Inflorescence a compact cluster, corollas bell-shaped, 3/8"-5/8" long, bright purplish-blue, 5-lobed, the lobes longer than the tube, stamens and style projecting well beyond corolla. Moist places at moderate elevations in Cascades, to AK and CA.

SHOWY POLEMONIUM
SKUNK-LEAVED JACOB'S LADDER

Polemonium pulcherrimum
(Phlox family, *Polemoniaceae*)
(Photo: Near Wrangle Camp, Jackson Co., early July)

Skunky odor. Stems rise only 6" or so, hairy. Leaves compound, about 3" long, with 13-21 small oval leaflets, hairy. Flowers in clusters, corolla 5/16"-3/8" long, bell-shaped, bright blue with yellow tube, stamens reaching to level of petals. Higher elevations in Cascades and Siskiyous, to AK and CA. **California Polemonium** (*P. californicum*) similar, corolla 3/8"-1/2", light blue with paler tube.

MONKSHOOD
COLUMBIA MONKSHOOD

Aconitum columbianum
(Buttercup family, *Ranunculaceae*)
(Photo: Imnaha Springs, Jackson Co., early August)

There is no mistaking a Monkshood, because the upper sepal, curving over and forming a protective hood, resembles nothing else. Plants range from 1'-5' high, usually with ascending stems, sometimes recumbent, with maple-like, deeply lobed leaves up to 6" across. Flower is formed of petal-like sepals, bluish-purple (sometimes whitish), with the "hood" above, 5/8" long exclusive of the sharp curved point, and lateral sepals about ½" long. Inside the "hood" are 2 whitish petals, looking at first glance like large stamens. Plant is **TOXIC**, and has caused death in livestock and humans. Streambanks and meadows at middle altitudes in Cascades and Siskiyous, to BC and CA.

TALL LARKSPUR
MOUNTAIN LARKSPUR
TOWER DELPHINIUM

Delphinium glaucum
(Buttercup family, *Ranunculaceae*)
(Photo: Grizzly Peak Trail, Jackson Co., mid July)

Often 6' and more, stems robust. Leaves to 6" across, deeply lobed, 5-7 divisions, the divisions incised. Flower spikes long and densely flowered, each flower about 1" long, purple, narrowly funnel-shaped, with spur 5/8" long. Wet ground at moderate to high altitudes in Cascades and Siskiyous, to AK and CA.

MENZIES LARKSPUR
FIELD LARKSPUR

Delphinium menziesii
(Buttercup family, *Ranunculaceae*)
(Photo: Near Table Mountain Road, Jackson Co., early June)

Stems 8" to 3' tall, with rather open flower clusters. Leaves typically not crowded toward the base, up to 4" across, many with long petioles, lobed 3-5 times, segments deeply incised. Petal-like sepals deep blue, ½"-¾" long, with spur 5/8" long, hairy. Two small whitish upper petals; 2 dark blue lower petals, inconspicuous, somewhat hairy. Meadows and woods, mostly west of the Cascades, to WA and CA. **Upland Larkspur** (*D. nuttallianum*) similar, but lower petals conspicuous, pale blue. **Low Larkspur** (*D. decorum*), in Josephine and Jackson Cos., grows to 20" tall, has somewhat smaller leaves and flowers; leaves few, and tend to be crowded toward the base.

MAHALA MAT

Ceanothus prostratus
(Buckthorn family, *Rhamnaceae*)
(Photo: Near Prospect, Jackson Co., early May)

Prostrate shrub, branches sometimes rooting, producing dense mats up to 10' across. Leaves evergreen, firm, 5/8"-1¼" long, spiny-edged. Flowers small, in clusters, 5 petals, with 5 incurved sepals resembling petals, blue to lavender to whitish. Coniferous forest, Cascades and Siskiyous, to WA and CA. A similar species, **Siskiyou Mat** (*C. pumilus*), in Southwestern OR, usually on serpentine, has smaller leaves, mostly not toothed.

BLUE BLOSSOM

Ceanothus thyrsiflorus
(Buckthorn family, *Rhamnaceae*)
(Photo: Harris Beach SP, Curry Co., mid May)

Shrub or small tree to 24' high, with green branchlets. Leaves oblong or elliptic, 1"-2" long, on short petioles, leathery, finely serrate, strongly 3-veined. Flowers small, 5 spoon-shaped petals, blue, fragrant, in dense clusters to 6" long. Along coast in Curry and Coos Cos., to CA. **Deer Brush** (*C. integerrimus*), found west of Cascades to coast, is shrubby, 3'-12' high, has light blue to white flowers in loose narrow clusters, and leaves that are entire, not finely serrate.

GIANT BLUE-EYED MARY
LARGE-FLOWERED COLLINSIA
LARGE INNOCENCE

Collinsia grandiflora
(Figwort family, *Scrophulariaceae*)
(Photo: Shale City Road, Jackson Co., late May)

Plants 4"-16" high, often in large patches. Leaves more or less oval, ½"-1" long, the upper narrower. Flowers often somewhat whorled. Corolla 3/8"-5/8" long, strongly 2-lipped, upper lip white or light blue, sharply bent back, lower one blue. Open, moist ground west of Cascades, to BC and CA. **Small-flower Blue-eyed Mary** (*C. parviflora*) has flowers about ½ the size. **Few-flowered Collinsia** (*C. sparsiflora*), in Josephine Co., has flowers 5/16"-1/2" long, solitary in the axils, pale to bright purple, upper lip mottled.

SISKIYOU PENSTEMON
TONGUE-LEAVED PENSTEMON

Penstemon anguineus
(Figwort family, *Scrophulariaceae*)
(Photo: Near Galice-Agness Road, Josephine Co., early June)

Plants to 30" high, broad pointed leaves 2"-4" long, dentate, upper leaves clasping, lower ones with long petioles. Inflorescence sticky-haired, flowers light blue to bluish purple, typically less than 1" long. Sterile stamen (staminode) projects conspicuously. Floor of lower petal may have slight hairiness, or none. Dry slopes in mountains of southwest Oregon, to CA. **Rattan Penstemon** (*P. rattanii*), in Coast Range, has larger flowers, floor of lower petal hairy, leaves narrower and longer.

AZURE PENSTEMON

Penstemon azureus
(Figwort family, *Scrophulariaceae*)
(Photo: Summit of Mount Ashland, Jackson Co., mid July)

Stems rise 8"-20" from woody base. Leaves entire, somewhat leathery, oblong to ovate, 1"-2" long, more or less petioled, shorter and clasping above. Inflorescence narrow, corollas about 1" long, bright blue (sometimes lilac), not hairy inside or out. Open forest, to 8000' elevation, to CA. Var. *parvulus*, shown in photo, is lower-growing, has smaller leaves.

MOUNTAIN BLUE PENSTEMON
GAY PENSTEMON

Penstemon laetus
(Figwort family, *Scrophulariaceae*)
(Photo: Near Olene, Klamath Co., early June)

Plant rises 8"-20", stems erect or decumbent below, stem hairy, inflorescence open. Leaves 1½"-3" long, entire, narrow, hairy, upper leaves clasping. Calyx about 5/16" long, hairy. Corolla ¾"-1½" long, the throat bluish-purple, dilated, lobes spreading, blue, the lower lip only slightly exceeding upper, and not reflexed. Corolla slightly hairy and glandular-tipped. Dry open areas, Josephine to Klamath Cos., and to CA.

SMALL-FLOWERED PENSTEMON
LITTLEFLOWER PENSTEMON
PINCUSION PENSTEMON

Penstemon procerus [*P. tolmiei*]
(Figwort family, *Scrophulariaceae*)
(Photo: Near Observation Peak, Jackson Co., mid July)

Flowering stems rise 4"-16", from a base which may be decumbent. Leaves generally crowded below, ½"-1½" long, narrow, with 3 or 4 pair of opposite leaves on stem. Flowers blue-purple, in 1 or 2 dense clusters, corollas about 3/8" long, the throats not much dilated, floors of corollas whitish, with sparse yellowish hairs. Mountain meadows in Cascades and Siskiyous, to CA.

MEADOW PENSTEMON
RYDBERG PENSTEMON

Penstemon rydbergii [*P. oreocharis*]
(Figwort family, *Scrophulariaceae*)
(Photo: Crater Lake NP Headquarters, Klamath Co., late July)

Stems erect, to 24" high, narrow leaves 1"-3" long, entire, upper leaves somewhat clasping, the lower on short petioles. Flowers about ½" long, purplish-blue, becoming blue on the lobes, in clusters on the stems. Corolla throat whitish deep inside, interior of lower petal hairy. Sterile stamen (staminode) has yellow hairs on the end. Meadows east of Cascade crest, to CA. **Ash Penstemon** (*P. cincicola*) is similar, but has smaller flowers, 1/4"-5/16" long.

SHOWY PENSTEMON
ROYAL PENSTEMON

Penstemon speciosus
(Figwort family, *Scrophulariaceae*)
(Photo: Cloudcap, Crater Lake NP, Klamath Co., early August)

Stems 2"-24", somewhat hairy, may be partially decumbent. Leaves leathery, 2"-4" long, narrow, entire, the basal leaves petioled, the stem leaves more or less sessile. Inflorescence long, showy, mostly on one side of stem. Calyx about ¼" long, segments pointed. Corolla purplish-blue, 1"-1¼" long, abruptly dilated to the throat, not hairy inside. Sagebrush scrub to dry open slopes in mountains, to WA and CA.

SNOW QUEEN
ROUND-LEAVED SYNTHYRIS

Synthyris reniformis
(Figwort family, *Scrophulariaceae*)
(Photo: Limpy Creek, Josephine Co., early March)

One of the first spring flowers. Leafless hairy stems rise 5"-8" above basal leaves, with loose clusters of flowers at the ends. Leaves heart-shaped and scalloped, 1"-2" long, on long reddish petioles. Corollas about ¼" long, deep to light blue, sometimes white, funnel-shaped, 4 petals, united half their length. Stamens stick out beyond the end of the corolla. Moist shady woods on west side of the Cascades, to CA.

BIRDSEYE SPEEDWELL
WINTER SPEEDWELL
PERSIAN SPEEDWELL

Veronica persica
(Figwort family, *Scrophulariaceae*)
(Photo: Valley of the Rogue SP, Jackson Co., early March)

Regarded as a weed, because it invades lawns. However, it has lovely little blue and white flowers that suggest Baby Blue-Eyes. Stems prostrate, forming bunches to 8"-10" high. Stem leaves mostly opposite, about 3/8" long, dentate or scalloped, with petioles of about same length. Flowers at tops of stems, each flower ¼"-½" across, blue with white center, with fine purple lines. Corollas 4-lobed, petals partially fused. Native to Asia Minor.

WESTERN BLUE VIOLET
WESTERN DOG VIOLET
HOOKEDSPUR VIOLET
WESTERN LONG-SPURRED VIOLET

Viola adunca (Violet family, *Violaceae*)
(Photo: Limpy Creek Botanical Area, Josephine Co., mid May)

Stems 2"-8" high, leaves both basal and cauline, oval, ½"-1½" long, generally scalloped, petioles ¼"-2½" long. Petals blue to violet, less than 5/8" long, with long, slender, often hooked spur, lower petals more or less whitish at the base, often dark-veined, lateral petals white-bearded. Wet meadows and damp woods, widespread, to AK and CA.

HALL VIOLET
OREGON VIOLET

Viola hallii (Violet family, *Violaceae*)
(Photo: Rough and Ready, Josephine Co., late March)

The flowers barely reach as high as the leaves, only 4" or so, and the plant is easily overlooked. Flower stems and leaf stems long, and both arise from the base. Leaves 1"-2" long, parted into linear segments. Flower is striking, with upper pair of petals deep purple, and the lower 3 white or cream color. Lowest petal yellow inside, with violet streaks. West of the Cascades, generally on gravelly soil, in open woods, to CA.

ENGLISH VIOLET

Viola odorata (Violet family, *Violaceae*)
(Photo: Valley of the Rogue SP, early March)

Fairly common in lawns and disturbed places, flowering early. Flowering stems and leaves rise directly from the spreading rootstocks. Leaves thick, leathery, more or less rounded, generally toothed, with long petioles. Flowers generally nodding, and rise above leaves on stems about 3" long. Petals deep violet, about ½" long, upper ones may be folded back. Lower petals generally bearded inside at the base and appear whitish; there may be fine white lines at the base. Native to Eurasia.

Siskiyou Fritillary

BROWN to GREEN FLOWERS

Brown, pinkish brown, and greenish brown flowers all go here. Even though the descriptions of the flowers may state that the color is "brownish-purple," or "brownish with green streaks," if the general impression is that the flowers appear brown, then they are placed here. In some cases, such as with California Ground-Cone and English Plantain, the true flowers may be some color other than brown, or may appear partly white because of prominent white anthers, but, since the overall impression of the color of the plant is *brown,* they are placed in this section.

WILD GINGER
LONGTAIL WILD GINGER

Asarum caudatum
(Pipevine family, *Aristolochiaceae*)
(Photo: Grizzly Peak Trail, Jackson Co., late June)

At first, you might not even know there is a flower there, because it is so well hidden by the leaves. Leaves are 2"-4" wide, rounded, slightly pointed, with long petioles, lying close to the ground. Push the leaves aside and there is the flower, brownish-purple, bowl-shaped, about 2" across exclusive of the tailed appendages, which may be 3" long. Moist shady forests, to 6000 feet, to BC and CA. **Marbled Wild Ginger** (*A. marmoratum*), found in southern OR and extreme northwest CA, is similar, but has conspicuous marbling on the leaves.

WESTERN HOUND'S TONGUE

Cynoglossum occidentale
(Borage family, *Boraginaceae*)
(Photo: Clover Creek Road, Klamath Co., early June)

(See, also, **Great Hound's Tongue,** p. 128.) Stems 12"-20", erect, leafy, very hairy. Leaves more or less oval, 3"-8" long, hairy on both surfaces, pointed, tapering to petioles, upper leaves clasping. Flowers in loose clusters, calyxes about ¼" long, with narrow, hairy lobes. Corollas tubular, about ½" long, with 5 lobes, brownish-pink or bluish. Open forest, east slope of Cascades, to Jackson Co. and CA.

CHECKER LILY
MISSION BELLS

Fritillaria affinis [*Fritillaria lanceolata*]
(Lily family, *Liliaceae*)
(Photo: Soda Mountain Road, Cascade-Siskiyou NM, Jackson Co., mid June)

Blends with the background, but generally stands up high enough to be readily visible. The stout stem is 8"-24" tall; the flowers, usually 1-3 in number, nod over, resembling bells. Leaves are narrow, to 4" long, arranged in whorls on the upper stem, then singly, above. Perianth 1" or more long, brownish purple, mottled and streaked with greenish yellow. Style deeply divided into 3 parts. Open fields, below 5000 feet, mostly west of Cascades, to BC and CA.

SISKIYOU FRITILLARY

Fritillaria glauca (Lily family, *Liliaceae*)
(Photo: Rough and Ready, Josephine Co., late March)

This little lily hugs the ground, and merges with the background. Stem is only 6"-8" high, flower is brownish and greenish. Leaves 3-4, thin, a few inches long, with no basal leaves. There may be only one flower, although 2-3 are possible. Perianth 1" or less long, the outside brownish with green streaks, and mottled brownish and greenish-yellow inside. Style is divided for half its length. Uncommon. Rocky slopes on serpentine, southern Josephine and Curry Cos., to CA.

CLUSTERED LADY'S SLIPPER
BROWNIE LADY'S SLIPPER

Cypripedium fasciculatum
(Orchid family, *Orchidaceae*)
(Photo: Near Applegate Lake, Jackson Co., late April)

Stems rise only 6"-8", with two fairly large leaves about 1" above the base, opposite, sessile. Flowers 1-4, with leafy bracts just below, perianth parts greenish-brown or somewhat purplish, sepals about 3/4" long, pointed, lateral petals smaller. Lip more or less oval, less than ½" long, greenish yellow. **Federal species of concern.** Coniferous forests, Curry, Douglas, Josephine, and Jackson Cos., below 5500', to CA.

CALIFORNIA GROUND-CONE

Boschniakia strobilacea
(Broom-rape family, *Orobranchaceae*)
(Photo: Near Applegate Lake, Jackson Co., late April)

Looks very much like a pine cone sitting on end. Parasitic on madrones or manzanitas. The above-ground "pine cone" part is the inflorescence, generally 3"-7" high, reddish-brown to dark purplish, with many more or less oval overlapping bracts, widest above the middle, about 3/4" long. Flowers peek out from among the bracts, corollas about 3/4" long, generally purplish, pale margins. Open woods or chaparral, at scattered locations in southwestern OR, to CA. **Small Ground-Cone** (*B. hookeri*) similar, but much smaller, often yellowish, parasitic on salal.

ENGLISH PLANTAIN
BLACK PLANTAIN
LANCE-LEAF PLANTAIN
BUCKHORN PLANTAIN

Plantago lanceolata
(Plantain family, *Plantaginaceae*)
(Photo: Near Pistol River SP, Curry Co., mid May)

Stems 8"-30" high, from basal clumps of leaves. Leaves narrow or oblong, 3"-10" long, tapering to petioles. Flowering spikes dense, egg-shaped at first, becoming cylindric. Flowers small, numerous, brownish, about 1/8" long, with conspicuous stamens that stick well out, and cream-colored anthers. Waste ground, especially west of Cascades. Introduced from Europe. **Seaside Plantain** (*P. maritima*), native, somewhat similar, has conspicuous stamens, but has narrow succulent leaves without petioles.

RATTLESNAKE GRASS
QUAKING GRASS

Briza maxima (Grass family, *Poaceae* [*Graminae*])
(Photo: Near Pistol River, Curry Co., mid May)

Members of the Grass family generally don't get looked upon as wildflowers, but this one is an attention-getter, because the "flowers" resemble the rattles of rattlesnakes. Stems are up to 24" high, with slender leaves. The "flowers," known as *spikelets,* bend over and hang down, usually with many in a cluster. Spikelets are 1/2"-3/4" long, green, with many overlapping bracts called *lemmas.* Widespread, at lower elevations. Native of Europe. A similar species, also called ***Rattlesnake Grass*** (*Bromus briziformis*), non-native, occurs at higher elevations, but has a small point on the ends of many of the lemmas, whereas *Briza maxima* has none.

BROAD-LEAVED CATTAIL
COMMON CATTAIL

Typha latifolia (Cattail family, *Typhaceae*)
(Photo: Denman WA, Jackson Co., late June)

Stems can be as much as 9' tall, with flat leaves 3'-4' long, ½" to 1¼" wide. The dark brown sausage-like spikes, about 1" dia., are composed of female flowers; the slender spikes above are composed of male flowers. Male and female sections are usually contiguous. Widespread in wet places, nationwide. A similar species, **Narrow-leaved Cattail** *(T. angustifolia)* has leaves ¼"-½" wide, and the male and female spikes are separated by ¼"-3".

Baneberry

BERRIES

The berries chosen for this section are those for which the berries are attractive, perhaps more ttractive than the flowers themselves. In some cases of species in this book, both flowers and their uits are attractive, as in the cases of blackberries, or thimbleberries. Note that the usage of the word ›erry" in this section is an informal one. The formal definition of a **berry** is a fleshy fruit in which the eds are not encased in a stone, and usually number more than one. Thus, the fruit of Pacific Yew is icluded, even though it is not a berry, but an aril. Likewise, the fruit of Western Juniper is included ecause it is berry-like in appearance, even though it actually is a fleshy cone. **(Note that some of the uits included here are toxic.)**

OREGON-GRAPE
HOLLYLEAF BARBERRY

Berberis aquifolium [*Mahonia aquifolium*]
(Barberry family, *Berberidaceae*)
(Photo: Beekman Arboretum, Jacksonville, Jackson Co., late July)

Oregon's state flower. (See photo of flowers on p. 58.) Shrub, to 15' tall. Leaves compound, 5-7 leaflets (sometimes 9), 1½"-3" long, leathery, spiny. Small yellow flowers in racemes up to 4" long. Berries deep blue, glaucous, more or less elliptic, about 5/16" long. Woodlands west of Cascades, to BC and CA.

DOUBLE HONEYSUCKLE
PURPLE-FLOWERED HONEYSUCKLE
RED TWINBERRY

Lonicera conjugialis
(Honeysuckle family, *Caprifoliaceae*)
(Photo: Near Mount Ashland, Jackson Co., late August)

Shrub, to 5' tall. Leaves 1½"-2½" long, lance-shaped to elliptic, pointed, short-petioled. Flowers in axils of leaves, corollas dark red, about ¼" long, peduncles about 1" long. Berries bright red, about ¼" diameter, typically with 2 berries incompletely fused. Higher elevations of Siskiyous and Cascades, to WA and CA.

BLACK TWINBERRY
BEARBERRY HONEYSUCKLE
INKBERRY

Lonicera involucrata
(Honeysuckle family, *Caprifoliaceae*)
(Photo: Harris Beach SP, Curry Co., late July)

Shrub, to 9' tall. Leaves 2"-3" long, leathery, more or less oval, entire. Flowers in axils of leaves, 2-flowered, yellow or reddish, 1/2" long, funnelform. Berries black, about 5/16" diameter, enclosed by a conspicuous red involucre with bracts that are united or nearly so. Widespread, to AK and CA.

BLUE ELDERBERRY

Sambucus mexicana [*S. nigra* ssp. *cerulea*]
(Honeysuckle family, *Caprifoliaceae*)
(Photo: Dead Indian Memorial Road, Jackson Co., late September)

Large shrub, sometimes tree-like, deciduous, to 24' tall. Leaves compound, 3-11 leaflets, narrow or elliptic, sharp-pointed, 1½"-8" long. Flowers small, white or cream-colored, in showy clusters, usually flat-topped. Berries bluish, but actually more or less black with bluish film. Woods and stream-banks throughout OR, to WA and CA.

RED ELDERBERRY

Sambucus racemosa [*S. callicarpa*]
(Honeysuckle family, *Caprifoliaceae*)
(Photo: Near Sunset Bay, Coos Co., late July)

The red berries and big compound leaves make this tree-like plant instantly recognizable. The tall shrub, sometimes a small tree, can grow to 15' high, with 5-7 leaflets on its compound leaves, the leaflets growing to as much as 6" long, sharply serrate. Flowers are in clusters, small, white or cream, and berries are bright red, about 1/8" dia., growing in bunches. Even though birds eat the berries, they can cause severe intestinal upset in humans. Damp woods west of Cascades, to CA.

SNOWBERRY
WAXBERRY

Symphoricarpos albus
(Honeysuckle family, *Caprifoliaceae*)
(Photo: Rocky Point, Klamath Co., late October)

Many-branched shrub to 4'-5' high, leaves generally oval-shaped, short-petioled, 5/8"-2" long, usually entire, but sometimes lobed. Flowers in clusters, less than ¼" long, bell-shaped, pinkish. Fruit round, white, waxy, ¼"-½" dia. In woods, widely distributed.

PACIFIC DOGWOOD
WESTERN FLOWERING DOGWOOD

Cornus nuttallii (Dogwood family, *Cornaceae*)
(Photo: Near Union Creek, Jackson Co., mid October)

(See photo of flowers on p. 16.) Small tree, usually less than 40'. At moderate elevations west of the Cascades, from BC to CA, the white flowers illuminate the woods in May. In fall, the rosy leaves do the same, when the sunlight falls on them. The true flowers are not the bright white "petals" that are so highly visible; these are modified leaves called "bracts." The flowers are the clustered yellow balls at the centers, that turn into clumps of red berries in fall.

WESTERN JUNIPER
SIERRA JUNIPER

Juniperus occidentalis
(Cypress family, *Cupressaceae*)
(Photo: Eagle Ridge, Upper Klamath Lake, Klamath Co., late October)

Tree, to 50' high. Often called "cedar" in much of the west. Leaves scale-like, closely appressed. Pollen cones small, seed cones fleshy, berry-like, blue-green, maturing black, ¼"-½" dia. East side of Cascades and as far west as Jackson Co., to WA and CA. Dwarf species, **Common Juniper** (*J. communis*), less than 3' high, with spreading needles, occurs at moderate to high elevations in Cascades and Siskiyous.

THIN-LEAVED HUCKLEBERRY
MOUNTAIN HUCKLEBERRY
BIG HUCKLEBERRY

Vaccinium membranaceum
(Heath family, *Ericaceae*)
(Photo: Near Fish Lake, Jackson Co., early August)

Shrub, 2'-5' high. Leaves thin, almost translucent, 3/4"-2" long, more or less oval, tapered to points at both ends, minutely toothed. Berries solitary in axils, 5/16"-7/16" dia, dark purplish red to black, slightly flattened, pedicels erect. Woods at moderate elevations in Cascades and Siskiyous, to BC and CA.

EVERGREEN HUCKLEBERRY
CALIFORNIA HUCKLEBERRY

Vaccinium ovatum (Heath family, *Ericaceae*)
(Photo: Harris Beach SP, Curry Co., late July)

(See photo of flowers on p. 89.) Evergreen plant to 10' tall, many-branched, thickly foliaged. Leaves small, dark glossy green above, paler below, thick and leathery, more or less oval shaped, finely serrate on edges. Flowers urn-shaped, pinkish, about 3/16" long, in clusters. Berries round, abundant, black, or glaucous with bluish film, to almost 3/16" dia. In the words of some, the glossy black berries sometimes look like "black widow bodies."

RED HUCKLEBERRY

Vaccinium parviflorum (Heath family, *Ericaceae*)
(Photo: Near Susan Creek, North Umpqua River, Douglas Co., late June)

Tall, open shrub, to 18' tall, deciduous. Leaves more or less elliptic, often pointed, 5/8"-1¼" long, sometimes slightly toothed on edges. Flowers solitary, globe-shaped, pinkish, about 5/32" long. Berries bright red, round, 1/4"-5/16" diameter. Woods, mostly along the coast, but also on the lower west slopes of Cascades.

SHINY-LEAVED GOOSEBERRY
SIERRA GOOSEBERRY

Ribes cruentum [*R. roezlii* var. *cruentum*]
(Gooseberry family, *Grossulariaceae*)
(Photo: Shan Creek Road, Josephine Co., late May)

(See photo of flowers, on page 94.) Shrub, 2'-4' high, with thorns. Leaves rounded, ½"-1" dia., 3-5 lobed, scalloped, dentate. Flower has conspicuous reddish-purple calyx with lobes that resemble petals, in tube about ½" long that spreads into the lobes. Petals white, about ½" long. Style deeply cleft, extends beyond the petals. Berries about ½" dia., with dense spines. Open woods, from Douglas County to CA.

BANEBERRY
RED BANEBERRY

Actaea rubra [*Actaea arguta*]
(Buttercup family, *Ranunculaceae*)
(Photo: Grizzly Peak Trail, Jackson Co., mid August)

In some locations in shady forests, Baneberry can dominate the understory. The plants are up to 3' high, with compound leaves that usually have 3 leaflets, each about 2" long and sharply toothed, somewhat resembling maple leaves. In May and June, tiny white flowers are in rounded terminal clusters, which become glistening red (sometimes white) berries by August, that are **TOXIC.** Woods, widely distributed, to AK and CA.

WESTERN SERVICEBERRY
SASKATOON

Amelanchier alnifolia [*A. florida*]
(Rose family, *Rosaceae*)
(Photo: Near Thousand Springs Sno-Park, Jackson Co., early August)

(See photo of flowers on page 38.) Large shrub or tree, to 30'. Leaves oblong or rounded, ¾"-1" long, serrate all around or only on outer half. Flowers white, 5 narrow petals, about ½" long, often twisted in appearance. Fruit berry-like, nearly round, 5/16"-1/2" dia, blue-black. Widely distributed in woods, to BC and CA.

MOUNTAIN STRAWBERRY
VIRGINIA STRAWBERRY

Fragaria virginiana [*F. platypetala*]
(Rose family, *Rosaceae*)
(Photo: Rogue-Umpqua Divide, early June)

(See also, p. 38.) Plants rooting from long stolons Leaflets mostly bluish-green and hairless on top sur face, teeth generally 7-11, leaves usually exceeding the inflorescence. Petals white or pinkish, about 3/8' long. Fruit red, about 3/8" dia. Woods and meadows more common east of Cascades, to AK and CA **Woodland Strawberry** (*F. vesca*) similar, but teet on the leaves generally 12-21, and inflorescence usu ally exceeds the leaves.

HIMALAYA BLACKBERRY

Rubus armeniacus [*R. discolor, R. procerus*]
(Rose family, *Rosaceae*)
(Photo: Lower Rogue River, Curry Co., late July)

(See photo of flowers on p. 40.) Stems long, trailing, sturdy, 5-angled, sometimes purplish, armed with large spines. Even the flower stems are spiny. Leaves palmately compound, 3-5 oval leaflets, with toothed margins. Flowers white or pinkish, 5/8"-1" across, 5 petals. Fruit 5/8"-3/4" long, black. Widespread in western OR. Old World native.

THIMBLEBERRY

Rubus parviflorus (Rose family, *Rosaceae*)
(Photo: Rocky Point, Klamath Co., mid July)

(See photo of flower on p. 40.) Plants to 6' tall, with woody stems and virtually no prickles, often creating thickets. Flowers white, to 1½" in dia. Leaves to 8" across, more or less resembling maple leaves, with 5-7 lobes, soft to the touch. Berries bright red, 1/2" dia. or more. When pulled from the vine, the berry has a shallow cup-like depression that resembles a thimble. Moist woodlands, AK to CA.

PACIFIC YEW
WESTERN YEW

Taxus brevifolia (Yew family, *Taxaceae*)
(Photo: North Fork Little Butte Creek, Jackson Co., late September)

Shrub to small tree, up to 75' high, usually smaller, with scaly, dark reddish brown bark. Flat needles, ¾"-1" long, 2-ranked, at first glance resembling leaves of a Coast Redwood. Fruit consists of a single seed almost completely surrounded by red fleshy pulp, resembling a berry, but called an **aril.** The fruit resembles a red huckleberry, but is **TOXIC.** Moist forests, often with Douglas-Fir, west slope of Cascades and westward, to AK and CA.

REFERENCES

Baumgardt, John Phillip. 1982. *How to Identify Flowering Plant Families.* Timber Press, Portland, OR.

Begnoche, Don. 1999. *Siskiyou Sundays: A Tour of Southwestern Oregon.* Don Begnoche, Ashland, OR.

Clark, Lewis J. (John Trelawny, ed.) 1998. *Wildflowers of the Pacific Northwest.* Harbour Publishing, Madeira Park, BC, Canada

Coffey, Timothy. *The History and Folklore of North American Wildflowers.* Houghton Mifflin Co. Boston, New York.

Crosby, Donald G. 2004. *The Poisoned Weed: Plants Toxic to Skin.* Oxford University Press, New York.

Derig, Betty B., and Fuller, Margaret C. 2001. *Wild Berries of the West.* Mountain Press Publishing Co., Missoula, MT.

Gilkey, Helen M., and Dennis, La Rea J. 2001. *Handbook of Northwestern Plants.* Oregon State University Press, Corvallis, OR.

Hickman, James C. (ed.) 1993. *The Jepson Manual -- Higher Plants of California.* University of California Press, Berkeley, CA.

Horn, Elizabeth L. 1993. *Coastal Wildflowers of the Pacific Northwest.* Mountain Press Publishing Co., Missoula, MT.

Jensen, Edward C., and Ross, Charles R. 1994. *Trees to Know in Oregon.* Oregon State University Extension Service, Corvallis, OR.

Jensen, E.C., Randall, W.R., Keniston, R.F., and Bever, D.N. 2000. *Manual of Oregon Trees and Shrubs.* John Bell and Associates, Corvallis, OR

Kingsbury, John M. 1965. *Deadly Harvest: A Guide to Common Poisonous Plants.* Holt, Rinehart and Winston, New York, NY.

Kozloff, Eugene N. 2005. *Plants of Western Oregon, Washington & British Columbia.* Timber Press, Portland, OR.

Niehaus, Theodore F., and Ripper, Charles L. 1976. *A Field Guide to Pacific States Wildflowers.* Houghton Mifflin Company, Boston, MA.

Oregon Natural Heritage Information Center. 2004. *Rare, Threatened and Endangered Species of Oregon.* Oregon State University, Portland, OR.

Peck, Morton Eaton. 1961. *A Manual of the Higher Plants of Oregon* (2nd ed.). Binfords and Mor Publishers, Portland, OR.

Pojar, Jim, and MacKinnon, Andy (eds.). *Plants of the Pacific Northwest Coast.* Lone Pine Publish ing, Vancouver, BC.

Porter, C.L. 1967. *Taxonomy of Flowering Plants* (2nd ed.) W. H. Freeman & Co., San Francisco, CA.

Pyle, Robert Michael. 2002. *The Butterflies of Cascadia.* Seattle Audubon Society, Seattle, WA.

Reyes, Chris. 1994. *The Table Rocks of Jackson County: Islands in the Sky.* Last Minute Publications, Ashland, OR.

Schaffer, Jeffrey P. 1983. *Crater Lake National Park and Vicinity.* Wilderness Press, Berkeley, CA.

Spellenberg, Richard. 1979. *The Audubon Society Field Guide to North American Wildflowers -- Western Region.* Alfred A. Knopf, New York, NY

Stewart, Charles. 1994. *Wildflowers of the Olympics and Cascades.* Nature Education Enterprises, Port Angeles, WA.

Strickler, Dee. 1993. *Wayside Wildflowers of the Pacific Northwest.* Falcon Publishing, Helena, MT.

Sudworth,George B. 1908. *Forest Trees of the Pacific Slope.* U.S. Department of Agriculture, Forest Service, Washington, D.C.

Taylor, Ronald J. 1990. *Northwest Weeds -- The Ugly and Beautiful Villains of Fields, Gardens, and Roadsides.* Mountain Press Publishing Company, Missoula, MT.

Thomas, John Hunter, and Parnell, Dennis R. 1974. *Native Shrubs of the Sierra Nevada.* University of Clalifornia Press, Berkeley, CA.

USDA Natural Resources Conservation Service. 2004. *The PLANTS Database, Version 3.5* (http.//plants.usda.gov). National Plant Data Center, Baton Rouge, LA.

Whitson, Tom D. (editor). 2002. *Weeds of the West.* The Western Society of Weed Science, Newark, CA.

Vos, Belinda L. 2003. *Lamb's tongue: the* Erythronium *species of Jackson County, and the botanists who collected and described them. Kalmiopsis,* vol. 10, 2003, pp. 11-22.

INDEX

INDEX

INDEX

INDEX

INDEX

INDEX